Journey to Mauritius

Lost and Found Series

New editions of the best in travel writing—old and modern—from around the world

Classic Travel
Writing

Journey to Mauritius

Jacques-Henri Bernardin de Saint-Pierre

Translated with an introduction and notes by Jason Wilson

Interlink Books
An imprint of Interlink Publishing Group, Inc.
New York • Northampton

This edition first published in 2003 by

INTERLINK BOOKS
An imprint of Interlink Publishing Group, Inc.
99 Seventh Avenue • Brooklyn, New York 11215 and
46 Crosby Street • Northampton, Massachusetts 01060
www.interlinkbooks.com

First published in French 1773
Translation, introduction and notes © Jason Wilson 2003

Library of Congress Cataloging-in-Publication Data

Saint-Pierre, Bernardin de, 1737-1814.
 [Voyage à l'isle de France. English]
 Journey to Mauritius / by Bernardin de Saint-Pierre ; translated by
Jason Wilson.
     p. cm. -- (Lost and found series)
"First published in French, 1773."
 ISBN 1-56656-447-6 (pbk.)
 1. Mauritius--Description and travel--Early works to 1800.
 I. Wilson, Jason, 1944- II. Title. III. Series.
 DT469.M429 S2313 2002
 969.8'201--dc21

                    2002008594

All illustrations courtesy of Jason Wilson

Cover Design: Baseline Arts
Typesetting: Devdan Sen
Cover Image: courtesy Oxford University Museum of Natural History

Printed in Canada by Webcom Limited

To request our complete 40-page full-color catalog,
please call us toll free at **1-800-238-LINK**, visit our
website at **www.interlinkbooks.com**, or write to
Interlink Publishing
46 Crosby Street, Northampton, MA 01060
e-mail: info@interlinkbooks.com

Contents

Acknowledgments

I would like to thank Professor Vinesh Hookoomsing of the University of Mauritius for his conversations and generous sending of crucial books and documents. I would also like to thank my cousin Paddy Rountree and his wife Liz for putting Andrea, Camila and myself up so stylishly at Bel Air and Pointe d'Esny, surely two of the world's most beautiful places. Thanks also to Anthony Edkins for his usual flair in finding off-beat references and books, to Andrea for pruning much self-indulgence, and to Jim Ferguson for so ably seeing this project through to its completion.

Finally, to my father and mother for memory excursions into their Mauritian days and my father's ancestry.

All opinions are mine, as are errors.

To Andrea

Introduction

Jacques-Henri Bernardin de Saint-Pierre reached the Île de France in the Indian Ocean, which I will anachronistically call Mauritius as it is called today, on board the frigate *Marquis de Castries* on 14 July 1768. He was not famous, nor rich, nor yet the best-selling author of *Paul et Virginie*. Later, this well-travelled military engineer, with a penchant for thinking that would, on his return to France in 1770, lead to a close friendship with Jean-Jacques Rousseau, won fame as a moral philosopher with his ambitious *Etudes de la Nature*. But in 1768, as he stepped ashore on the tropical, volcanic island of Mauritius, Bernardin's anonymity and poverty were complete. Without a protector, heart-broken by his affair with a Polish princess[1] while working as a spy for France in Warsaw, he at least enjoyed the freedom of thinking against the grain. Suffering, vulnerability, and a sense of spite regarding his fate had paradoxically enriched him.

On his return to France after two years in Mauritius, Bernardin became an author, albeit anonymously. His first book was the Amsterdam-printed *Voyage à l'Isle de France* of 1773, rapidly translated by John Parish into English in 1775 as *A Voyage to the Island of Mauritius*. At the time, England had its eye on Mauritius, and this travel book described the strategically important island in detail.

The combination of fortuitous circumstances that led Bernardin to Mauritius can be unravelled, for there is no doubt that this tropical island made his name and fame as the setting of his bitter-sweet romance *Paul et Virginie* of 1787. Mark Twain, on the spot in Mauritius, quipped in 1896: "Apparently, there has been only one prominent event in the history of Mauritius, and that one didn't happen. I refer to the romantic sojourn of Paul and Virginia here."[2] Bernardin de Saint-Pierre had put Mauritius on the world literary map, at some cost, as we shall see.

Île de France

Before his arrival on the island, not much had "happened" to call Europe's attention to what was in essence a stopping-post for sailing ships on their way to the Indies. Although possibly visited by Arab traders who named it Dina Arobi,[3] and then by Portuguese navigators who called it Cerné (a corruption of Ilha do Cisne, meaning island of the swan, in reference to the swan-like dodo), Mauritius was first claimed by Dutch sailors in 1598. The Dutch finally settled, building in 1638 a modest fort at Grand Port in the southeast in what has rightly been called "a beautiful harbour".[4] These Dutch found the island uninhabited, and they were uninhibited in ransacking its natural splendour. The island was named Mauritius after Prince Maurits of Nassau, at the time Stadholder of the Netherlands. The Dutch governed the island, felled its precious ebony trees, brought in slaves from Madagascar and convicts from further afield because there were no native islanders to do the dirty work. (The slaves and convicts soon ran off and hid in the woods, ushering in white fears of *marron* attacks throughout the period of slavery.) The Dutch also introduced sugarcane, manioc/cassava from Brazil, rats and Javanese deer, and slaughtered the island's heavy, flightless dodos. They clung to the island from 1598 to 1658 when they left to return again from 1664 to 1710, this time definitively evacuating because the Cape of Good Hope offered the Dutch East Indies Company better resources on trade routes to and from Indonesia. Although the Dutch did try to colonize the island, they were unable to resist the food shortages, the rats, and the cyclones. Perhaps the absence of destructive human beings on this island, before the Dutch arrived, was the origin of the claim that it was paradise; the arrival of human beings in the form of Dutchmen triggered the "fall" and a history of ecological destruction that only today is being countered. The slaves (in 1706 there were 71 of them) ran off into the forests, and even burned down the wooden Dutch fort in 1695. If these runaway slaves survived after the Dutch left, they could be called the original inhabitants of the island.[5]

After a gap of eleven years when the island belonged to nobody, the French arrived in 1721–1722 to establish an overflow colony of the nearby island of Réunion (or Bourbon as it was called then), although this brand-new French colony was first claimed by a passing French sailor in 1715 who named it the Île de France.[6] It was governed by the Compagnie Française des Indes (the East India Company), which had a monopoly of trade with India, and then, from 1767 (a year before Bernardin's arrival), after the Compagnie collapsed, as a French crown colony and a free port with power shared between a governor and an *intendant*. A hostile view of why the French needed Mauritius comes from Edward John Trelawny, who took part in the English blockade of the island between 1808 and 1810: "The French found the Mauritius of essential importance, enabling them to harass the English commerce, and to preserve a footing in India."[7]

The society that developed in these early colonial years was based on the island as a staging post, supplying boats and crews. The island was not self-sufficient, as Jocelyn Chan Low noted, and suffered a chronic dearth of basic supplies.[8] Mauritian historian Auguste Toussaint quotes from a report written in 1765, three years before Bernardin arrived: "the inhabitants of the Île de France are not much interested in farming; all they think of is making their fortune as fast as they can by any means. Their one aim is to enrich themselves and bring their money back with them to France."[9] Pierre Sonnerat was on the island in 1768 at the same time as Bernardin and wrote: "no European intends to remain here; he comes for three or four years during which he tried to get rich as quickly as possible."[10] However, despite this mercantile ethos at the heart of colonialism, the right man appeared, and sought to implant a more efficient colony, if only to suck more money out of it.

Bertrand-François Mahé, Comte de La Bourdonnais (1699–1753), the greatest of all the French governors of the island, first landed in Mauritius in 1735 and stayed for four years. Back again on the island in 1741, he created a shipyard, built the first ships there and sailed to Pondicherry, India, freeing the town of Mahé (named after him) and conquering Madras in 1746. He was then ordered back to France in 1746. Over his years in the new colony he transformed the little island. He lived at Mon Plaisir, today the Sir Seewoosagur Ramgoolam

Botanical Garden at Pamplemousses (honoring the island's first post-independence prime minister). The governor re-introduced manioc from Brazil as food for the slaves in his attempt to see that they were well fed, both to ensure they worked, and for humanitarian reasons. He also introduced sugarcane (the "Otaheite" variety), indigo and cotton, rebuilt the hospitals and built the aqueduct that brought fresh water to Port Louis. It was largely his efforts that implemented the plans first made by Jean François Charpentier de Cossigny (1690–1780) to fortify and convert Port Louis into a proper capital.[11] Labourdonnais (as he is known) also tried to quell the runaway slaves, reducing them, according to Nwulia, to some twenty male *marrons* by 1740 (although they increased again). An anonymous English officer wrote in 1811, about Labourdonnais, thus: "...to him these beautiful colonies owe everything."[12] More recently, a Mauritian historian, Pierre de Sornay, called Labourdonnais the colony's real founder.[13] Sadly, Labourdonnais fell foul of the King, was accused of treachery by his enemies and imprisoned in the Bastille in 1746. Freed in 1751, he died in disgrace in 1753.

The best summary of Labourdonnais' activities comes from Michael Malim:

> He was a man of charm and wit, of quite amazing energy and versatility, administrator, legislator and diplomat, a first-class marine and civil engineer, and as bold and capable a soldier as sailor. His massive forts, barracks, warehouses and other buildings survive in Port Louis to this day [1952]. Within four years of his arrival he had changed a squalid palm-leaf settlement into a stone city, powerfully fortified. The difficulties he had to contend with were prodigious...[14]

I have dwelled on Labourdonnais as governor because he reappears as himself in Bernardin's romance *Paul et Virginie* (the date given was 1746, his last year), brainwashed by widowed Madame de la Tour's wicked, rich aunt back in France. Under pressure, he obliges Virginie to travel there to be "properly" educated and married in Paris. He leaves a bag of money to pay for her expenses and speaks directly to the reader, defining the reason why people leave France for colonies such as Mauritius and must return to the metropolis: "'Why do people come to the island? Isn't it to get rich?'"[15] Bernardin could not have invented a more succinct justification of colonial intentions. In the novel Labourdonnais appears again with help during the wreck of the *Saint-Géran* off Île d'Ambre where Virginie drowns (in fact on 24 December 1744, but Bernardin muddled dates in the novel).

The French name Île de France lasted from 1715 until the loss of the island to the British in 1810, following two years of sea-blockades and several skirmishes. The island then reverted to its original Dutch name of Mauritius as confirmed in the Treaty of Paris in 1814.[16]

Since Labourdonnais' days Mauritius has undergone several transformations, none more dramatic than its population explosion. In 1999 the island was reckoned to contain 1,168,256 people with a population density of 639 people per square kilometer (population density is 244 per sq. km. in the UK and 30 per sq. km. in the United States). The whole island is only 1,860 square kilometers (about the size of Greater London, or Rhode Island in the USA), and this population density must be related to the fact that its land-use and economy were essentially agricultural, primarily sugarcane. In the population census of 1735 under Labourdonnais there were 1,922 people, whites and slaves. When Bernardin de Saint-Pierre jumped ship in 1768, this had risen, but there were still only some 26,000 people, including the slaves, who represented 83 percent of the population.[17] In fact, in his romance *Paul et Virginie* he evoked the island as "almost deserted".[18] As already noted, manioc and sugarcane had been successfully introduced, and the first primitive sugar-mill began working in the 1740s under the enlightened Labourdonnais; by 1786 there were 10 sugar factories, by 1863, 303 mills. During Bernardin's time, over-population was not a worry; the problems were more to do with slavery and squeezing maximum profits out of the slaves' work. Bernardin was a witness to this far-off slave colony, at a turning point in its economy as French landowners, the sugar oligarchy (*les blancs*), were beginning to dominate social and economic life. (They would continue to do so for the next 200 years, despite the island's belonging to Britain from 1810 until independence in 1968.)

A Restless Life

Bernardin arrived on this island, which meant nothing to him, when he was 31 years old. Born on 19 January 1737 in Le Havre into a family that aspired to nobility but lacked the documents to prove it (hence the fake "de"), he was the eldest of a family of four (later a younger brother languished, deranged, in the Bastille, accused of treason). Most biographies agree that his Le Havre childhood was unhappy, with an absent post-master father leaving his education in the hands of mean-spirited priests. When his mother died, his father remarried, and when the latter died in 1765 he left little in his will for Bernardin. Throughout his life Bernardin projected happiness into the future, sometimes even combining this psychological need with dreams and actual plans of founding utopias. Patterns emerge from this childhood of an intense anticipation of future happiness collapsing into despair. Some biographers have speculated on a family neurosis; Bernardin does seem to have suffered from depression.[19] The earliest biographer, L. Aimé-Martin (who married Bernardin's widow, and was ousted as unreliable by Maurice Souriau),[20] traced Bernardin's nomadic restlessness to an early passionate reading as a twelve-year-old of Daniel Defoe's *Robinson Crusoe*, published in 1719 and based, as is universally known, on the true story of Alexander Selkirk's marooning on the Pacific island of Juan Fernández off Chile. The idea of the island as a self-enclosed paradise did not begin with Defoe, nor even with More's earlier *Utopia* (1516), as the idea is clearly archetypal, a place of deep and obscure desires merely given verbal felicity by Defoe.

Dreams of tropical islands led Bernardin to accompany a sea-captain uncle on a voyage to the island of Martinique, in the West Indies, when he was twelve. From then on, travel beckoned and he became a "misfit and a wanderer" for over 15 years, gaining as well a reputation for insubordination.[21]

Bernardin was trained in the scientific tradition of his times; he won a first prize for mathematics in 1757 and joined the prestigious École des Ponts et Chaussées for one year before it was closed with the outbreak of the Seven Years War. In 1760 he became an *Ingénieur du Roi* and joined the French army. During the seven years from 1760 until his sailing for Mauritius, Bernardin was on the move, part mercenary, part spy for the Polish against the Russians (he was caught and spent nine days in prison but did not squeal). He was also on the lookout for a life-opportunity not offered him in France, where he was poor and without patrons. He travelled to Malta in 1761, on to Amsterdam, then to St. Petersburg, where Catherine II was on the throne (she corresponded with Diderot and Voltaire) in 1762–1763, where he won her favor and learned Russian. He then moved during 1764–1765 to Warsaw, where he fell in love with a Polish princess and was deserted, then to Vienna, Dresden, Berlin, and finally back to Paris in 1765, empty-handed. His wandering exile over, he was still penniless. Finally in 1767 he was offered a job as military engineer ("capitaine d'infanterie, ingénieur du Roi") to accompany the Count de Maudave, a native of Mauritius, to re-establish the harbor at Fort-Dauphin in Madagascar as a new colony to be administered on utopian principles. In the event, Bernardin fought with Maudave during the voyage and decided to abandon ship in Mauritius in July 1768 after a terrible storm at sea and the death of eleven sailors from scurvy.

In Mauritius Bernardin had no real job awaiting him, so he worked as a master mason, but did not receive the pay he deserved as a royal engineer because someone had forgotten to sign his *brevet*. He did, however, make some money on the black market and pay off some debts in France.[22] He lived in a one-room house at the edge of the capital Port Louis, with two slaves, and became a vegetarian to save money.

But luck was on his side, for another recently arrived passenger was the *intendant* for Mauritius, Pierre Poivre, who quickly became Bernardin's mentor in matters of hostility to slavery, science and knowledge, though Bernardin excluded his name from the first edition of his *Journey to Mauritius* (in fact Souriau detected that he had scratched out all references to Poivre in his manuscript).[23] In any case, Bernardin was proud of excluding names from his first edition of the *Journey*, as it protected the living.[24] Poivre (1719–1786) was an enlightened official, who introduced spices and rice, tried to civilize the island-colony with science, revitalized the economy, brought nuns out in 1770 to run the first hospital and allowed the first Hindu temple to be built in 1772. The historian Auguste Toussaint examined Poivre's ambitions and declared that the latter had initiated a remarkable agricultural development.[25] As *intendant*, Poivre was in charge of the police, justice, and finances, as well as being the Commissionaire

Général de la Marine, dealing with supplies and the harbor, which he cleared of silt. But he was in open animosity with Governor Dumas and then his replacement Desroches, who controlled the army and navy. When Bernardin arrived, Poivre and Dumas had actually come to blows. Bernardin would suffer the consequences of befriending Poivre by inheriting his enemies, the governors.

Poivre was a well-travelled, seminary-trained, all-rounder who first landed on Mauritius in 1740, meeting Labourdonnais. He went on to explore the Far East from 1741 to 1748, was there again on a secret mission to steal plants from 1748 to 1757, with part of that time spent on Mauritius. He was finally sent back to Mauritius by the King from 1767 to October 1772 where, like Labourdonnais before, he lived at Mon Plaisir. He wrote many official reports, including a factual travel account, *Voyage d'un philosophe ou Observations sur les Moeurs et les Arts des Peuples de l'Afrique, de l'Asie et de l'Amérique* (1769, translated into English by Oliver Goldsmith).[26] Crucially, he was director of the Jardin Botanique des Pamplemousses from 1767 to 1772. It was the botanist Poivre who persuaded Bougainville's naturalist, Philibert Commerson (1727–1773), to stay on in Mauritius on his way back from sailing around the world, which he did on landing there in November 1768.[27] Commerson, who died on the island, brought breadfruit from the Pacific islands with him, and befriended Bernardin.[28] In an addendum prepared for the second edition of his *Journey*, Bernardin confessed that Poivre was the most attractive man he had ever met, and that he owed his keenness for studying nature to him, having seen him "fertilize rocks, so to speak".[29] However, something cooled in Bernardin's relationship with Poivre, and back in France they did not see each other (documents at Le Havre convinced Maurice Souriau that Bernardin had fallen in love with *Intendant* Poivre's far-younger wife, who rejected him).[30] It is also true that Poivre was well-known to be quarrelsome, perhaps aggravated by having lost his right arm to a pirate's cannonball and by being much older than his young wife; whatever the cause, he was involved in perpetual quarrels.[31]

During his two years of self-exile on Mauritius, Bernardin took copious notes, wrote letters home and observed everything around him from a compassionate angle. His budding religious philosophy, a kind of Deism, was derived from a belief that purpose in the world was the result of a benign Providence (God's will), that Nature was not a blind force, but the source of all knowledge and self-knowledge, contacted through feelings, not reason. It was a philosophy that would later appeal to female readers, but with the advent of Darwinism would also be ridiculed. For the literary historian Gustave Lanson, Bernardin's later work on nature revealed a complete "scientific ineptitude".[32] But his ability to notice things in the natural world had evolved from his scientific training and was broadened by concerns for the social and political world emerging from his absorption of Jean Jacques Rousseau's then recent *Discours sur l'origine de l'inégalité* (1755) and his thrilling *Le Contrat Social* (1772). Rousseau's opening battle cry "Man was born free, and he is everywhere in chains. Those who think themselves the masters of others are indeed greater slaves than they"[33] became a manifesto for rebels like Bernardin. When Bernardin first read Rousseau is not clear, though Rousseau's notoriety (condemned in Paris, his novel *Emile* and *Le Contrat Social* burned in Geneva in 1762, a warrant issued for his arrest, etc.) would have led Bernardin to take note of his thought. There is no doubt that Rousseau's thinking informed Bernardin's and runs through all his works as an interlocking structure of beliefs and opinions. These range from notions of freedom from tyranny, a loathing of the corruption of the aristocracy and the rich who perpetuate their rights through the law, ideas about natural virtue and freedom as linked to moral duty and justice, to the need to have "teachers" and to let feelings and "conscience" rule man. Closest to Bernardin's Mauritian experiences were Rousseau's views on slavery, when he argued in *Le Contrat Social* that the right of slavery was "void". In fact, like Rousseau, Bernardin was deeply religious, possibly a Unitarian, even a Calvinist.

An ability to step outside of himself and notice the world about him (an aspect of the scientific mind) led a specialist on Bernardin's work, Jean-Michel Racault, to call this travel account "the most scrupulously documentary possible".[34] Right from the first readers this was the common view. In 1775 Oliver Goldsmith was reported to have admired Bernardin's travel writing "for the accuracy and ingenuity of the observations".[35] In France, the philosopher Condorcet noted of the *Journey* that it dealt with slavery "with complete truth".[36] That is,

Bernardin saw Mauritius with a cold eye; he did not write picturesque, exotic stuff.

Bernardin was finally forced to quit Mauritius by the arrival in 1769 of Governor Desroches who brought his own engineers with him and further ostracized Bernardin (already jilted by Madame Poivre). Granted permission to return, he left Mauritius on the *Indien* on 3 December 1770.

Back in Paris, the years 1771 to 1780 were marked by extreme poverty and hard work; he completed his travel book, partially re-inventing the genre. The French *philosophe* D'Alembert arranged for the manuscript to be sold for a thousand francs but Bernardin did not see a *sou* and sued the publisher. It was published anonymously "par un officier du roi" in two volumes in 1773, in Amsterdam to avoid censorship. When Charles Darwin read the book in 1842, he did not know it was by Bernardin, yet he knew who Bernardin was, for *Paul and Virginia* inspired Darwin's irony in a letter of 1836: "We proceed to the Isle of France... Oh that I had a sweet Virginia... A person not in love will have no right to wander amongst the glowing bewitching scenes. I am writing most glorious nonsense..."[37] Later, in the 1790s, when Bernardin was preparing the second edition of the *Journey*, he wrote: "When I printed it, I was not free to say everything. The censor cut out many innocent items."[38]

Nevertheless, his book became a scandal, especially the passages on slavery and corrupt colonial society, and that despite the censorship. Aimé-Martin wrote in 1826: "The whole of Europe shuddered at the picture he traced of the slaves' suffering,"[39] and Bernardin became a hated figure for the powerful French landowners on the island. According to Robert Chaudenson, these white colonials banned the sale of the book in Mauritius.[40] The second edition Bernardin prepared for press in 1796–97 never appeared, and, despite Chaudenson's research, nobody knows why.

A fascinating example of the subversive influence of Bernardin's book in Mauritius can be seen in the way his name reappeared in association with a political party, the People's Movement, which promoted radical Hinduism along Gandhian lines in the 1940s and set about reversing the terrible illiteracy of the Hindus on the island through local schools. Its founder, Basdeo Bissoondoyal, bracketed

Bernardin with Gandhi (the latter visited Mauritius in 1901) as heroes for the Indian indentured laborers (brought in to replace slaves on the plantations) in their struggle against white domination on the island. Bissoondoyal translated *Paul et Virginie* into Hindi, wrote many articles on Bernardin and edited a cheap edition of the *Voyage* (which I have not been able to locate). He also wrote on Gandhi (who loved Bernardin's parable about wisdom and a caste-less worker, *La chaumière indienne*, 1790, translated as an appendix here), and on Tagore (who eulogized *Paul et Virginie*) as well as on the *vedas*, Hinduism in general and his own island in *The Truth about Mauritius* (1968).[41] A curious detail about Bernardin's respect for Indian culture, epitomized in *La chaumière indienne*, is that he advocated vegetarianism ("people who live off vegetables are, above all others, the most beautiful, the most robust, the least exposed to diseases and passions, and those who live longest").[42] What I find moving is that Bernardin still spoke across race and culture to the downtrodden Hindus in twentieth-century Mauritius. As Basdeo Bissoondoyal pointed out, "some of the whites would not forgive Saint-Pierre for sympathizing with the slaves."[43]

Following the anonymous publication of the *Journey*, Bernardin befriended Jean-Jacques Rousseau, whom he met in June 1772 and continued to see until the latter's death in 1778. He became his secretary, accompanied him on long herborizing talks and walks, and wrote about him.[44] Living in poverty in Paris, he researched his own preferred masterpiece *Etudes de la nature*, arguing that the natural world was God's gift to man. It was published in 1784; its third edition in 1787 included the romance *Paul et Virginie* as the fourth volume; its sixth edition contained *La chaumière indienne* as an appendix. When the Revolution broke out, Bernardin became, for a short while from September to November 1792, a member of the Popular Assembly in his district. The same year, he was appointed by King Louis XVI (just before his execution) as Buffon's successor as director of the Jardin des Plantes in Paris. He managed to keep his post during the revolutionary turmoil, in a balancing act between the Jacobins and the aristocrats (in fact, Bernardin was a convinced monarchist who loathed the aristocracy).[45] Dismissed, he was then elected as the first professor in the newly founded École Normale Supérieure in Paris in 1794.

It was during this hectic time that Bernardin planned a second edition of his *Journey to Mauritius*. His love life flourished with success. He first married Félicité Didot in 1793 (she was 36 years younger), and they had a daughter named, inevitably, Virginie, and then a son, Paul. After the death of his wife in 1799, he married Desirée de Pellepore, who was 43 years younger than him. In 1803 he was elected to the Académie Française, becoming its president in 1806 when he read an elegy to Napoleon (whom he revered, even though the latter re-introduced slavery in 1802). Thus he became a highly esteemed public figure with a penchant for polemics, for going against the grain, an auto-didact and outsider who always sought the difficult middle-ground, with public enemies among the *philosophes* and the atheists. Bernardin lived from 1804 to 1814 at Eragny-sur-Oise, where he died in his garden pavilion, aged 77, a famous writer.

Slavery

The young poet Charles Baudelaire reached Mauritius on 1 September 1841, aged twenty, supposedly sent to India by his step-father to cure him of "literature", but he jumped ship, stayed there two weeks, and found another ship to bring him back to France via the island of Réunion. On Mauritius he wrote a sonnet to a local man's wife that refers to Mauritius as the "pays parfumé que le soleil caresse" [scented country caressed by the sun], with its palm trees and its beautiful Creole women (a rhyme "caresse/paresse" [caress/laziness] he re-cycled in further poems). It ends on a conceit about slaves; the woman's looks, he writes, could make poets more submissive than black slaves.[46] Baudelaire's most vivid memory of his brief stay on the island was seeing a black woman publicly flogged in the Port Louis market place.[47] Slavery, then, was the dark and nasty side to this paradise island. In fact, Anthony Barker noted that Mauritius was one of the largest slave colonies in the British Empire at the time of the Emancipation Act of 1833.[48]

Like Baudelaire later, Bernardin de Saint-Pierre was equally disturbed by what he saw on the island. In an autobiographical piece written in 1809, he claimed that his stay in Mauritius was ruined by the "deplorable fate of the wretched blacks" that left him in a "profound melancholy".[49] Isabelle Vissière has studied this aspect of his work and believes that his travel account was a "violent" indictment of slavery, choosing her adjective carefully. She offers figures for the years he was on the island. In 1766 there were 2,400 whites to 18,000 black slaves; this rose in 1776 to 3,400 whites and 25,000 black slaves, a constant ratio of 1 to 7. Moses Nwulia produced these figures for the rise in slaves in Mauritius: in 1767 there were 15,027; in 1787, 33,832.

Slavery had already been denounced back in Paris by the main *philosophes* like Diderot, Voltaire and Montesquieu, but as Hugh Thomas noted about these Enlightenment figures, "not even the most powerful intellects knew what to do about the matter in practice."[50] Count Buffon in an essay on blacks of 1749 digressed personally from the matter at hand, writing that he could not but feel sad and revolted about their state of slavery and the current "avidity for profit", but was pleased that laws had put a stop to "the brutality of masters". Such laws, however, were not put into practice, and Buffon never saw this misery on the spot.[51] Bernardin was one of the first to denounce slavery from actually seeing the system in operation. Vissière classes Bernardin as unique for his time in his understanding that slavery profoundly dehumanized everybody involved. Hollingworth summarizes: "His vehement hatred of slavery was exceptional for the time."[52] Hugh Thomas saw the anti-slavery writers of that period as new and radical.

In a farsighted way, Bernardin cursed sugarcane as the cause of slavery. He blamed avidity for the sweet stuff back home in Europe as a way of enlivening dull food, giving quick energy and forming the basis for rum, chocolate, jam and preserves. The vast profits derived from growing it were accrued, he saw, at the expense of the slave's health and life. In a postscript to a letter he wrote: "I do not know if coffee or sugar are necessary for happiness in Europe, but I do know that these two plants have led to misery in two parts of the world. We have depopulated America in order to clear land to plant them and we are depopulating Africa to find workers to harvest them." In his 1759 work, Voltaire's Candide meets a black slave in Surinam without his right hand or his leg and asks him who had treated him so cruelly. The slave answers: "When we work in the sugar mills and the grindstone catches a finger, they cut off the hand; when we try to run away, they cut off a leg. Both these things happened to me. This is the price paid for the sugar you eat in Europe." Montesquieu in his *L'Esprit des lois* (1748) had earlier linked sugar and slavery: "Sugar would be too expensive if one could not get slaves to produce it."[53] Historian Hugh Thomas calculates that some eleven million Africans were sequestered to the New World estates, over two-thirds of them to sugar plantations.[54] Strong suggests 1750 as the date for the awakening of social protest over the stigma of slavery attached to sugar, and quotes Helvétius: "No cask of sugar arrives in Europe, to which blood is not sticking."[55]

It was on the basis of his comment linking sugar and slavery that Vissière reads Bernardin's travel account as one of the Enlightenment's most vibrant anti-slavery manifestos.[56] The surprise is that this view is not more widespread. With time, Bernardin's denunciation of slavery has become documentary evidence (used by Nwulia in his archival study of slavery in Mauritius). Bernardin's testimony to the abuses of slavery in Mauritius has even influenced later travellers to the island, despite the attempt of Mauritians to suppress it. For example, Julian Mockford, in 1950, cited Bernardin on maroons and slaves, to conclude: "Almost every cave and dense forest region in Mauritius is haunted by the memory of such cold-blooded murder and callous Christianity. It does not do to inquire too zealously into curious place-names which are neither French nor Dutch, for they will be Malagasy or African, and the gruesome past will unbury itself."[57]

One can read Bernardin's later best-selling romance *Paul et Virginie* as an anti-European colonialism work, grounded in his horror of slavery.[58] There are two well-known incidents in the novel involving runaway slaves. The first is when an old slave woman, barely a skeleton, arrives at Paul and Virginie's huts up on the hill above Port Louis begging for food after running away from a plantation on Rivière Noire where she has been whipped. Virginie takes her back and pleads for her release. The slave owner pretends that he will do what she asked, but later Paul and Virginie learn that the runaway slave woman was chained and whipped even more. The second incident comes when Paul and Virginie are lost in the forests and are rescued and carried home by a gang of runaways who, far from the colonial view of them as murderers, are depicted by Bernardin as humane and caring for the lost white children. The final irony is that the fatherless children, with their single mothers and well-treated servants, are all dressed in rough Bengal blue linen, "like slaves".[59] In fact, one could say that the little mountain slope "bassin" or nest where Paul and Virginie live in a communal utopia is like a runaway slave colony, except that these whites are running away from the corrupt values of colonial Port Louis and the Europe it mimics. Many contemporary readers sided with Bernardin's portrayal of slaves in the novel; its success increased the stagnant sales of the earlier *Journey* and led to Bernardin being proposed by the Marquis de Condorcet as secretary to the newly founded Société des Amis des Noirs in 1788. Souriau even claimed that black slaves were better treated by Mauritian planters, thanks to the novel.[60]

Throughout the eighteenth century, slaves represented four-fifths of the total population of the island. These slaves had been first brought over from Madagascar (today the Malagasy Republic), then mainly from today's Mozambique (Portuguese East Africa), with some from Senegal, from Malay and from Pondicherry, French India, while the Compagnie des Indes ran the island. The slaves were used for domestic service, to clear the red earth of volcanic rocks and boulders (mounds visible today everywhere in the cane fields), and to work the fields, as sugarcane slowly came to dominate the economy. The slaves lived in *camps des noirs* and were supposedly protected by Jean-Baptiste Colbert's *Code Noir*.[61]

It is around this *Code Noir* that some of the limitations of Bernardin's anti-slavery opinions have been located. The 1685 Code was not abolitionist, but religious. It expelled Jews from the recent colonies and ensured that slaves should be baptized, raised as Catholics, buried in holy ground and given Sundays and feast days off (articles 2, 6, 14). It detailed diet with portions of manioc, salted beef or fish (article 22) and tried to force planters to look after old slaves (27). However, it also listed punishments, for example, for stealing food, to be branded with a "fleur de lis"; for running away, to have an ear cut off and be branded with a "fleur de lis", and a second time, to be ham-strung (article 38).[62] In 1723 the Code was amended to control relationships, especially sexual relationships, between white and non-white in the French colonies, given the imbalance between men and women in emigration to the colonies and the general lack of women. But more had to be done, and

Intendant Poivre and Governor Dumas rewrote the *Code Noir* in 1767 to ensure (on paper) that slave-owners carried out the original articles, with some rights of complaint. But the reality was different, as Bernardin realized on arrival in 1768. That is why his book has an engraving on its frontispiece of Bernardin with a copy of the *Code Noir*. If Bernardin was ahead of his time, he also argued, quoting Pliny, that whites were superior to blacks and suggested that whites have more spirit and courage than blacks and Asians (but he recanted this view in his proposed second edition). But if he was inevitably racist, as were all thinkers of the time, one thing he loathed, which modified his racism, was cruelty.

Two stories contradict each other during Bernardin's stay on Mauritius: one was that slaves were happy in Mauritius; the other that the white landowners lived in constant fear of *marrons* or runaway slaves. Colonial Mauritius was, according to Blair Allen, plagued by problems of *marronage*.[63] He cites an English naval lieutenant in 1772 (two years after Bernardin left the island) who reported three to four thousand runaway slaves, while a French navy controller calculated in 1775 some 1,200 runaways. Blair Allen surveyed the capture-books listing runaway slaves and found 465 for 1773 and 510 for 1775. He concluded that *marronage* was a widespread and constant feature of Mauritian colonial life through the eighteenth and early nineteenth century.[64] However, as the island was so small, most runaways were re-captured within a month. In the 1870s there were still maroon hunts, but now for indentured Indian runaways. Over the colonial period there were specially-trained maroon hunters, and slaves could be graded according to their propensity for running away (those from Madagascar fled most, often trying to get back home by pirogue, while the Indians escaped least). The fear of maroon vengeance was a powerful motive for keeping the slaves in order.

So necessary was slavery for economic prosperity that it lasted beyond the French Revolutionary Convention's emancipation of the slaves in 1794 (releasing some 70,000 slaves in the French colonies). This Mauritius ignored, becoming a rebel colony between 1794 and 1802, when Napoleon restored slavery in the colonies, until the British took over in 1810. Even then, illicit slave trading, crucial to work on the thriving sugar plantations, continued, as Nwulia and Barker have shown. The powerful French landowners managed to have the agent for the Anti-Slavery Society, John Jeremie, expelled from the island twice, in 1832 and in 1834.[65] Slavery was only finally abolished in Mauritius under the British in 1835. Huge compensation was paid out, thanks to Mauritian Adrien d'Epinay's negotiations in England. And the slavery void had to be filled and was with workers brought in from India as indentured labor. Though these migrant workers were given contracts and were able to return to India, indentured labor was all but slavery in name. However, in time, indentureship would completely transform the ethnic balance of the island. Between 1834 and 1909, 451,786 laborers arrived in Mauritius from India, and some 294,197 stayed on to become the dominant ethnic group on the island today. Bernardin, who admired the Malabars as they were then called, would have been delighted with this change.

According to Basdeo Bissoondoyal, the sufferings of Indian immigrants in Mauritius were worse than those of the black slaves,[66] and he fought politically to give them back their dignity. The history of this fight (with the Labour Party equally involved) for a voice and a vote is the history of Mauritius itself, with key events like the 1885 Constitution, the 1937 strike and the 1943 hunger march as milestones towards final independence. Toussaint, in his short history of Mauritius, noted in 1971 that the most serious deficiency of Mauritius lay in its social conditions, and that the laborers and the poor in general lived in "utter misery".[67] So Bernardin's exposure of "slavery" continued to be pertinent, attested by Basdeo Bissoondoyal's inspiration in his writing.

Resistance to Bernardin's revelations about the horrors of slavery ran parallel to fear that abolition would scupper the planters' privileges. C. Thomi Pitot, in the name of his fellow plantation owners, gave a speech in 1805, published serially in 1842 in the newspaper *Le Cernéen* and in full in 1888–89 (i.e. reprinted throughout the nineteenth century), voicing rage at the way Bernardin had drawn false attention to their treatment of slaves. Pitot combs Bernardin's famous Letter 12 (of 1769) in his *Journey* concerning the fate of the blacks, and, reading him closely, refutes him point by point. Pitot's stance is that of the local witness against the European passerby; he asserts his eyewitness experiences to counter Bernardin's fictions. He also defends his colonial honor, feeling like a David against the Goliath of Bernardin, who was still alive and famous at the time of the speech (1805). Pitot was writing against the French Revolution's abolition of slavery (never applied in far-off Mauritius), and offers Haiti as an example of the mayhem that comes about when slaves are freed. He makes several interrelated points: the colony was very recent; slaves were happier in Mauritius than peasants in miserable Europe; so-called debauchery was not as bad as prostitution in Europe; in all, slaves were happy and well-looked after. He points out lies (slaves were *not* executed every day), mistakes (Bernardin confused "fête banane" with "fête de bonne année"); mocks Bernardin's hypocrisy in buying and overloading his two slaves when touring the island, picks on an odd adjective used by Bernardin who called tropical vegetables "monstrous", and puzzles over why Bernardin showed such bitterness. Pitot does catch Bernardin out in some contradictions; there might be some truth to an obscure "*personal resent*"[68] driving Bernardin's jaundiced view, for in later writings like *Paul et Virginie* he turns the Mauritian tropics into a paradise. In confirmation of Bernardin's prestige, Pitot called that other abolitionist Bishop Wilberforce, the "Bernardin of England".[69] According to d'Epinay, Bernardin read this refutation, but did not answer.

More or less at the same dates, the young, reckless Edward Trelawny (1792–1881), who years later would burn Shelley on a pyre in the Bay of Spezia, Italy, claimed he was working for an American privateer called De Ruyter (now established as modelled on the fearsome pirate Robert Surcouf), who had a grand plantation house in Mauritius. He arrived on the island with his Moslem princess Zela who had been offered him in marriage by a dying father during one of their raids on Madagascar to eliminate pirates, and with whom he had fallen in love. In his autobiographical *The Adventures of a Younger Son* (1831), now confirmed as largely fictional (he did not desert, never met De Ruyter/Surcouf, nor fell for Zela), he lands at Port Louis after the English invasion and witnesses the slaves:

> *While they are talking of humanity, they will lash the bare and festered back of an overloaded female slave, her tender nature one animated mass of ulcers and cancers, half consumed by flies and maggots... I have seen men with*

their spines knotted like pine trees and their skin as scaled and callous, the flesh cracked into chasms from which the blood oozed out like gum. I have seen hundreds of these poor wretches undergoing their daily toil in the dockyards of Port Louis and the pity and pain I felt at the sight of these poor slaves could only be equalled by the deep and overwhelming damnation I invoked on the heads of their oppressors forever.[70]

Trelawny is not the only supporting witness to Bernardin's claims. *Intendant* Poivre's cousin, Pierre Sonnerat, arrived in Mauritius in 1768, the same year as Bernardin, and also saw that most landowners exercised a "cruel and revolting tyranny" over their slaves.[71]

So much for Pitot's pleadings of 1805. In fact, Pitot, who ignores Sonnerat, absurdly claimed that Trelawny was an adventurer who took revenge on Mauritius because he had failed to sell his cargo of skinny buffaloes and mangy donkeys.[72]

In the 1830s the newspaper founded by Adrien d'Epinay, *Le Cernéen* (after the Portuguese name for the island), published a letter from one of Pitot's slaves called Pèdre, addressed to the English MP Mr. Buxton, where this literate slave of 110 years ironically asked if he could be cared for in England as well as he was in Mauritius. Clearly no slave could have written that letter, and it tapped into that plantation-owner self-justifying myth of "treating slaves so well that they are happy with being slaves". That the newspaper owned by d'Epinay could publish such a letter under British rule is confirmed by the fact that it was d'Epinay who travelled to Britain twice to negotiate adequate compensation after the abolition of slavery in 1835, which was awarded, to the delight of the French land-owners (d'Epinay died in France in 1839).

A later descendant, also called Adrien d'Epinay, continued to malign Bernardin in 1890 by calling him bitter, morose and disillusioned, daring to pay back his island hosts by casting a gratuitous slur on the Creoles; all in all, a "spiteful philosopher".[73] Another Mauritian descendant, this time of Pitot's, continued Bernardin's character assassination. Albert Pitot, in what purports to be a historical sketch, repeated the allegations of Bernardin's "dark and hypochondriacal character of a spoilt child", his colossal egoism and excessive rancor to discount the writer's witnessing of colonial slavery.[74]

A hostile tone concerning Bernardin's account was still displayed in

1939 when the Mauritian historian Auguste Toussaint outlined Bernardin's years on the island, accused him of being a misanthrope,[75] writing banal notes, too much satire, and ignoring the beauty of the island to concentrate on the condition of slaves. Toussaint's position is that of the hurt patriot; the *Voyage à l'Isle de France* was only written to make Europe take pity on the destiny of the slaves.[76] For Toussaint it was a wicked piece of work, with gross calumnies motivated by Bernardin's rancor.

In 1954 Alix d'Unienville attempted, as a Mauritian, to give a balanced view of Bernardin's critique of the land-owning, slave-owning whites. He argued that Bernardin owed his fame to Mauritius, not the other way round, and confirmed that Bernardin wrote with bitterness and was himself a nasty little man, with a wicked character and detestable morals. He also accused him of his greatest crime, that of trying to seduce Poivre's virtuous wife. The key to d'Unienville's biased summary is that those slave-owners Bernardin criticized in 1773 were the ancestors of those (French landowners) of pre-independence Mauritius. Bernardin's final sin was to illustrate his thesis, distorting facts that did not fit (but no examples are given).[77] There is a long history, then, of local irritation with Bernardin's anti-slavery sympathies (stretching from 1805 to 1954).

Yet Bernardin's portrayal of slavery in Mauritius has stood the test of time, and his eyewitness recording has become a document. The frontispiece of the first edition of the *Journey* gives his intentions away: you can see a naked slave in chains, with his severed leg resting on one of Bernardin's charts, beseechingly showing a copy of the *Code Noir* to a writer at a table, with a spaniel at his feet and shells and botanical specimen on the ground, under the roof of a typical verandah looking out to Port Louis harbor. The writer, of course, is none other than Bernardin himself. Charles Pridham, in 1849, in a section on the slave trade and slavery in Mauritius, cited pages from the "horrid" cruelties related by Bernardin. Pridham praised Bernardin as the only French writer to have the courage to touch upon the condition of slaves and concluded that "we cannot but place the greatest reliance on his truthfulness."[78] That Bernardin himself bought a slave has been used against the truth of his testimony, and this is a crucial point to bear in mind, for he was shocked more by the inhumanity of the treatment of

slaves, hoping to apply the *Code Noir* justly, rather than wishing to abolish slavery altogether.

In 1903 the Abbé Ducrocq still felt that Bernardin needed defending from the "cruel hatred" of the Mauritian descendants of those who felt insulted by him. Despite Bernardin being attacked with senseless violence, Ducrocq called him a martyr to the truth in the anti-slavery movement, corroborated by all the documents he had consulted, and claimed that that blood had stained all plantation owners in Mauritius. Ducrocq defended Bernardin's virtue, his honesty concerning money, sexual and political favors and religion during the Revolution, arguing that he was a truly "good" man whose testimony can be trusted.

The actuality of Bernardin's travel writing is mirrored by this sad history of slavery, starting with the original maroons left behind by the Dutch in 1710, through the century of African slavery and on to indentured laborers from India. Behind this story of abuse and indignity runs the thread of racism, of class disgust by *blanc* for black still alive today. In 1952 Michael Malim met few educated Mauritians free from color-prejudice, and discovered that it was "deep and bitter".[79] History has left the island divided into ethnic groups where racism is not solely color-determined, for Creoles despise Hindus and whites, who despise them in turn.[80]

But this racial tension and blending has also created the lively multiculturalism of Mauritius today. After all, as Anthony Barker has argued, Mauritius was an "ethnic melting-pot in the era of slavery" as slaves came from all over the Indian Ocean rim, from Indonesia, Malaya, India, Zanzibar, Mozambique, Madagascar, and even further afield. This "ethnic variety" was the most striking feature of slavery in Mauritius when compared to the New World.[81] Charles Darwin in 1835 found in the various races Port Louis' most interesting spectacle.[82] Alexandre Dumas set his novel *George, or, The Planter of the Isle of France* in this "strange mixed population".[83] Mark Twain saw the consequence of slavery's miscegenation in 1896 when he described Port Louis as having the "largest variety of nationalities and complexions we have encountered yet", listing French, English, Chinese, Arabs, Africans "with wool", blacks with straight hair, East Indians, half-whites, quadroons etc., thus making Port Louis genuinely multicultural years before that word was bandied about.[84] The outcome of slavery, together with the island's strategic position, led the Hindu educator Basdeo Bissoondoyal to claim that the truth of Mauritius was its "mosaic" of races.[85] Malim speaks for many observers of this Mauritian uniqueness: "Kipling was wrong. Evidently he never came to Mauritius. East and West *have* met here. And South. Lord knows what sort of a hotch-potch is being brewed out of it. It looks fascinating."[86]

Paul et Virginie

This romance put Mauritius on the literary map forever (and also made Bernardin famous and rich). Through writing the novel he returned in memory to the island some seventeen years later, the same island that he had so severely criticized, and where his unhappiness and sense of abandonment in a backwater had colored his vision of the place. But passing time and a hard life in Europe had mellowed his critique of the island in the earlier travel book, and in his romance he converted an area above Port Louis on the slopes of the Pouce mountain into a paradise, a *locus amenus*. The story of the intimate and ideal relationship between Paul and Virginie tells of a fulfilling happiness ruined by Virginie being bribed and sent back to France to complete her white colonist's education, and by nascent sexuality. The tragedy is completed on her return by a shipwreck and a decisive moment of outrageous modesty (Virginie refuses to let a sailor touch her and thus save her), making the story a bestseller all over Europe, especially with women readers. From Europe it was read as a heartrending exotic dream, even by a *maudit* reader like the poet Isidore Ducasse, Comte de Lautréamont, who asserted that *Paul et Virginie* shocks our deepest aspirations for happiness (though this pessimistic novel once irritated him).[87]

However, those who had actually been to the island read it in a different way; closer to a travel-novel. The anonymous officer, who narrated the published account of the English victory of 1810, noted the pleasing and minutely accurate picture in the admired story of *Paul and Virginia*;[88] it was "minutely accurate" because he was on the spot, testing the novel. In 1859 the Rev. Patrick Beaton praised Bernardin's "faithful and comprehensive picture of the natural scenery of the island"; this reverend's five years on the island confirmed an "air of reality" throughout the work "which owes little to the author's imagination".[89] Mauritian historian Auguste Toussaint in 1939 preferred the novel to the travel account in terms of it being a better, more accurate description of tropical nature, with smells, sounds and sights. In one sense, the real protagonist of the romance is Mauritian landscape; it is an immense hymn to tropical nature.[90]

Another way of testing Bernardin's accuracy can be seen in how the travelling scientist Alexander von Humboldt[91] eulogized this novel in *Kosmos* (1845–62) "for the wonderful truth with which [it] paints the power of nature in the tropical zone". Humboldt admired Bernardin "because he knew nature not as a scientist, but because he felt it in all its harmonious links." Humboldt's ability to "test" the novel came from his own five years in the tropics of South America (from 1799–1804). While on the banks of the great Orinoco river and looking up at the Southern Cross, Humboldt was reminded of that "moving scene where Paul and Virginie, seated near the source of the Lataniers river, chat together for the last time, and where the old man, at the sight of the Southern Cross, warns them that it is time to separate!" Humboldt, on the banks of the vivid Orinoco, was transported in his mind to another river, the Lataniers in Mauritius, which disembogues near Port Louis and whose source is below the Pouce mountain. Humboldt travelled through South America for five years with a pocket edition of *Paul et Virginie* always accompanying him.

Bernardin himself read his own "novel" in the same way. In the "avant-propos" to the 1793 pocket edition (the one Humboldt owned, and the one I cite from), he outlined his intentions. The first was to "paint a soil and vegetation different from those of Europe." He wanted to set his doomed lovers where he himself had sat, by the sea, under rocks, shaded by coconut and banana trees. He then wanted to embody in his characters moral truths about nature and virtue, but did not need to invent anything: "I can assure you that those who I am going to talk about really existed, and that their story is true." It is that old Cervantine subterfuge, it seems, of claiming fiction as history, but Bernardin scorns fiction; after all, *Paul et Virginie* first appeared in a book of essays, and he self-deprecatingly called this story a "faible" (weak) essay.[92] Souriau quoted a draft version of this foreword, found in the Le Havre archives, where Bernardin added that he had often walked up to the little valley on the slope and seen the ruins of two little huts.[93] Why, in 1806, Bernardin removed this "avant-propos" from all further editions of his romance I cannot guess.

Bernardin intended a two-level reading. The first I would call a traveller's tale, a geographic evocation of a small tropical island during Labourdonnais' governorship on to which the second level is fitted: two lovers embodying values of happiness, love, virtue and tenderness (utopian day-dreams) fast disappearing from Europe. (Fascinatingly the pocket edition first appeared in 1789 as Paris exploded into mob rule and revolutionary passion.) The opening of the romance confirms how essential topographical accuracy was to Bernardin, and prolongs the accuracy of his earlier travel book: "On the Eastern slope of a mountain that rises behind Port Louis in Mauritius, you can see two ruined huts on a piece of land that was formerly cultivated."[94] This opening narrator is clearly Bernardin himself, writing from when he was on the island, exploring the *ruins* of Paul and Virginie's huts and then listening to the old man's story of their ill-fated love, set some thirty years before.

The story then is rooted in place, as if taken from a travel book, with the hillside bowl where widowed Madame de la Tour and her daughter Virginie live with the ostracized Marguerite and her bastard-son Paul. This nest high on the hill above Port Louis offers a view on to the Morne de la Découverte, on to Pamplemousses (now the Botanical Gardens), its church, and the Baie du Tombeau and Cap Malheureux. This protected bowl is the source of the Lataniers river. In 1801, J. B. G. M. Bory de St. Vincent (1780–1846), the naturalist on Baudin's voyage who was forced to remain in Mauritius, walked up to where Bernardin placed Paul and Virginie's huts, still half-wild.[95] Looking for the remains, he exclaimed: "How often have I wandered in this valley reading Bernardin's novel," weeping as he walked up the Lataniers river. He located two coconut trees, like the ones planted by Paul and Virginie, whose leaves intertwined. The murmur of their leaves seemed to tell him that Paul and Virginie really existed. For Bory de St. Vincent, as for many others on the island, this novel was a historical fact. In 1802 the artist M. J. Milbert (1766–1840), also forced by illness to abandon his ship under Captain Baudin and remain in Mauritius for three years

(1801–1804), climbed up to this site. In his *Voyage pittoresque à l'île de France* (1812) he quoted the opening of the novel as a description of the site, adding notes to show how this site had changed over the lapse of thirty years. The first note refers to the cutting down of the forests for sugarcane fields; the second to the logging of the now rare *latanier* palm trees in the bowl, leading to a drying-up of the area; and the third refers to the cutting down of the two palm trees, due as much to a need to clear the ground as to greed for the succulent "coeur de palmiste".[96] Milbert then drew the hillside site with the two palm trees re-instated.

Edward Trelawny lived an idyll close to that of Paul and Virginie when he claimed that he rested in Mauritius in De Ruyter's plantation house up on the plains. De Ruyter, rich and cunning from privateering, refused to have slaves, and Edward and Zela avoided Port Louis society,

walking about barefoot in imitation of the fictionalized lovers Paul and Virginie. That Zela would die poisoned by a jealous widow in Edward's arms as they reached Mauritius in 1810 mocks the coincidences between life and fiction, and confirms that the whole episode was a fantasy on Trelawny's part, spawned by his reading of Bernardin's book. Zela was burned in a pyre on a Mauritian beach (as Shelley would be later incinerated on an Italian beach, while Trelawny ripped the poet's heart out in front of Byron). Even the Malay slave girl Adoo died in grief, as did the faithful servants in the romance. Trelawny had read *Paul et Virginie* and Rousseau while at sea, and invented his ill-fated love affair with Zela while blockading Paul and Virginie's tropical island with the British fleet.

Sea-Voyages and Writing

When Bernardin returned to France in 1770, he set about publishing the letters, diary entries and dialogues he had written but not sent home as a book, in what would be a quasi-epistolary travel account. Keeping mainly to the letter-genre allowed Bernardin to establish his sincerity, an aesthetic term promoted by Jean-Jacques Rousseau. Epistolary novels were all the rage in eighteenth-century France; Rousseau himself had published *La nouvelle Héloïse* in letter form so that letters grouping topics became "an outlet for his own opinions".[97] Bernardin followed Rousseau's lead by also collecting his opinions in letters with sub-headings. Bernardin thought the letter form the most sincere of all genres.

In Letter 28 Bernardin laments that he has no travel-writing models to imitate: "We lack a model in such a fascinating genre," he wrote. Not much earlier, in 1755, in his *A Discourse on Inequality*, Rousseau had complained, with examples, about how badly travellers observed, and how prejudiced they were, only confirming what they already knew. "The real features which distinguish nations, and which strike eyes made to see them, have almost always escaped their notice," he concluded. The point of travel for Rousseau was to "shake off national prejudices" and to learn to study "man and customs". After travelling the world, this new kind of philosophical tourist would then write up his experiences and the reader would see "a new world spring from under their pens" and "learn thereby to know our own world".[98]

Bernardin took up this challenge. For him at that time, travel writing was a new, unexplored genre. In pondering how to write about his experiences, he offered several interrelated critiques and problems. One concerned the contents of the travel book. It pre-supposed what he called "universal knowledge"; the traveller needed to know a little about everything, to have a Renaissance breadth of learning. A travel book also needed order and a plan, if not a plot. Then there were stylistic problems of excessive wit taking over from factual observing. Further, the reader needed to trust the writer, whose main virtue should be "sincerity". However, Bernardin was faced with one overwhelming problem: "You must speak about everything" and yet avoid diffusion; too many isolated facts, unrelated incidents would create an aesthetic mess. He solves these problems by simply publishing his letters home, and interpolating them with mini-essays; often the letters have subtitles, like an essay.

Bernardin had done his homework; he lists previous travel writers and reveals their defects and limitations: too bookish, too cultural, or ignorant of nature. He states his credo quite nakedly: "I prefer the tendril of a vine to a column; and I would have preferred to have enriched my homeland with one nutritious plant than with Scipio's silver shield."[99] He laments a lack of vocabulary for evoking nature in comparison to the vocabulary developed for describing architectural monuments. Worse, all countries tend to blend into similarities: "... travellers render natural objects so poorly. If they paint a country, you will see towns, rivers, mountains: but their descriptions are arid like geographical maps: India is no different to Europe." Somehow, language cannot capture the "peculiar characteristics" of place. This problem is intrinsic to the nature of words, of course, but good travel writing depends on the inner quality of the traveller, and this Bernardin calls his "sincerity", his open feelings, his vulnerability.

This critique of travel writing suggests that it is the mind of the traveller that makes his text interesting, not where he has been. Samuel Johnson, writing at much the same time, thought the same: "Books of travels will be good in proportion to what a man has previously in his mind; his knowing what to observe; his power of contrasting one mode of life with another." It is Bernardin himself who holds our attention with his gripes about colonial society.

His last area of criticism concerns the perverse lure of abroad. After ten years travelling, Bernardin objected to travellers placing happiness elsewhere, abroad. This is a psychological critique. For Bernardin, Paris was the centre of the world because it embodied the freedom to be. Bernardin defined this freedom as "he who loves freedom depends on nobody but heaven itself." To depend on slavery in Africa, in America, in Mauritius, was depraved. Thus, he argued, Europe was more precious, its peasants more resourceful, its food, its wheat, its vines more nutritious. In that home versus abroad conflict, Bernardin chose the familiarity and happiness of home and saw travel as a journey into guilt: "the sight of one single person in misery can poison happiness." Bernardin closed his letter on the vicissitudes of travel writing, of travelling away from beloved home, pleading that his book might wipe away the tears of the "unhappy black slave weeping on the rocks at Mauritius" and make the tyrants regret and repent. His work, he concludes, will have a moral purpose; it will incite its guilty readers to fight slavery by wounding their hearts, by making them cry—as he so successfully made them do in his romance *Paul et Virginie*.

Bernardin was not alone in finding the travel account in its tricky infancy. While he was mulling over these problems, a man he met in Mauritius in 1768, Louis-Antoine de Bougainville, found himself faced with identical issues as he prepared his *Voyage de la frégate La Boudeuse et de la flute l'Étoile autour du monde*, which appeared in Paris in 1771. In his "discours préliminaire" Bougainville enumerates the 13 round-the-world journeys that preceded his (like Bernardin, he had done his library reading). In a note to the second edition, Bougainville thanks M. Forster, his translator into English, for referring to three further round-the-globe trips, including Forster's own under Cook.[100] Bougainville states that not one of these previous journeys was by a Frenchman. He then lists all those others who had sailed to foreign parts. This recount allows Bougainville to claim himself, with Cook, as the first moderns to circle the earth.

What does "modern" mean? First, that his account is not "a work of amusement"; he was trained as a scientist and not as a writer, and at the age of 25 had published a two-volume treatise on integral calculus (*Traité de calcul intégral*), being something of a mathematical prodigy.[101] This claim to modernity is to his advantage, because what he is really saying is that he is writing the "truth": "I am now far from the sanctuary of science and literature; my ideas and my style have more than taken the imprint of the wild, errant life that I have been leading for the last twelve years."[102] From this rough sailor's life (true to real experiences overseas), Bougainville then attacks armchair philosophers and vicarious travellers (he constantly mocked Rousseau) in his concluding outburst: "I am a traveller and sailor, that is a liar and a fool in the eyes of that lazy, superb class of writers, who in the shadows of their studies, philosophize until the cows come home about the world and its inhabitants and imperiously submit nature to their fantasies."[103] A traveller is by definition a liar, telling tall tales that cannot be disproved by the stay-at-homes, and both he and Bernardin argue their ways to reversing this prejudice by exposing the defects in previous travel accounts and claiming to tell the truth. Bernardin's earlier critique of travel writing is more detailed, but both grapple with accuracy, based on having been there as "moderns".

In 1804 Bory de St. Vincent continued to discuss a travel writer's problems. He felt constrained by having been at sea and abroad for so long that he had not been able to keep up with "sedentary learning in Europe";[104] like Bougainville, simply being on ship prevented him improving his style of writing, as there was no library on board. He also felt that his readers back home in Europe would doubt everything that was extraordinary. Further, there are so many ways of seeing and describing any one thing or incident, and worst of all, that a travel writer has to talk incessantly about himself; despite Montaigne's famous dictum that "the I is odious," the phrase "I have seen" is repeated endlessly. Such constant doubt about travel writing ensured that there was no blind confidence in the genre and made the writing fresh, alive, unpredictable.

At a more technical level, Bernardin censured the Abbé de Choisy for skipping the tedium of the actual sea journey out. Bernardin contradicted what the young sailor Trelawny would later claim: "Ordinary events during a voyage do not bear relating."[105] If we compare Bernardin's log of events at sea to that of another famous sea-traveller, namely Captain Cook, who had his account of his first voyage on the *Endeavour* ghosted by Hawkesworth and published in 1773, then we can see what he meant, for Cook does not convey the daily experience of sea-journeys and reaches his destination in a few paragraphs, while Bernardin takes pages and ages. Finally, one last contrast with Bernardin: Joseph Banks had accompanied Cook and kept a long, impersonal journal that was partially used by Hawkesworth. Finally published in 1962, the book was, in the words of a biographer, the work of "a voyaging eye, and this eye was turned perpetually outwards."[106] Extreme reticence and an awareness of public scrutiny (his journal was copied out and passed among friends) ensured that this account was also laconic about the intimate Banks. In comparison, Bernardin gained from not being an *official* writer.

So much for the travel account. What about travelling itself? As already noted, Bernardin spent some ten years on the move around Europe and the Indian Ocean, and meshed his views on the benefits and penalties of travel into his travel book, forming part of his frame of perception. The crucial point is that Bernardin deflated travel as mind-broadening. In many places in his *Journey* the restless, rootless life of the traveller is subverted by a powerful nostalgia for a quiet, stable and rural home. This nostalgia for stasis and human warmth, away from society and aloof from corruption, forms the bedrock of his romance *Paul et Virginie;* in Guyot's words, it reveals a constant "nostalgia for an idealized French countryside".[107] In his author's preface of 1773 to the *Journey*, Bernardin hoped that his book would prevent all emigration and cajole his readers into cultivating their own patch of land at home. Yves Bénot has called the book an "anti-voyage", a travel book that advises against travel. Travelling had awoken Bernardin's patriotism, his unconscious love of French soil. It was this discovery that made it impossible for him to love Mauritius.

Yet had he not travelled, he might not have found his roots. Bernardin is clear: "To truly love your country, you must quit it." This he has probably learnt from his mentor Rousseau, as Guyot pointed out, who in his novel *Emile*, made his character travel as part of his education for two years before returning to a quiet corner of France. Only travel abroad allows you to find your real roots. And as we saw, this Candide-like moral includes finding the right woman, and having children.

Natural History and the Dodo

Bernardin laid no claims to being a natural historian, although Charles Darwin called his travel writing "extremely interesting".[108] There are many asides in the *Journey* about this deficiency: "Please note that I know nothing about botany"; or "I have read all that has been written on the formation of shells and do not understand anything." Back in Paris, Louis Leclerc, known as Count Buffon, was churning out, from 1749, his systematic taxonomies, without bothering to travel himself; the work was titled *Histoire naturelle, générale et particulière* and had reached volume 36 before he died, leaving it uncompleted (Bernardin would succeed him as Director of the Jardin des Plantes). In Sweden Linnaeus, the Latinized version of Carl von Linné, a traveller himself (but mainly around Sweden), was building up his new classification system from 1735 (*Systema naturae*) thanks to wide-roaming botanists like fellow Swede Dr. Daniel Carl Solander (1736–1783) who accompanied Joseph Banks on Cook's first world tour, 1768–1771 and who sent him back specimens.[109] The mapping of world natural history was in its infancy. In fact, Cook's, with Bougainville's, could be called the first scientific sea-voyages, and these voyages coincided in time with Bernardin's.

The writer who gives the best sense of this new period of outdoor research is Gilbert White, whose *The Natural History of Selborn* (1788) covers the same ground and reveals the same mind-frame as Bernardin's. Bernardin knew that nobody had described Mauritius, even though *Intendant* Poivre was a leading figure in the taxonomic revolution, and was Bernardin's mentor, especially in botany. Bernardin suffered severe defects in his descriptions of fish, trees, animals and flowers (and later critics would find it hard to know to what exactly he was referring).[110] Part of the problem was due to the age he lived in, one of incipient, stuttering sciences (Allen noted that the first reference to a geological hammer was in 1696, to a butterfly net in 1711),[111] and part was intrinsic to the nature of words themselves. Bernardin did not draw or illustrate his plants and trees (although the few illustrations in his book were from his hand); he could not tag Latin names to anything as he had not studied the new Linnaean system; and he did not collect and bring home his natural history booty in cabinets for specialists to ponder over, as Cook and later Humboldt had (for example, Cook returned in 1771 with over 1,000 new plant species). He even concocted his own system, based on a design developed from his engineering days, as in his section on seashells and his corresponding engraving. A modern reader is hence left struggling with imprecise words and analogies, unable to capture particularities. Bernardin was still a classicist, and ransacked Pliny, Plutarch and others for equivalents in nature; he was not alone in this failure to see that words are generic and Platonic. What is clear is that he tried to use his five senses to capture each item described (he tastes, bites, relates tales and superstitions) so an updating of his scientific endeavour would need to include visual and scientific descriptions in the notes, as well as local Creole names.

Bernardin developed a notion that science and feeling could be combined; he insisted to the point of public ridicule that the tides were created by the melting and freezing of the poles;[112] he thought telescopes kept the observer emotionally distant from the stars under observation. His later *Etudes de la nature* are more a "religious manual", as Souriau pointed out back in 1905, than a contribution to science; this would explain his phenomenal success with readers.

The oddest omission in the first edition of Bernardin's *Journey* was that of the dodo, which he remedied in the projected second edition. The dodo, totemic bird of Mauritius, embodies a sad ecological allegory about European expansion, for whether it was Dutch sailors or the hordes of rats, pigs and monkeys that finished off this heavy, flightless bird (with a sharp, powerful beak) is irrelevant because all its predators came from outside the island, together. Buffon called the dodo a "dronte" and gave an accurate description of it in his *Histoire naturelle*, claiming that it had died out because it was flightless, stupid and ugly.[113] But the name dodo came to represent this large bird, not "dronte"; dodo, claimed to be from the Portuguese *doudo* for stupid (though not in my two-volume Portuguese dictionary), was used by sailors because the bird was so stupid and so easily killed, and this name stuck. Masauji Hachisuka tried to establish that the last living dodos were described in Benjamin Harry's visit to Mauritius in 1681, though Perry Moree found a reference in a sailor's journal about capturing two live dodos in 1688.[114] By 1693, some eighty years before Bernardin's account, François Leguat enumerated many Mauritian birds, but did not mention the dodo.[115] By 1755 the dodo at the Ashmolean Museum in Oxford, though partially destroyed by fire, began to intrigue specialists, who even questioned whether it had really existed or not (no complete specimen survives). Only in 1828 did J. S. Duncan at Oxford prove that the dodo (*Raphus cucullatus [Didus ineptus]*) had existed, and from then it entered popular mythology as one of nature's freaks. Popularized by Lewis Carroll in the opening of his *Alice's Adventures in Wonderland* (1865), with a famous drawing by Sir John Tenniel, the bird became a verbal cliché ("dead as a dodo") and was finally exported back to Mauritius as an imperial emblem on stamps, in tourist brochures, and as the name of an elite white French club.[116] In 1874 George Clark found a skeleton in Mauritius, symbolically preserved in the "La Mare aux Songes" near today's airport, where "songe" is not a dream, but the edible *Calidum esculentum*, added to the best Creole dishes. David Quammen made the dodo the symbol of the way man has caused, and is causing, so many species to disappear; according to Carl Jones in Mauritius, its extinction made man realize for the first time that he had caused the loss of a species. Interestingly, he suggests that the word dodo was the bird's song, its swan song, "doo-doo".[117] In a recent television programme (*Extinct*), a DNA test proved that the dodo was from the Asian pigeon family.[118]

Another species mentioned by Bernardin, but on the verge of extinction by the time of his stay was the giant Mauritian tortoise of which there were two species: the *Geochelane inepta* and the *Geochelane triserrata*. According to Quammen, sailors stacked hundreds at a time upside down in the holds of their boats, thus keeping them alive to be eaten at sea. By 1780, soon after Bernardin's stay, they were extremely rare. Today the Aldabra giant tortoises are being bred on the island at the Vanille Crocodile Park, Rivière-des-Anguilles, and there is a scheme to restore these tortoises, which live for hundreds of years, back to the island of Rodrigues.

Colonial Society

In a draft version of his book called *Voyages de Codrus*, Bernardin summed up his view of colonial Mauritius: "I found more discord in that island than with the Phoenicians, more poverty than with the Scythians, a despotism that was harsher than that in any barbarian's court. Most of the people were reduced to slavery and were more miserable than animals. There was no freedom, no society, nor emulation of honesty. Any mental talents made you enemies."[119] In

Letter 11 Bernardin gave a very critical account of white colonial life on the island. This society was based on Mauritius being a staging post on the long, slow journey to India and the Far East. Like any port, the capital Port Louis abounded in whores, who sexually serviced the sailors and soldiers. The moral state of the colony was affected also by the fact that eighteenth-century colonists only endured the distant island to make or remake their fortunes as quickly as possible.

Auguste Toussaint called the island the El Dorado of its day,[120] and described the ravages of cheap alcohol and tropical weather, the constant hunger and lack of effective agriculture (everything was imported from France, as Bernardin noted), and the scarcity of respectable European women (men preferred black mistresses).

Toussaint relied on Bernardin's account as his principal source (without here criticizing his "jaundiced" views as he would in a later article in 1939), and borrowed Bernardin's image of the island as a huge "auberge" (tavern). Toussaint backed up this view, and justified Bernardin's, by quoting a letter written in 1774 by the then governor of the island, Chevalier Desroches (appointed in 1769) to *Intendant* Poivre. He mentions the "disgusting disorder" that reigned in Port Louis, the gambling, the duels, the free black women, the soldiers and sailors who had deserted, and the fugitives from Europe. In all, there was a scandalous licenciousness, which he as governor intended to crush (according to Toussaint he failed, for the port's role as vice den lasted until well after the Suez Canal opened in 1869).[121] Even Poivre was tainted by this state of affairs in the capital, and was relieved of his post in 1772. When Bernardin showed part of his manuscript to Madame Poivre, she made the astute point that Bernardin had confused Port Louis with the rest of the island: "It is only after a long stay in Port Louis that you can depict this island: Port Louis has nothing to do with the rest of the island."[122] For her, the rest of the island was beautiful, always green, with two harvests a year and lovely woods. Edward John Trelawny echoed this view of the capital as different to the rest of the island in 1831: "The scum that the French revolution has boiled up, domineers at the Isle of France, a Botany Bay to which France transports her lawless felons."[123]

Bernardin's negative description of early white society (corroborated by Trelawny and the Dutch writer Jacob Haafner, in Mauritius during 1786–1787),[124] if linked to how slavery mixed up the races, reveals another side to the coin. For Mauritius, in Professor Vinesh Hookoomsing's words, became a "unique natural laboratory" which continues to restore the balance of power between the diverse and fused races and religions in its post-colonial years.

The Journey Home

Bernardin's journey home was beset with misfortunes, losses and delays. He spent time at Réunion, the Cape Colony and Ascension Island. Although Bernardin supplies the reader with some background information on these stopovers, I have thought it helpful to say a little more.

First stop was Réunion, like Mauritius a volcanic island (but with one active volcano) and without an indigenous population. Unlike Mauritius it has no natural harbors and has very high, snow-covered peaks (the highest is the Piton des Neiges at 3,069 meters) about which the Réunion-born Parnassian poet Leconte de Lisle (1818–1894) wrote a poem. Its area is 2,512 square kilometers, slightly larger than Mauritius (1,860 square kilometers). Also discovered by the Portuguese and used by pirates until the French flag was hoisted in 1638, it was named Bourbon in 1649. The Compagnie des Indes, which ran the island through Labourdonnais, settled colonists in 1665. It then reverted to the Crown in 1764, as did Mauritius. Bourbon, as Bernardin knew it, was renamed Réunion in 1792, and I have kept it that way in my translation. Although occupied by the British from 1810–1815, it was returned to France where it became a *département* in 1946, with all the economic and cultural consequences. Saint-Denis is the capital, with the man-made harbor at La Pointe des Galets constructed in 1884. The first export crop was coffee, followed by sugar, and finally tourism. Only about 35 percent of the land is arable. At the time of Bernardin's six-week visit in 1770, Réunion was more populated than Mauritius, which anyhow had begun, as noted, as an overflow colony. Today, though, the population is around 598,000, roughly half that of Mauritius. The best account of Réunion, and fairly close in time to Bernardin's visit, is that given in incredible, even tedious, detail by Bory de St. Vincent in 1801 and 1802. He characterized the island as a "burnt country with a volcano always on fire", and climbed and travelled beyond the inhabited coast.[125] La Fournaise is still active, as is the cone named Bory, after this French naturalist-traveller.

After Réunion, Bernardin found himself landing at the Cape of Good Hope. Though the Cape was discovered in 1488 by Bartolomeu Dias de Novais, it was Vasco da Gama's arrival in 1498 that led to Portuguese control of this area, though the Portuguese did not settle. The Dutch East Indies Company also used Table Bay as a supply depot for fresh water and meat. From 1652, when Jan van Riebeck landed, until 1795, when the British finally invaded, the Dutch settled and controlled the Cape. By 1707 they numbered 1,779 whites, with some 1,107 slaves, but only reached some 15,000 by 1795. Bernardin saw the colony, especially family life and the treatment of slaves, as an idyllic foil to Mauritius.

Captain Cook arrived at the Cape in the *Endeavour* a few months after Bernardin in March 1771 and assessed it in much the same way. He wrote:

> *Cape Town consisted at this time of about a thousand brick houses, the outside of which were generally plastered, and had a pleasing appearance; the streets, which cross each other at right angles, were spacious and handsome, the inhabitants chiefly Dutch, the women beautiful in a high degree and possessing those blooming countenances which denote the most perfect health; they were most of them mothers of many children, and Captain Cook says, they were the best wives in the world. The air of the Cape of Good Hope is pure and salubrious.*[126]

Last stop on the way back to France was Ascension Island, 88 kilometers square, and first visited by the Portuguese Juan de Nova in 1501. It was barren and uninhabited, with Green Mountain its highest peak at 875 meters. It was visited by ships to hunt turtles. William Dampier was wrecked there in 1701, and Cook visited the island not long after Bernardin, in 1775 on his second voyage. He described it as "composed of barren hills and valleys, on the most of which not a shrub or plant was then to be seen, but stones and ashes in plenty." He noted that a ship from Bermuda had caught 105 turtles, leaving many more to rot, "an act as inhuman as injurious to those who came after."[127] From 1815 Ascension Island was a British dependency. In July 1836 when Charles Darwin landed it was settled with British marines. He climbed Green Hill and remarked on the island's "naked hideousness".[128] The island is now a tracking station, with a floating population of some thousand, part of the Saint Helena Dependencies under the British Crown.

La chaumière indienne

In Letter 12, Bernardin eulogized the Malabars as "a very gentle people". He categorized them as sober, thrifty and adoring women, qualities that one could apply to Bernardin himself; he ended his description with a prophecy (made real by indentured labor): "It would be desirable to have a great number of Malabars established on this island, especially the worker caste." He lived near their quarters and had been able to observe them. In 1835 Darwin noticed the 800-odd Indian convicts in Port Louis and found them "noble-looking figures", with "fire" in their expressions and imposing. They were quiet, well behaved, clean, religious, showing "plenty of intellect". Not long after in 1839, when slavery was finally abolished and no freed slave dreamed of working in the fields, the British government began the Indentured Labour contract system that transformed Mauritius into an Indian country and fulfilled Bernardin's wish.

The short story *La chaumière indienne* recreates Bernardin's perceptions about the Mauritian Malabars so succinctly that Gandhi found inspiration in the story. In the foreword to the first edition of 1791 (published as an appendix to the sixth edition of *Etudes de la nature*), Bernardin revealed that he had intended to add it to his *Voyage à l'Isle de France*, linking these Malabars back to India itself (which he did not know).[129]

The story concerns a search for truth, as the English translation of 1796 declared (*The Indian Cottage or, a Search after Truth*) at the expense of the officially wise, the *savants*, the scientists and Academicians. Partly a satire on pedantry, both European and Hindu, the searcher finds the truth in an untouchable Indian in his secluded valley shack (no wonder Gandhi loved it). This shack could be linked back to the huts Paul and Virginie lived in on Mauritius, and Bernardin's own modest house in Port Louis. In fact, the subtitle of the first English translation of *Paul et Virginie* (*Shipwreck, or Paul and Mary*), which senselessly changed Virginie into Mary, was "An Indian Tale" (presumably a tale from the Indies?). Basdeo Bissoondoyal commented on this to decide that *Paul et Virginie* brings "Mauritius nearer to India than to any other country".[130] And all this when Bernardin never reached India himself and based his descriptions on what he had known in Mauritius, and on close readings of earlier travel writers to India like François Bernier and Sir Thomas Roe.[131]

There is also a biographical reading in Bernardin's mocking of the Academies because, as he claimed in his foreword, he had been ridiculed in Paris for not having a list of academic titles after his name, and saw himself simply as a "solitary" out to help the unhappy, and in this case, the afflicted in India.[132] The Academicians, in contrast, were blinded by ambition, jealousy, prejudice: all obstacles to finding truth.

This story also reveals Bernardin's constant praise of women in his quest for happiness. *La chaumière indienne* closes with the most crucial truth discovered by the seeker in India: "One is only happy with a good woman." For Bernardin, the mother was the founder of human societies.[133] According to a recent critic, this constant interest in woman's lot best defines Bernardin's thinking.[134] The little community in *Paul et Virginie* was run by ostracized women without husbands. In a "Note" to the 1806 edition of *Paul et Virginie*, Bernardin bursts into this elegy:

> *But women have contributed more than philosophers to form and reform nations. Women will not grow pale at night composing long moral treatises; they will not climb into the gallery to boom out laws. It was in their arms that men first tasted happiness, in life's cycle, being happy children, faithful lovers, constant husbands, virtuous fathers. Women placed the first base to natural law. The first founder of a human society was the mother of a family... Men are born Asian, European, French, English; they are farmers, merchants, soldiers; but in all countries women are born, live and die as women...*[135]

Women remind men of the natural laws; their tenderness has a divine source; they invented bread, the arts etc. "O women," Bernardin intones, "your sensibility has checked male ambition." And so he continues, claiming that woman has civilized the human race, until he gets to women's tears. There Bernardin finds both his muse and his ideal reader, a woman crying. The mini-matriarchy of *Paul et Virginie* is aimed at women readers, whose tears are proof to Bernardin that he is morally right. The "Note" ends with praise of the French Revolution and Napoleon ("powerful star...").

Lastly, in his quest for the right genre, Bernardin has switched back to fiction from essay, as he did in *Paul et Virginie*, to dress his arguments, for fiction perhaps "makes men more attentive to truth."

Mauritius Today

Bernardin's critical picture of Mauritius remained relevant through the prolongation of slavery into indentured labor in the nineteenth century. His stay coincided with the beginning of the sugar boom, which hit its peak in the decade 1850–1860. Sugar brought Polish novelist Joseph Conrad, then master in the British merchant navy, to Mauritius on his ship the *Otago* to fetch 500 tons of the sweet stuff. He was on the island from 30 September to 22 November 1888, and fell unrequitedly in love.[136] Further sugar booms in 1920–1923 allowed the white land-owning, essentially French minority to consolidate its power and live the grand colonial life, albeit in the tropics with its diseases and cyclones far from Europe, and always with the fear of mass revolts. But, as Toussaint has shown, Mauritius' wealth ensured that by 1789 it became a terminus, no longer a port of call. In 1769 (when Bernardin was there in melancholic exile) only 78 ships called at Port Louis; by 1803 there were 347.[137]

For the white colonials, the opening of the Suez Canal in 1869 reduced the journey home to one month at sea. In 1956 the sea journey took two weeks. You can now fly non-stop in eleven hours. Bernardin took four and half months to get there in 1768, and Charles Baudelaire, the Parisian *flâneur*-poet, three and a half months in 1841. Now with Internet and email, distance is no longer a crucial factor in defining social life. (You can read *Le Mauricien* on the web free, and Mauritians support Manchester United with the same fervor and insider knowledge as anybody in Britain.)

Sugar remained the monoculture on the island throughout the twentieth century, with Commonwealth preferential treatment, though sugar mills declined and continue to decline. Some have modernized with computerized factories, a skilled labor force and mechanical cane cutting, quite unrecognizable to Bernardin or his enemies like Pitot. The island's landscape is dotted with brick cooling towers standing upright in cane-fields, attesting to the many abandoned mills, and are protected by law. However, land has been slowly broken up and Indian small-holders, known as *sirdars*, own most of it (they already owned more than thirty per cent by 1900). Still, when the Nobel-novelist V. S. Naipaul visited the island in 1972, he found a tiny, sad agricultural colony, with everybody longing to leave, a prison, with "sugar-cane and sugar-cane, ending in the sea".[138] He closed his dystopian vision with the observation that "the barracoon is overcrowded", the title of his piece. But something happened to contradict Naipaul and the many like him who saw no future for the island.

The decline of sugar in Mauritius as the prime export crop, in a world market saturated with cane sugar, has been compensated by two success stories: the skilled workers in textile factories, and the tourist beach-hotels. The shacks the cane-cutters lived in up to the 1970s were no different to the palm huts that Paul and Virginie inhabited, inevitably destroyed by the same recurring cyclones that Bernardin described in such vivid details, but the Mauritian government has rebuilt many flattened homes in cement. It is less picturesque for the tourist, as many of these new cement houses have not been painted, and straw shacks romanticized poverty, but workers are better off today with satellite TV and decent work. Mauritius even imports labor in the textile factories. In 1997 *The Economist* described Mauritius as the Singapore of Africa, with unemployment dipping below two percent.[139]

So Bernardin did not predict today's Mauritius, though it would be pertinent to ask whether this economic success is the whole story, and whether it has percolated into the whole social fabric. Up to the 1960s and independence there was a tolerated level of poverty, close to its Indian version (a vision that would not have surprised Bernardin). Nowadays, the rich, of whatever background, live in their lovely houses, with chauffeurs and servants, while the tourists stay locked in tropical beach-compounds (however luxurious), closed to locals. Perhaps Bernardin's sense of the island as a kind of "auberge" or inn remains valid; a place of surprising co-existences, of race, of culture, of religions.

At the end of 1999 Vinesh Hookoomsing took an impulsive drive into the interior of this "almost-India" island from the university campus where he works. He turned past the Mahatma Gandhi Institute, evoking India on land donated by a sugar estate and incorporating a Centre d'Etudes Mauriciennes. He passed a textile factory on his way to Saint Pierre and then veered towards Laura-Malenga, giving a lift to an old woman who spoke to him in Bhojpouri, on her way to the Venkateswara Mandir. Laura-Malenga is not in guidebooks like *The Spectrum Guide* or the *Globetrotter* and has no center. With a population of 1,154, of whom eighty percent are Indian, there is a school named after Adolphe de Pleuritz, defender of Indian laborers, a shop and an old sugar factory closed in 1921. A local pandit tells his "story". This village has its Shivala, as well as a Hare

Rama Hare Krishna center dating from 1993. Hookoomsing sees a clash between the old rural Hindu world and the modern, urban-based one. There is a temple modeled on one from Tirupati, near Madras. Driving on to Belle-Rive, he passes the private medical college, named after the island's first prime minister, Sir Sewoosagur Ramgoolam. Near a small village, where the "tea" plantation failed, he picks up more people, who now speak Creole to him. On his way to Vacoas, he passes the Divine Life Society's headquarters, the Indira Gandhi Cultural Centre, and a huge shopping mall or supermarket, with Pizza Hut and traffic jams. Later he visits a family in Rose Hill and talks to a Christianized Indian woman who still speaks Bhojpouri; Vacoas is today home to the largest concentration of Hindus in the island. In this journey, then, we can see and hear the "new" Mauritius grow from the "old" one whose origins Bernardin had anatomized in what should be seen as the nation's founding text.

The Translation

Why a new translation? The first edition of Bernardin de Saint-Pierre's *Voyage à l'Isle de France* was published anonymously in Amsterdam in 1773. In French it has been in and out of print in edited versions since then, including Maspéro-La Découverte (1982) and Chaudenson's Mauritian edition of 1986, without contradicting the sense that the *Voyage* seems to have "slipped into oblivion", as a critic wrote in 1994.[140] John Parish's English translation appeared in 1775, with the title *A Voyage to the Island of Mauritius*, and was re-edited suppressing the translator with another title and some additions in 1800. There has been nothing in English since then. So my new translation recuperates this eclectic, honest and vivid book as a description and indictment of Mauritian society in the mid-eighteenth century and beyond. It can be read into *Paul and Virginie*, which Bernardin wanted to include with his second edition, as it leads to his wonderful parable *La chaumière indienne*. Read as part of one overlapping work-in-progress, the travel book, the romance and short story interpret each other and offer a firm geographical and historical grounding to Mauritius that is still valid today.

Why I re-translated rather than re-edited the 1775 translation is simply that translations date. I have remained more faithful and literal in regard to Bernardin's French and the way his mind works, confirming him as a "modern" in his attempt to fuse science with feeling and his quest for an open form or fluid genre that captures all he wants to say.

NOTES

[1] According to Bernardin's first biographer, Aimé-Martin, she was born Marie Lubomirska but called herself Princess Miecznik. She had been married to Charles Radziwill.

[2] Twain, 1925, pp.292-293. Twain was told that *Paul et Virginie* had sold more than any other book in Mauritius except for the Bible.

[3] For a reasoned refutation of this Islamic claim, see Shawkat Toorawa, "Imagined Territories: the pre-Dutch History of the South-West Indian Ocean" in Evers and Hookoomsing (eds.), 2000, pp.31-39, where Mauritius only appears on Cantino's map of 1502, not on al-Idrîdî's one of c1165.

[4] By Shelley and Byron's pirate friend Edward James Trelawny in his fictional memoirs, *Adventures of a Younger Son*, p.169.

[5] See the articles by Robert Ross, Daniel Sleigh and Jocelyn Chan Low on the Dutch inheritance in Evers and Hookoomsing, 2000.

[6] The document is reproduced in Régis Fanchette, *Ile Maurice. Mauritius*, naming Guillaume Dufresner, captain of the vessel *Le Chasseur*, as the man who claimed the island for France after finding the island "inhabité" (p.36).

[7] Trelawny, p.183.

[8] Evers and Hookoomsing (eds.), p.63.

[9] Toussaint, 1977, p.33.

[10] Sonnerat, 1782, vol. 2, p.363.

[11] See note 71 in the main text.

[12] *Account of the Conquest of Mauritius*, 1811, p.25.

[13] Sornay, p.35.

[14] Malim, p.6.

[15] Bernardin de Saint-Pierre, *Paul et Virginie*, 1793, p.100. My translation. This symbolic scene with the lure of money is the first step in the souring of happiness that is the theme of the novel.

[16] The British, "with little sense of imagination or history, resurrected the Dutch name of Mauritius. They would have done better, one feels, to have revived the old Portuguese name *Ilha do Cirne*..." Malim, p.13.

[17] Appendix in Charles Pridham, 1849, on population: in 1767 there were 3,163 whites and 15,027 slaves to give a total, with freemen, of 18,777 with slaves as 83% of the population; in 1777, 3,434 whites and 29,761 slaves, which leaps in 1842 to an estimated 174,699 in total. See also Sornay, 1950, and Nagayen, 1996.

[18] *Paul et Virginie*, p. 71.

[19] Argued by Duchêne, for example. See Lanson's (p.176) unflattering thumbnail sketch of Bernardin: "C'était un nerveux, inquiet, chagrin, pétri de fierté et d'amour-propre, ambitieux, aventurier..."

[20] It is not up to me to enter into this debate, but Maurice Souriau's long

introduction demolished Aimé-Martin's standing as a trustworthy biographer; on the other hand, Aimé-Martin knew Bernardin so well that he could speak, and write for him. See Souriau, 1905, pp.vii–lix.

21 Robinson, p.13.

22 Souriau, p.94. For more details on his pay, see d'Unienville, 1973.

23 Souriau, p.113. Following Chaudenson, I have restored what Bernardin would have included on Poivre in his second edition.

24 In a letter of 1780, cited by Souriau; the reason, not to ridicule people in print, not even blacks. For example, he left out the *Marquis de Castries* captain's name (Jean-Baptiste Christy de la Pallière, a naval companion to Labourdonnais).

25 Toussaint, 1936, p.63

26 *The Travels of a Philosopher, being Observations on the Customs, Manners, Arts, Agriculture, and Trade of Several Nation in Asia and Africa.* London. Poivre was ahead of his time, for example: "the Isle of France was covered with woods, and they have been quite rooted up by the colonists," p.35.

27 Bougainville, 1981, p.284.

28 Philibert Commerson smuggled aboard Bougainville's ship, the *Boudeuse*, somebody who appeared to be his servant or butler, but who was discovered to be his mistress, Jeanne Baré. According to d'Epinay, 1890, she was the first woman to sail around the world. Commerson was also a Rousseau-disciple who had edited a list of Mediterranean fish for the Swedish botanist and taxonomist Linnaeus, to give him his Latin name. He also wrote about Tahiti in the *Mercure de France* in November 1769, in what Neil Rennie calls the "first published account by a scientist of Tahiti."

29 Chaudenson, p.201.

30 Souriau calls it the "novel" of his ill-fated affair, pp.101–114. Her name was Françoise Robin.

31 Toussaint, 1936, p.64. See also Nagapen, 1996, and Toussaint, 1977.

32 Lanson, 1923, p.176. Lanson berated Bernardin's "essential imbecility", and listed some of this "piteous philosopher's" views, such as that cows had four udders in order for man to drink milk as well as the calves etc., p.177.

33 Rousseau, 49.

34 Racault, 1986, p.18.

35 Quoted by Chaudenson, pp.25–26.

36 Quoted by Little, p.xviii.

37 In Burkhardt and Smith, 1985, p.493.

38 Chaudenson, p.35.

39 Aimé-Martin, p.117.

40 Chaudenson, p.15.

41 See Unnuth, 1988, who reveals how Bissoondoyal (1906–1991) "worshipped" Gandhi, and met him and Tagore when in India studying between 1933 and 1939. Unnuth outlines his four prison sentences in Mauritius, compares him

to the radical Brazilian educationalist Paulo Freire, calls him a Hindu missionary (he founded over 300 Hindi schools) and shows how his Hindu movement was based on Bapu's (Gandhi) methods of fasting, dissent and passive resistance. Bissoondoyal argued, rightly, that Indian immigrants were treated just as badly as slaves, and that mill-owners were cruel and oppressive. See also U. Bissoondoyal, 1990, on Bernardin ("who gave a dignified portrait of the slave") and on his uncle, Basdeo Bissoondoyal. Although Bissoondoyal's influence peaked between 1944 and 1949, Sir Seewoosagur Ramgoolam and his Labour Party recognized the important work he had done in ushering in independence.

42   Cited in Ngendahimana, 1999, p.227. Bernardin's eulogy of vegetarianism echoed Rousseau: "For as prey is almost the only thing carnivorous animals fight about, and as frugivorous animals live among themselves in perpetual peace, it follows that if the human race were of this latter genus, then manifestly it would have had much greater ease subsisting in the state of nature and much less need and occasion to quit it." *A Discourse on Inequality*, p.143.

43   Bissoondoyal, 1968, p.74. For more on Bissoondoyal, the "professor" and the personality cult that grew around him, as well as on his more politicised brother Sakdeo Bissoondoyal (founder of the Independent Forward Bloc in 1958), in the context of Mauritian independence, see Smith Simmons, 1982, pp.86–90.

44   For example, see his "La vieillesse de Jean-Jacques" in a collection on Rousseau published by H. Georg in Geneva, 1878. Bernardin took careful notes and recreated them, with dialogues. We see a very domestic Rousseau who, adoring coffee, is gifted some from Réunion by Bernardin. Bernardin's favourite works by Rousseau are his opera *Le Devin du village*, first performed in Fontainbleau in 1752, and the third volume of the novel *Emile*.

45   See Ngendahimana's clear exposition of Bernardin's political views.

46   Baudelaire, 1973, pp.89–90. The local Mauritian was called Autard de Bragard (1808–1876).

47   *Ibid*, p.40.

48   Anthony Barker, 1996, p.1.

49   Quoted by Abbé Ducrocq in Bernardin de Saint-Pierre *et al*, *Ile de France. Voyage et Controverses*, p.182.

50   Thomas, pp.462–463.

51   Georges-Louis Leclerc, known as Count Buffon (1707–1788), never travelled outside Europe. See Buffon, 1984, p.142.

52   Hollingworth, p.35.

53   Thomas, p.463.

54   *Ibid*, p.447 and p.863.

55   Strong, p.105.

56   Vissière, pp.62, 64, 79.

57 Mockford, pp.13–116. Mockford also wrote *Khama. King of the Bamangwata*, Cape: London, 1931.

58 Anna Neill examined the lack of reference to the slave question in 1993, but ignored Bernardin's travel account. She opened: "It is difficult to know how to read *Paul and Virginia*," and closed with the romance's inability to face the historical, economic and political status of the blacks on the island, thus sidelining "the complexities of the antiabolitionist colonial history." Countering this superficial reading, I can quote Maurice Souriau, in 1905, who saw the novel as a "plaidoyer vigoureux" in favour of the black slaves.

59 *Paul et Virginie*, p.16.

60 Souriau, p.249.

61 Colbert (1619–1683) was Louis XIV's Superintendant of Finance, who encouraged trade, protected the arts, founded the Compagnie des Indes Orientales in 1664, as well as putting the *Code Noir* together.

62 Ngendahimana includes the whole *Code*.

63 Blair Allen, p.22.

64 *Ibid*, p.26 and p.35.

65 See John Jeremie, *Recent Events at Mauritius*. Bagster: London, 1835.

66 Unnuth, p.52.

67 Toussaint, 1977, p.77.

68 In Bernardin de Saint-Pierre *et al*, *Ile de France. Voyage et Controverses*, p.158.

69 Pitot, reproduced in *Ibid*. Many thanks to Professor Vinesh Hookoomsing for sending me the book.

70 Trelawny, 1974, p.187. Anne Hill first argued that this autobiography was fantasy by checking Trelawny's naval career and the muster books, and establishing that he served in 12 ships between October 1805 and August 1812, when he was honourably discharged just before his twentieth birthday. He never deserted. He was at Mauritius during the naval blockade in August 1810 and the English invasion of November/December 1810. Earlier, Margaret Armstrong's *Trelawny. A Man's Life* (1941) had taken Trelawny at his word that his book was "not a novel... but a faithful record of my early life." See Hill, 1956. For an up-to-date biography, see St. Clair, 1977.

71 Sonnerat, vol. 2, p.363.

72 Quoted by Barnwell, p.252.

73 In what purported to be a factual chronology of Mauritian history, D'Epinay could not help but accuse Bernardin again, pp.194–196.

74 Pitot, 1899, pp.86–87.

75 Toussaint, 1939, p.176.

76 *Ibid*, p.179.

77 D'Unienville, 1954. Thanks to Professor Vinesh Hookoomsing for suggesting this book.

78 Pridham, p.164.

79 Malim, p.121 and p.193.

80 Just to stick to a recorded example from a conversation between Malim and Paul "X" in 1952: "You don't know, my friend, how deep and bitter colour-prejudice is, on *both sides*. The creoles despise and dislike the Hindus, the *Malabars, une nation tripe,* they call them. But they like the Whites even less. And there are Whites, believe it or not, who are blind enough to prefer the Hindus to the creoles. The Hindus, you see, were never slaves... After all, even creoles are human. Though you'd better, perhaps, not quote me as having said so..." *Ibid,* p.125.

81 Anthony Barker, p.167.

82 Darwin, 1845, p.484.

83 Dumas, who never travelled to Mauritius and borrowed much from Saint-Pierre, mentions *Paul et Virginie* and describes a hurricane. Dumas, 1846.

84 Twain, pp.291–292.

85 Bissoondoyal, 1968, p.2.

86 Malim, p.38.

87 Comte de Lautréamont, *Poésies I* in *Oeuvres complètes,* 1973, p.291. By reading *Paul et Virginie* through the earlier *Journey,* you can recover a romance grounded in a vivid geography and a historical rejection of slavery, colonialism and male values of commerce and competition, so that far from being "the worst novel ever written" (James Fenton, *New York Review of Books,* 14 August 1997), it is a "really heart-breaking book, and makes no concessions to consolation" (Albert Camus, *The Rebel.* Penguin: Harmondsworth, 1962, p.226).

88 Anon, 1811, p.49.

89 Beaton, p.43.

90 Toussaint, 1939, p.180.

91 See my edition and translation of Alexander von Humboldt, *Personal Narrative of a Journey to the Equinoctial Regions of the New Continent,* 1995.

92 Bernardin, 1789, pp.iii, v and vii.

93 Souriau, pp.237–238.

94 Bernardin, 1793, p.1.

95 Bory de St. Vincent, 1804, pp.204–207. Bory de St. Vincent (1780–1846) became a member of the Académie des Sciences, explored Africa, particularly Algeria, and published extensively on natural history. He was noted for his originality.

96 Milbert, 1812, pp.56-59.

97 Jean J. Seznec on Rousseau in *The Listener,* 10 March 1966.

98 Rousseau, 1984, pp.154-161.

99 A similar sentiment is echoed by Paul in his philosophical dialogue with the wise old guru: "Oh! She who planted this pawpaw tree has made a more useful and sweeter present for those who live in the forests than if she had donated a

library." (p.161); Paul refers to Virginie.

[100] Forster (1754-1794) had accompanied Cook on his second voyage around the world and published an account, *Voyage round the World on the Resolution*, 1777.

[101] See Edward Goodman, 161.

[102] Bougainville, p.18.

[103] Quoted from Bougainville, p.19. See also Rennie, pp.116-117.

[104] Bory de St. Vincent, p.viii.

[105] Trelawny, p.437.

[106] O'Brian, 1987, p.71.

[107] Guyot, p.113.

[108] Darwin, 1842, p.73. Darwin quotes from this "interesting pedestrian tour" in Bernardin's French, from the first anonymous edition of 1773.

[109] Aspects of Linnaeus' influences are discussed in several essays in Miller and Reill, 1996, especially Lisbet Koerner, pp.117-152, and Alan Bewell, pp.173-193.

[110] Baudry, p.784.

[111] Allen, p.6.

[112] This theory of tides led to a book in English, culled and translated from Bernardin's writings, called *The Theory of Tides*, Bath, 1795, aimed at a scientific readership. In a note, the author apologized for a digression by Bernardin lamenting the slave trade.

[113] The entry by Buffon is quoted in full by Bory de St.Vincent, vol. 2, pp.302-307, who called the dodo "un oiseau monstrueux".

[114] In Evers and Hookoomsing, 2001, p.6. See also Frances Staub's essay in same edition, arguing with Kitchener's report in the *New Scientist* (18 September 1993) about the dodo's seasonal fatness, what it fed on (vacoas seeds, wild figs, palm dates), its famous gizzard stone etc.

[115] Leguat, p.65.

[116] See Laetitia van den Heuvel's excellent essay, "Dodo's Virtual Reality", in Evers and Hookoomsing, 2001, pp.77-89, and Geneviève Dormann's novel *Le bal du dodo*, 1989. Thanks to Prof. Hookoomsing for sending me a copy.

[117] Quammen, p.267.

[118] See also "Dodo Flew to its Grave", in *Natural Science*, 3 March 2002.

[119] Cited in D'Unienville, 1973.

[120] Toussaint, 1936, p.55.

[121] *Ibid,* pp.67-68.

[122] Quoted in Souriau, p.107.

[123] Trelawny, p.183.

[124] See Paul van der Velde, "Jacob Haafner in Mauritius, 1786-1787", in Evers and Hookoomsing, 2001. Haafner attacked that depraved colonial society, backing his arguments with quotations from Bernardin.

125   Bory de St. Vincent, p.244.
126   Captain Cook, 1932.
127   *Ibid*, p.224.
128   Darwin, p.493.
129   Bernardin, 1791, p.v.
130   Bissoondoyal, 1968, p.228.
131   On Bernier as having exercised some influence on later constructions of the Orient, see Peter Burke, "The Philosopher as Traveller: Bernier's Orient", in Elsner and Rubies, 1999, pp.124-137.
132   Bernardin, 1791, p.xxxv and p.ix.
133   Bernardin: "La première fondatrice d'une société humaine fut une mère de famille." Quoted by Ngendahimana, p.157.
134   Ngendahimana, p.158.
135   *Paul et Virginie*, 1989, pp.57-58.
136   Her name was Eugénie Renouf. See Barnwell, 1948, and Hollingworth, 1963. Conrad's fiction *A Smile of Fortune-Harbour Story* reflects his stay in the "Pearl of the Ocean" (Mauritius is not named), where "first-rate sugar-cane is grown... Sugar is their daily bread, as it were."
137   Toussaint, 1971, p.41.
138   Naipaul, p.279.
139   See my piece on Mauritius in the *Times Literary Supplement*, 12 January 2001.
140   Malcolm Cook, 1994, p.845.

VOYAGE

A

L'ISLE DE FRANCE,

A L'ISLE DE BOURBON,

AU CAP DE BONNE-ESPÉRANCE, &c.

Avec des Observations nouvelles sur la nature & sur les Hommes,

PAR UN OFFICIER DU ROI.

TOME PREMIER.

A AMSTERDAM,

Et se trouve à Paris,

Chez Merlin, Libraire, rue de la Harpe, à Saint Joseph.

M. DCC. LXXIII.

Author's Preface to the First Edition, 1773

These letters and diary entries were written to my friends. On my return I placed them in the proper order and had them printed as a public testimony of friendship and gratitude.

I have written on plants and animals, but I am not a naturalist. Natural history should not be locked up in libraries. This book is intended to be read by everybody. I believe that I have seen the visible character of Providence, and I have spoken about it not as a system that entertains my intellect, but as a feeling that fills my heart.

Besides, I hope that I can be useful to mankind if my feeble picture of the fate of the luckless blacks can save them from one single lash of a whip, and if Europeans, who cry out against tyranny in Europe, and who write such pretty treatises on morality, cease being barbarous tyrants in the Indies.

I believe that I will have rendered a service to my own country if I can prevent one single honest man from emigrating, and if I can persuade him to cultivate one more acre in some abandoned wasteland.

To truly love your country, you must quit it. I am attached to mine, though neither by my fortune, nor by my rank, but I love those places where, for the first time, I saw the light and loved, spoke and felt alive.

I love this soil that so many foreigners adopt, where all that one needs abounds and which is preferable to both Indies by its temperature, the excellence of all that grows there, and the industry of its people. Indeed, I love this nation where human relationships are more numerous, where esteem is more enlightened, where friendship is more intimate and virtue more lovable.

I well know that one finds in France, as before in Athens, what is best and what is most depraved. But it is the nation that produced Henri IV, Turenne and Fénelon. These great men who governed, defended and guided France, also loved it.[1]

Prospectus for a New Edition of the Journey to Mauritius[2]

Forced to suspend my work on the elements of morality to provide for my family's needs, I propose to publish a new edition of my *Journey to Mauritius* that many people have often asked me to undertake.

Above all, I wish to take my book out of the hands of speculators and forgers. Speculators have taken over my works like any other commercial object. If I want to sell, they give me paper and if I want to buy, they demand money. Forgers, on the other hand, pirate my books and mock the laws. I had one of them arrested when he dared to advertise my books in a catalogue. This affair has been dragging on for two years... But not only speculators and forgers steal the fruit of my work, but also booksellers themselves to whom I entrusted the sale. They have sold for their own profit what I gave them to sell for me...[3]

The first edition of my *Journey*, with illustrations, consisted of but two slim volumes in large print which were sold for 7 *livres* and 10 *sols* and which today have reached 20 *écus* in cash. The second edition will only have illustrations linked to the understanding of the text. It will be composed of two large volumes of 600 pages and will be the sixth and seventh volumes of my *Studies on Nature*.[4]

It will have doubled the contents of the first edition. I have cut nothing out of the old text, but have added passages that are related to it and that have been for a long time in my desk, incidents that were personal to me, criticisms of others and above all of myself. There has been a special interest in Cook's Second Voyage, interpolated with Forster's. We like reading that account written by two men who had the same aims but whose way of looking and character were different. It seems as if we journey round the earth not with one traveller but with two. If one can compare small ventures with great ones, my new *Journey to Mauritius* will combine this kind of pleasure. I made the journey in 1768 and published it for the first time in 1773. The second edition will appear in 1797. There has been an interval of 29 years. It is almost the length of a generation. It will thus be written by two people, one aged thirty-one and the other sixty; one a bachelor, the other a father of a family. However, it will be drafted by the same person because those two men are me. Life's course presents at its two extremes two quite different perspectives; that of the start reveals objects in the future, that of the end, those in the past. I have seen Europe from Mauritius, now I will see Mauritius from Europe. I will try to join the flowers of my spring to the few fruits of my autumn. I hope that readers will find in this account some interesting subjects. Among these will be the historical elegy of my friend, a small dog to whom I was extremely attached. He made the crossing with me and I lost him on the island of Réunion. I wrote his elegy in an academic manner. This joke pleased some women but got me into trouble with some serious philosophers and contributed to the hate their leader vowed me.[5] I will also deal in my book with important questions of trade and navigation for our Republic, among others, the colony that was intended at Fort Dauphin on Madagascar for which I was destined, as well as the cultivation of spices on Mauritius, unfortunate enterprises about which nobody has spoken the truth, although something about this has been recently written. This journey will end with what would be a very touching subject were it treated by a better pen than mine. It is a play in prose of five acts set in Africa. The main character is a black called Empsaël who was the first minister of Emperor Moeli Ismaël of Morocco. It is well known that the blacks are all-powerful in that empire. Having found on my voyage that blacks are enslaved by Europeans, I thought it just to present Europeans as slaves under blacks to better convince you of our injustice towards them and how Providence reacts...[6]

Preamble to the Journey to Mauritius[7]

In 1790 it occurred to me to publish my *Journey*, victim for many a year of forgers. Several reasons led to this decision. The first was that when it was printed, I was not free to say everything. Censorship excised quite innocent items. The second is that I myself did not dare say everything, thus my closed style excluded all that was personal. But later I felt that what is personal in a traveller is what makes a journey most interesting. What gives the illusion that makes things present is that the reader is in company. From that it can be stated that travel accounts are, without contradiction, more interesting than geographical descriptions of the same country. My studies of nature have also broadened my mind. Public indulgence has approved them. Objects change according to the point of view...

I will thus not change anything in the form of my letters. I will simply add my personal adventures, my reflections, as stories or narratives that will bind my letters together all the better. The letter form seems to me the most favourable in all cases. I prefer the most straightforward forms. If I were to write another journey, it would take the form of a journal and rather than tell someone else about things, I would write to myself...[8]

We have had several voyages round the world but it is harder to travel round oneself, to know the poles on which we spin and how with the same organs and the same passions we are so different from each other. Exacting travellers will give us, as I did, the dimensions of their boats and the members of their crews; for myself, I would offer those of my inner self, and by writing some of my adventures down, I would be thrown back into my infancy.

I do not wish to write a confession of my life for I do not have enough faith in men; I will say both what is good and bad. I will say enough to let myself be known exactly as I was and am. That will help others to be happier.

Before describing a journey, it is pertinent to introduce the traveller. The storyteller is really the hero of any book. The world is a mountain that each person describes not according to nature, but following his way of seeing it, some in the morning, others at evening. It is the moment the painter chooses and the time of day that makes the journey. When I set off on my travels in 1768 I was a novice: I did not dare to unfold my ideas, I had to remain cautious; now twenty years later, free, and calmer from passions, I like to review the differences that the years have brought with them in the progress of several things so that a reader can enjoy the same country and the same man of twenty years before.

I come from an honest and humble background. My life has rolled on the two pivots of ambition and love, but in such a way that I have spent my life far from intrigues and unmarried. I was born the most confiding and credulous of men, but having had a typical education I was surprised to find in those who preached goodness and sweetness such strange acts of cruelty that suspicion and shyness grew in me when faced with such people, so much so that I have never been able to heal myself. I would have become wicked if I had not had trust in God. There was a time when I was unhappy enough to grope between vice and virtue: in the end my confidence in God won out: having nobody to complain to, it was in Him alone that I could place my trust.

My sensibility is extreme: I have never forgotten a good turn nor an insult.[9] I seek to acknowledge the former. I have often forgiven the latter, but never forgotten. Jean-Jacques Rousseau used to tell me that man's first impulse was very good, but that thinking made him malicious; however, contradicting him, my first impulse is to be malicious, but thinking makes me good.

It seems to me that my soul lives on several levels. I naturally like the valley floor where tired by the world's evils I enjoy resting, but if anybody rises above me and tries to upset me, then my soul rises above his; if the misfortune involving me increases, I climb to another level until I reach the mountain's peak and am far from the sight of men, finding solace in a world where they no longer have power over me. Happiness pulls me down into the valley and malice forces me to hide on the mountaintop. As for my ambition, I direct it as much as I can towards the happiness of others, and dwell in my own as little as possible, preferring an ounce of happiness to a quintal of reputation, treating others as I would like to be treated.

As for my inclination to love, the older I get the more difficult I become. The more difficult to love I become, the less I deserve it. However, I cannot give up this illusion which has charmed my life, persuading me that, like Seneca, I might find a Pauline in my old age.[10] I had overheard my father say that we are descended from a noble family, perhaps even from Eustache de Saint-Pierre, but there was no proof. As for the nobles of Lorraine, we have a patent signed by the Marquis de Laigle who witnessed it, but with a clause that one of my ancestors had managed the affairs of his house. Thus ambition soon finds its punishment within another ambition. With this document I left for the north, having lengthened my name with the title of knight given to me by friends and which I had adopted, for in the service of Russia you are nothing without some certificate. One mistake leads to another. I had no coat of arms and I dared not give myself a fake one: I had a seal engraved according to my whims. Later, this contradiction often troubled me whilst I travelled for I was not born to deceive. When asked about my ancestry, if I was related to the Abbé de Saint-Pierre, I answered no, but that I was descended from a noble family in Lorraine, but did not dare show the title, which humiliated me. It is the only mistake I committed, forced to by circumstances of work and time, and encouraged by my friends; a mistake that I soon confessed but that friends still attribute to me despite myself, perhaps out of self-love rather than respect for me.

With my fortune so much at odds with my ambition, I had to become a schemer and adventurer in order to survive and I was not that by nature. I was attached to my duties, very frugal, poor. I had to die of hunger for I was proud with men and difficult about how to make my way. The trust I have had in God since infancy has always kept me on the honest path and I owe it to this that I found work in Russia at a time when I felt abandoned by everybody and was without money.

However, these ordeals gradually softened my ambitions. I turned pity for myself towards other people. As for love, I had tasted its charms, mixed with those of ambition, in the arms of a princess, but I was looking for a simple, sweet woman. Thus I insensibly drew closer to nature, but my life was passing by without work and without marriage.

What can I say? My interest in man had led to much distress. Although very reserved in society, if I see someone suffering, I draw near; I give myself to this person, sympathetically, trustingly. The result is that I have made many enemies, for attaching myself to the weakest and fighting the strongest meant that I was surrounded by both enemies and ingrates. I found in my own country many who were jealous, envious and wicked: some were jealous of my youth, others of my health, others of the way I was treated by friends. Others, seeing me as simple and honest, for I have never adopted the light and impertinent tone of high society which seems to me to be the worst tone that anybody could assume, thought that my honesty and modesty were weaknesses and they never ceased being insolent with me. Or when they suddenly realized that this simple man was rising above their level, I would make implacable enemies who quietly employed the means of the feeble and wicked, namely calumny...

I was the unhappiest of men in society. What had remained of my education was that indelible vice of seeking the approval of others: they had but to say one word and I related it to myself. You had to get close to the rich and those who hand out fortunes, and I just couldn't please them for I first had to become wicked like all those around them. I saw that society was a perpetual succession of slander, and that slander was just indirect praise for oneself. Society seemed to me to be a gathering of wicked people who did not have the guts to attack each other head on and so set traps and ripped apart reputations in secret. I saw them all infected with that vice of our education: the need to be first or best. I was just as sullied, but tried to divert the vice towards virtue. I sought out what was honest, trying to distinguish myself through my studies or my observations, but could never find the right moment to speak. Thus my silence and my modesty were taken for timidity. Add to that the distress of my poor birth: I saw that I would never achieve anything. I admit that I have several times blushed about my birth.

I found myself, then, caught between my education in vanity and my principles. That endless struggle made me the most unhappy of men. My education and the world told me that I had to push forward, court women without whom nothing could be attained, flatter the powerful, slander my equals, boast constantly about my talents and thus benefit from the advantages of my person and my experience. On the other hand, a natural impulse told me that I should not do to others what I did not want done to myself. I was thus respectful towards women, sincere and frank with the powerful, waiting to speak in turn, avoiding wounding whomever it might have been. This reserve made people think I was shy; it was made worse by the melancholic look that worrying about my fortune gave me. Add to that my dark clothes, my serious demeanour, while those with wealth on their side were alive, supple, pleasing, bowing almost to the ground...

I was recovering from a bout of melancholy which I had cured myself with a diet and water. After nine days in bed, followed by another relapse of nine days, I went outdoors to take the air: I was frail, it was summer and I went into a café to have something refreshing. I was without wealth, without a patron, and was spending what little remained of an inheritance. I glanced at a newspaper and saw that a nobleman that I had met in Russia was back in Paris after his mission. The next day I went to visit him. He received me in a friendly way, which intensified my friendship. I had a little dog that I had locked inside the carriage, asking the driver to look after him, but I was surprised when, after the first compliments, I saw my dog leaping at me with joy at having found me. I blushed and wanted to show the dog out when the nobleman said, "Why send the dog away?" and he started to stroke him. My friendship grew ever stronger: who loves me loves my dog. After that he spoke to me about my business and scolded me for not having contacted him before. I told him of my woes. "What are your plans?" he asked me. I had been so unlucky with making any progress in France that I said that if there was any opening, then I wanted to go to the colonies. He said to me: "You have done the right thing coming to me. I am intimate with the Minister for the Navy. In a few days you will see a result." One of his subalterns, whom I had met in Russia and then seen in Paris but who had ignored me, now lavished his friendship on me, and at the mention of colonies, began to say that there was only a place for me in the Indies, for all posts in Europe had been taken, and exalted my genius which, he said, needed a great stage. A few days later I got a message from the grandee. I went to see him that evening and he said: "Your affair is settled; you are off to Mauritius as an engineer; go and see a ship's officer and he will introduce you to a landowner from that island; it will be most pleasant for you."[11] This captain was staying with a Duchess. I went in the morning, a Sunday at nine. A woman told me through the uniformed guard that I should return between eleven and midday. I returned at half past twelve, my head full of worries. I passed through the door, distracted, walking towards the house across the courtyard when I heard a vulgar and insolent voice shouting: "Where are you going? Who are you?" in a tone that you wouldn't even use to a Savoyard. I turned around and saw a tall young uniformed Swiss guard all bedecked in silver striding towards me with the same insolence with which he had addressed me. I told him as directly as possible that I was visiting the captain. "Do you think you can enter a private house without first speaking to the guard? Who are you?" As his insolence increased in proportion to the lowering of my voice, and especially because of some people about to climb out of a coach, I said: "Wretch, are you talking to me?" and moved my hand to my sword. "Wretch or rogue?" he said. "You are the wretch," I said, "to have spoken to me in such a way." At the same time, I strode towards the house. Then, as the Duchess was climbing into her coach, I climbed the staircase, and a servant announced me to the captain who was getting out of bed. I had barely begun talking to him when the uniformed Swiss guard, on my heels, said to him, hat on head: "How is it that people who come to see you can insult the Duchess's staff?" The noble captain lowered his eyes, troubled. I said to him: "Sir, I have no desire to compromise myself with your uniformed guard: I will tell you what happened." The guard then left: I explained the misunderstanding. The captain, upset, said: "My intention was to introduce you to a very influential landowner but after this, all my good intentions would be useless." I withdrew, more struck by the attitude of a Knight of Saint Louis than by the cheek of a uniformed guard, and went and told my protector what happened. He joked about it at first: "The Duchess's guards think they're the pope's mustard pot; don't worry about it." I have dallied over this trifle because this, as we shall see, was the cause of my problems in Mauritius.

At last I managed to meet the landowner. I found a grandee, sporting the Saint Louis cross and an inane expression and smoking a pipe. He approached me in an affectionate way and began a magnificent paean to all my qualities. He said he had been instructed to tell me that I had a secret commission of the greatest importance, that the Court had picked me out to rebuild the walls of Fort Dauphin in Madagascar, an island of 800 leagues all round and far more important than our other possessions Réunion or Mauritius, some 500 leagues from there. He also said that thanks to the nature of its produce this island could combine all Asia's trade, that one could impose an empire on its warring people. He based his observations on several passages from Tacitus. He said that the Court had instructed him to take charge of this enterprise as governor: he told me of his plans for humanity, for civilization. He would take all the seeds he could and several arts from Europe. He had with him men of rare merits who would benefit from my intelligence, and he congratulated himself on having me to accompany him. Now all my ideas sprang back to life, all my projects revived. I dreamed only of Madagascar, of its sweet climate, of the happiness of civilizing its people. I got hold of the *Voyage* by Flacourt, who had been the last governor. I thought that religion is the basis of all societies. I raised a temple dedicated to nature and as I knew that the means of our colony would be scant, I recall that I drew a temple in a jungle with palm trees whose trunks supported a framework and whose leaves would cover the roof. Finally, blacks and whites would live in perfect harmony.

I had to prepare for the journey. I had almost no money at all, and the first thing I did was buy books and mathematical instruments. My purse was empty and I still had to buy linen and clothes for a voyage that would last five to six months and a stay of several years. My protector told me that he would send me to his shirt-makers and tailor who would give me the credit I needed. The baron lent me his chamber valet to drive me there. These shirt-makers were three rich sisters, rather old and ugly. I told them about my proposal to pay for what I needed with a third of the amount in cash and the rest within a year. The two younger sisters were happy, but the eldest asked me on what capital I would base my payment. "On my appointment," I told her. "It will have to be on your property." "I don't have any," I answered, "but I will write my promissory notes so that if I died, the sale of my belongings would pay you back." Most others, in my place, would have easily obtained credit. I had been recommended by a very reputable nobleman; I had an important job, but my frankness removed any chance of credit the moment I said I had no property. The younger one accepted, the middle one doubted, but the eldest rejected my offer. "What if you died?" she said. So, I was facing the prospect of packing books and instruments but not having any clothes on the island until the tailor, who had agreed to my terms for my uniforms, said as I returned: "Your honesty does you harm; that is not the way to get credit in Paris, but I will furnish you with all you need on your conditions."

All I had was my salary of 100 *louis* and my expenses were owing. I had received an advance. I reached Lorient where I took a furnished room, having no funds and living very frugally. Soon the governor arrived with two secretaries, one of his friends I had seen in Poland, one of his cousins, his favourites, and a retinue of servants. The governor held an open table. The people around him did not seem at all suitable for founding a colony as they were libertines, thirsty for wealth and pleasure. As for the chief, I was told that he was a bankrupt landowner from Mauritius who had tried to buy black slaves cheaply, that it was impossible for Europeans to live in Madagascar for six months of the year because of the awful climate, that he was a very bright but wicked man who would muddle God up with the angels.

This gave me plenty to think about during the six weeks that we stayed at Lorient. I saw that his conversation and that of his friends was extremely salacious, that they mercilessly tore everybody apart, and ridiculed all society. Soon my turn came and I did not take to his jokes.[12]

Letter 1

Lorient, 4 January 1768

I arrived at Lorient in the freezing cold. Everything was frozen from Paris to within ten leagues of Rennes. That city, which was burnt down in 1720, has now a certain grandeur that it owes to this catastrophe. Noticeable are several new buildings, two rather beautiful squares, the statue of Louis XV and, above all, that of Louis XIV. Inside, the Parliament is well decorated, but, in my view, with too much uniformity. The panelling of the wainscot is painted white, with gilt mouldings. Most of the churches and public buildings are in this taste. Otherwise, Rennes struck me as a sad town. It is situated at the confluence of two sluggish rivers, the Villaine and the Isle. Its outskirts are composed of dirty houses, with badly-paved streets. The people dress in a coarse brown cloth, which makes them look poor.

In Britanny I saw a great deal of wasteland. Nothing grows there but broom and a plant with yellow flowers which seemed to be composed solely of thorns that the peasants call *lande* or *jan*; the peasants crush it to feed their animals. The only use for broom is to heat ovens; more could be made of it, especially in a maritime province. The Romans made excellent rope out of it, which they preferred to hemp for their ships. I owe this observation to Pliny, who was known to have commanded the fleets of the Empire.[13]

In these heaths, couldn't one successfully plant potatoes, an assured survival crop at risk neither from inclement seasons nor the storehouses of hoarding profiteers?

Industry seems stifled by the aristocratic government or the rule of the states. The peasant, who is without representatives, is likewise without protection. In Britanny, he is poorly dressed, drinks but water and lives off black bread.

Human misery always increases with dependence. I have seen rich peasants in Holland, peasants at their ease in Prussia, in a bearable situation in Russia, and in extreme poverty in Poland. I will soon see the black, the peasant of our colonies, in a deplorable state. Here, I believe, is the reason. In a Republic there is no master, in a monarchy there is but one, but an aristocratic government provides each peasant with a particular tyrant.

From liberty industry is born. The Swiss peasant is ingenious, the Polish serf cannot imagine anything. This stupor of the soul, which lends itself better than philosophy to endure great misfortunes, seems to be a blessing from Providence. "When Jupiter," said Homer, "reduces a man to slavery, he takes from him half his understanding."[14]

Excuse these reflections. It is hard to see great misfortunes without seeking a remedy or the cause.

Towards Lower Britanny, nature seems somewhat stunted. The hills, the valleys, the trees, the men and animals are smaller there than elsewhere. The landscape, divided into wheat fields, into pasture surrounded by ditches and shaded by oaks, chestnuts and hedges, has a neglected and melancholic aspect which should please me, but for the season, which makes all sorts of countryside sad.

In several places we found quarries of slate, of red and black marble, and mines of lead mixed with a very ductile type of silver. But the true wealth of this country lies in its linens, its threads and its cattle. Industry is reborn with freedom, with proximity to seaports. That is probably the sole benefit produced by maritime commerce, which is hardly anything more than avarice guided by law. How peculiar is man's condition, that he should derive greater benefit from his passions than from his reason!

The peasant in Lower Britanny is contented. He considers himself free, close to an element on which all the roads are open. Oppression cannot stretch itself further than his fortune. If he is too hard pressed, he boards a ship. On the ship where he has taken refuge he finds the oak wood of his enclosures, the linen woven by his family, and the wheat of his fields, household gods who have abandoned him. Sometimes he recognizes the Lord of his village in the officer on the ship. In their common misery, he sees that the officer is but a man, more to be pitied than himself. At liberty concerning his reputation, he becomes master of it, and from the tip of the yardarm where he is perched, he can judge, in the middle of a storm, the man whom on shore he would never have dared to scrutinize.

Letter 2
Lorient, 28 January 1768

Lorient is a small town in Britanny which has thrived from its trade with the East Indies. Like most new towns it is regular, with unfinished streets in straight lines. It has mediocre fortifications. There are some fine warehouses, the unfinished Hôtel del Ventes, a lookout tower, wharves under construction, and ground plans for future buildings. It is located at the end of a bay formed by the rivers Blavet and Ponscorf, which deposit a lot of mud in the harbour. The entrance to the bay is narrow and defended by Port Louis, whose citadel is too high so that shot fired from it falls short. The sea washes the foot of the ramparts.[15]

Port Louis is an old, deserted town. It is like an old gentleman with a financier as a neighbour. The nobility lives in Port Louis, but the merchants, the muslin and silk warehouses, the money and attractive women are all at Lorient. Their manners are the same here as in all other commercial ports. Everyone's purse is open, but money is only lent in order to make more; interest on a loan for the Indies is twenty-five or thirty per cent a year. The borrower is far worse off than the lender; his profits are uncertain, his obligations are not. Law authorizes this lending of money by contracts and this gives the creditors a claim to the whole ship's cargo, a power that spreads over the entire fortune of most seafaring people.

There are three ships ready to sail to Mauritius, the *Digue*, the *Conde*, and the *Marquis de Castries*. Others are being fitted out and some more are being built. The din of the carpenters and caulkers, the crowds of foreigners, and the incessant movement of ships, stimulate everybody into the giddiness that is the sea-life. The lure of riches that is associated with the Indies increases the illusion. You would think yourself a thousand leagues from Paris. The people here no longer speak French; those in town know no other boss than the East India Company. The better sort of people talk of Mauritius and Pondicherry as if they were next door. You'd be right to think that the aggravations of business arrive alongside the bales from India, for dealing in money divides man from man rather than uniting them.

Letter 3
Lorient, 20 February 1768

We only await a fair wind in order to sail. I have booked my passage on board the *Marquis de Castries*, an 800-tonner with 146 men, laden with naval stores for Bengal.[16] I have just seen my accommodation, a little canvas recess off the great cabin. There are fifteen passengers, most of whom are lodged in the Sainte-Barbe, a gun room where they store the cartridges and artillery instruments. The master-gunner is in charge of this area and lodges here, with the secretary, the chaplain and surgeon. Above this is the great cabin where the passengers dine with the captain. The second floor has the council chamber and the captain's cabin; it is decorated on the outside with a gallery and is the finest room on board. The officers' cabins are also there, so that they can more easily watch over activities on deck. The chief pilot and the chief petty officer are accommodated there too, for the same reasons.

The crew is lodged under the forecastle and between the decks, a dismal prison where you can see nothing. The forecastle runs the length of the whole ship which is level with the great cabin and has a gangway before it, as has the cabin. The kitchen lies under the forecastle. Provisions and merchandise are in the hold, and the powder room is under the gun room.

This, in outline, is the ship's design, but to evoke its disorder is impossible. You cannot move around for the casks of Champagne, trunks, chests and boxes strewn around. Sailors swear, cattle low, birds and poultry scream on the poop and the wind howls. There is the din of the whistling wind in the rigging and the creaking of the timbers. Several other ships are at anchor near us and we are deafened by officers hailing crew through loudspeakers: *hard a starboard, cast off moorings…*Tired by this uproar, I got into a boat and went ashore at Port Louis.

It was very windy. We walked through the streets but met nobody. From the citadel walls I saw a black horizon and the Ile de Groix covered in thick fog. On the shore crowds of women chilled to the bone and a sentry on the walls astonished at the endurance of the men fishing in the middle of the tempest.

Tightly buttoned up and soaked through, holding on to our hats, we hurried to get back. Passing through Lorient, we saw the whole market square covered with fish: white and purple skate, others covered with prickles, dog-fish, enormous conger eels twisting on the paving stones, huge baskets full of crabs and lobsters; piles of oysters, mussels, cockles; cod, sole and turbot… in short, a miraculous catch, like that of the Apostles.

These good people live in faith and piety. When they fish for sardines, a priest goes on the first boat, and blesses the water. It's the conjugal love of the olden days: whilst the fishermen are arriving back, their women and children hang from their necks. It is thus among people in need that we can still find virtue: as if man retains his morality only while living between hope and fear.

This part of the coast abounds in fish. The same species of fish are, in general, larger than elsewhere, but their taste is inferior. I was assured that the sardine haul brought in four million *livres* to the province. It is rather odd that there are no crawfish in the Britanny rivers; perhaps because the waters do not run fast enough.

Back in our inn again, with the din of the wind and sea still buzzing in our ears. Two Parisians, Messrs. B..., father and son, who were due to board ship with us, without so much as a word, ordered a carriage and have returned to Paris.

Letter 4

On Board the Marquis de Castries, 3 March

I have no time to say goodbye: we are setting sail. Please look after the five letters enclosed: there are three for Russia, Prussia and Poland. Wherever I have travelled, I have left behind someone I miss.

Our vessel is at peak. I hear the sound of the whistles, the hissing of the capstan, the sailors heaving the anchor. The last gun is fired. We are under sail and I see the shore, the ramparts and roofs of Port Louis disappear. Goodbye friends, more dear to me than the treasures of India! Goodbye, forests of the North, which I will never see again! Tender friendships! Times of rapture and happiness sunk like a dream! Goodbye! One lives but for a day, to die the rest of one's life.

Log

March 1768

We left on the 3rd at a quarter past eleven in the morning. The tide was not high enough and the wind very nearly pushed us on to a rock to the right of the channel. When we reached the Ile de Groix we lay to, waiting for some passengers, but only one joined the boat, due to the foul weather.

A violent storm arose on the 5th. The ship was on her way under its two lower sails. I was terribly seasick. At half past ten in the morning, still in bed, I felt a great shudder. Someone shouted that the ship had struck the bottom. I climbed on to the deck where I found everybody in a panic. A wave struck us on the starboard side and carried off the yawl, or little launch, with the chief officer and three men. One of them remained entangled in the shroud of the main mast from where he was taken, his shoulder and hand crushed. It was impossible to save the others, and we never saw them again.

This disaster happened because the ship did not respond to its helm. The poop was too low in the water, which damaged the action of the rudder. The bad weather lasted all day and the ship's motion killed most of the poultry. I had a dog on board that constantly and anxiously panted.[17] The only birds that seemed impervious were the sparrows and canaries, used to perpetual motion. We are taking these birds to India out of curiosity.

I was incredibly sick, as were the other passengers. There is no remedy against this evil, which causes dreadful vomiting. However, it is useful to eat some dry food, and especially acidic fruit.

The weather turned fine on the 6th. We prayed to God for those poor sailors. The chief officer was a really decent man. The chaos of the day before was made good. When the wave crashed on to the ship, it broke the beam that goes round the hatchway, although it was ten inches thick. On the 7th we reckoned ourselves to be near Cape Finisterre, where gusts of wind and a rough sea are common, as with all capes. On the 8th a beautiful sea and fair wind. We saw some white birds with black borders round their wings, called Velvet Sleeves.

The air felt much hotter and the sky more pleasant on the 9th and 10th. We approached the Fortunate Isles, the Azores, if it is true that heaven has placed good fortune in any particular island. On the 11th the wind dropped and the sea was littered with *bonnets flamands*, a kind of viscous creature shaped like a cap, which moves forward in the water.

On the 12th and 13th some regulations came into force. It was decided that each passenger would have but one bottle of water a day. Breakfast was fixed at 10 o'clock and would consist of salted meat and dried vegetables. The evening meal, at four o'clock, was a little better. We put out all the fires at 8 o'clock. On the 14th we expected to glimpse Madeira but were too far to the west. It was calm. We saw two brown birds the size of pigeons flying as high as the masts. We took them for land birds. These signs are important but sailors' methods of observing them are imprecise. They confuse all the species on the European coasts under one name.

On the 16th, at dawn, we saw the island of Palma ahead of us. On the left, Tenerife with its peak in the shape of a dome topped by a pyramid. These islands were covered with mist all day, and at night there were flashes of lightening and thunder, a spectacle that terrified the first sailors who discovered them in modern times. It is known that the Romans had heard about these islands, for Sertorius dreamt of withdrawing there. The Carthaginians, who traded in Africa, knew them. The historian Juba counted five islands and gave a detailed description of them.[18] One he called the island of snow because it remained covered with it all year. We did indeed see the peak under snow, even though the air was hot. These islands, so they say, are the ruins of the large island of Atlantis that Plato spoke about. By the depths of the ravines from which the mountains rise, one could believe that they are the debris of that original world, turned upside down by an event preserved as tradition among all people. According to Juba, Canary Island took its name from the large dogs bred there. The Spaniards, to whom the islands belong, make excellent malmsey there.

On the 17th, 18th and 19th we passed between these islands, with Tenerife on the left and Palma on the right. Gomera was to the east. I sketched these islands with their deep ravines or furrows.[19] We saw a flying fish. A lapwing perched on our ship and flew westwards. It was an orange-red colour, with wings mottled black and white; its bent beak was ebony black. On the 20th we left the island of Ferro behind, and lost sight of the Canaries. The sight of these islands, situated in such a fine climate, excited many a fantasy in us. We compared the tranquillity and abundance, the satisfaction and pleasures experienced by the islanders to our own agitated lives. Perhaps some unhappy Canarian on a burning rock spotted us and wished to be himself on board on the way to the Indies.

On the 21st we saw a land swallow and a shark. We were becalmed all day. On the 22nd the heat was so strong that it caused a number of bottles of Champagne to explode, although they were encased in salt: this is the system used by many officers outward bound for India; each bottle is sold there for one *pistole*. The flood of Champagne soaked everything, destroyed the lettuces and cress that I had sown in wet moss where these plants grow amazingly well. This salted liquor was so corrosive that it completely spoilt those papers of mine that it had wet.

On the 23rd a fresh wind. The sea appeared to be greenish. We saw a ship on its way to Senegal. On the 24th the trade wind prevailed from the northwest; the ship rolled very much.

The 25th and 26th, the weather fine and a good wind; we passed the latitude of the Cape Verde islands, which we did not see; they belong to the Portuguese. Fresh provisions can be found there, but water, the most precious, is found with difficulty. We saw flying fish and a land swallow. We noticed that the buckwheat in the holds heated to such a degree that we couldn't cup it in our hands. We brought it up on deck. Ships have been known to catch fire by this means. In 1760 an English ship loaded with hemp was burnt in the Baltic Sea. The hemp caught fire by itself. I saw the wreck on the coast of the isle of Bornholm.[20]

On the 27th an awning was erected to shelter us from the heat. On the 30th we got ready to fish and hooked ten tuna fish, of which the smallest weighed sixty pounds: we saw a shark. The heat increased and the crew suffered from thirst impatiently. On the 31st we caught a bonito; during the night desperately thirsty sailors pierced and opened the water jars of several passengers, who as a result found themselves, like the crew, reduced to one pint of water a day.

Observations on the Customs of Sea-faring People

I will only speak of the influence of the sea on sailors, in the hope of inspiring some indulgence in respect of the defects usually ascribed to them.

The speed of response that seamanship demands makes them coarse in their expressions. As they live far from land, they think of themselves as independent: they often speak of princes, of laws and religion with a freedom equal to their ignorance. Not that they aren't, according to circumstances, devout or even superstitious. I have known more than one who would not so much as touch a rope on a Sunday or a Friday. In general their religion depends on the weather.

The idleness of their lives makes them fond of scandal and stories. The quarter-deck is the place where the officers spin out their fables and tall stories.

The habit of constantly confronting new experiences makes them capricious concerning friends and tastes: at sea they long for land; on land they miss the sea.

On long voyages, it is prudent not to confide in anybody and never to argue. The sea naturally sours tempers. The slightest answering back turns into a quarrel. I have seen one arise from a question of philosophy. It is true that such questions have sometimes caused philosophers to fight each other on land. For the most part, sailors are taciturn and moody. Can one be gay in the midst of dangers, and deprived of the basic things of life?

One must not forget their good qualities. They are open, generous, brave, and, above all, good husbands. A seafaring man looks on himself as a stranger on land, especially in his own house. Amazed at the novelty of furniture, of the customs of home-life, he leaves the running of a world he knows little about to his wife.

Sailors add to these good and bad qualities the vices of their education. They are addicted to drunkenness. Every day a ration of wine or brandy is issued. There are seven men in a mess and I have seen them agree among themselves to drink alternately the allowance of all seven. Some are given to stealing. Some are clever enough to fleece their comrades while they sleep. In this class of wretched men, you can sometimes find individuals of extreme probity. Usually the master and the gunner are men you can trust, and they run the crew. You then could add to them the chief pilot who does not hold among us the rank that his merit deserves. On these three men depends the good behaviour of the crew and often the success of the navigation.

The lowest man on the ship is the cock or cook. The cabin boys are children, often treated barbarously. There is hardly an officer or sailor who does not make them feel his bad temper. The crew even amuse themselves on some boats by flogging them when it's calm to make the wind rise up, so they say. Thus man, who so often complains of his weakness, nearly always abuses his power.

From all this you will conclude that a ship is a place of dissension; that a convent and an island, which are kinds of ships, must be filled with discord and that Nature's intention, which is so openly understandable, is that the earth be peopled with families and not with societies and fraternities.

Having censured the manners of seafaring people, it would be right to extend some criticism to myself.[21] I made an essential mistake in my log for this month in forgetting to write down the names of the mate and the two other wretched sailors who were swept by a wave from the ship's deck on the 5th near Cape Finisterre. They might have been mere sailors, but they were human beings, companions, and, even more, worked hard together on a ship where I was but an idle speculator, and useless in practical matters.

I have often noticed in the accounts of voyages by Dutch and English ships that if the lowest sailor perished, his name, his age, where he was born, were noted down; to which were added some of his personal characteristics. You can find frequent examples in the accounts written by vice admirals, commodores, commanders. Captain Cook, above all, is very precise in his *Voyage around the World*.[22] This habit is proof of patriotism and of the depth of humanity that reigns among nations. Moreover, in a ship's log, the name, character and family background of a sailor who dies on board should be at least as interesting for men as the name, characteristics and family of a fish or a sea-bird caught in the open seas, which our sailors never forget to note in their logs whenever the occasion arises. Besides, there is not a broken yard or a snapped rope about which they do not make notes; all this to give a learned and scientific air to matters of the sea. That's what I have striven to imitate in my log, enticed by national precedents and by my country's education system, which leads each of us to want to be the best wherever we are, and thus to despise all who are beneath us, and often to hate those who are above us. As I had the honour of being an officer to his Majesty, with the grade of Captain-Engineer, I had not thought that sailors were sufficiently important to mention by name when they died. Even though I could plead that my heart was constantly busy with a grand human objective, in a journey that I had only undertaken to aid the happiness of the blacks in Madagascar, it is likely that I deceived myself by proposing, when all is said and done, that I too wanted the glory of being the best, even among savages. I was like many men I have known, who decide to create republics and yet who insist that they not be created in the place where they actually live. They want to create a republic in order to become legislators; but they would be very annoyed to live in them as mere citizens. We are trained for nothing more than vanity.

For me, adversity has so often told me that I was but a man often more wretched than a sailor, by the flaws in my health and prejudices, which have since childhood made me base my happiness on other people's fickle opinions. And if I could rewrite the account of a similar long-distance voyage, I would record not the measurements of a badly-constructed ship such as ours, unless the ship in question was remarkable for its speed or some other quality, but the names of all the men in the crew. I would not forget the lowest cabin boy, and instead of observing the habits of fish and birds that live outside the ship, I would study and note those of the sailors who make it move. For these human traits would not only be more interesting to note down than those of animals, but also more so than the traits of those people who never leave their corner of the earth, and especially those in high society, at whom all philosophers seem to aim their observations.

The manners of sea-faring people are far more varied thanks to their cosmopolitan and amphibious life, and more open through the rigours of their job and their frankness, than those of princes. This is where we can know man in the raw, ceaselessly struggling, without art, with his vices and virtues, against his passions and those of others, against fortune and the elements. Despite his defects, through which it would be unfair to characterize him, I would like to make this class of men interesting. Moreover, there is no character so depraved that he does not reveal some good qualities as compensation for his vices. Often, behind the grossest vices such as drunkenness and swearing, sailors hide excellent qualities. You find daring and generous men who without a moment's hesitation, throw themselves into the sea to save some wretch about to drown. Some have plenty of imagination, and during a watch of six hours tell marvellous stories to their comrades where they link incidents with as much art and interest as in *The Arabian Nights*; others, extremely taciturn, listen intently, expressing themselves in signs, and pass days without speaking a word. Most of them are fascinating for their misfortunes, their shipwrecks, by their way of looking, by their religion, their opinions about science, war, the court and government in the countries they have seen or by the wars which they have seen, or by their love life, so different to those of shepherds. But if instead of limiting oneself to studying their manners, we could busy ourselves in softening them, one would find extremely grateful friends. I think that a traveller, in deciding to observe the society of his travelling-companions, could banish for himself and for his readers the monotony of his long journey. But we are so accustomed to despise what we think to be beneath us that I can say in a journey of four and a half months where one saw but sky and water, there were not half of our poor sailors whose names were known by the passengers and by the officers: and when one of them came into a room, we paid less attention than if it had been a cat or a dog. Thus is the poor and wretched man turned into a stranger to his fellow man by our heartless institutions!

I return to my journal.

April 1768
On the 1st we saw sharks and caught one; a bonito also. I intend to continue my observations on fish at the end of my log for this month. On the 2nd, calm weather and then squalls. We are at the limits of the southern trade winds. In the afternoon a squall forced us to reef all our sails. We approach the Equator and now have little twilight. On the 4th we had a stormy sky. We heard thunder in the distance and then we had a squall. A sailor who died of scurvy was buried at sea; several others are affected. This disease shows itself early and spreads alarm through the crew. We caught bonitos and sharks.

The 5th and the 6th. At three o'clock in the morning there was a terrible storm which forced us to reef all our sails except the mizzen. I have always noticed that the rising of the moon dispels the clouds in a conspicuous way. Two hours after it is above the horizon, the sky is perfectly clear. We had two days of calm, mixed with rainy squalls. On the 7th we hooked bonitos. I saw some glass easily cut with scissors under water: I cannot explain the cause.

On the 8th and 9th we caught a shark, some remora and two tuna fish. Although near the Equator, the heat did not bother me as the air is cooled by the storms. On the 10th the Crossing of the Equator baptism, or ducking, was announced. A sailor, disguised in a mask, went and asked the captain to follow the ancient custom. These are rituals invented to dispel melancholy in the crew. Our sailors are very sad. Scurvy gains ground bit by bit and we have not yet covered one third of the journey. On the 11th the baptism ceremony. The principal passengers were lined along a rope, to which their thumbs were tied with a ribbon. Some drops of water were poured on to their heads. We gave some money to the pilots.[23]

On the 13th crossed the Equator. The sea at night seemed covered with luminous phosphorous. The lower deck is cleaned every Sunday; the chests and hammocks of the crew are brought up on to deck and pitch is melted between the planks; a third of our water jars were found to be empty, though we have not travelled a third of our journey. The 14th, 15th and 16th, variable winds; very hot. We were continuously surrounded by bonitos, tuna fish, porpoises, and *bonnets flamands*, and saw a huge shark.

On the 17th, 18th and 19th the calm and heat continued. Pitch melted from the rigging. Irritation and impatience increased on board. It is not rare to lie becalmed a whole month near the Equator. I saw a whale swimming westwards. On the 20th, 21st and 22nd the distressing calm continues, as do our jitters. The ship was surrounded by sharks. Some tuna fish, bonitos, five or six sharks and a porpoise, with a very pointed head, were all caught. Sailors claim that a porpoise promises wind: accordingly, at midnight the wind picked up. On the 24th and 25th some squalls, and changes in the wind. Towards the evening the moon was ringed by a large colourless circle.

On the 26th a white bird, which the sailors said was a booby. In the evening, in full sail, we were hit by a violent squall that turned us on our side for a few minutes. Our ship sails slowly. When the wind is fair, we make but two leagues an hour. On the 27th high seas, fresh wind, and squalls of rain. We saw a petrel, which the English call the Bird of Storms. On the 29th fine weather with more squalls. At sunset we saw a ship to windward, steering the same course as us. On the 30th a fine fresh wind and beautiful sea. The air cooled. We saw last night's ship, a little ahead. She had a crowded sail as we had. She hoisted English colours, we ours. We caught tuna fish and saw a flying fish.

Observations on the Sea and Fish

There is no sight sadder than the open sea. You soon become very impatient at occupying the centre of a circle, the circumference of which you never reach. There are, however, some interesting moments: I do not only mean storms; during a period of calm, and especially at night in the torrid zone, one is surprised at how the sea sparkles. I took in a glass some of those luminous points of which the sea is full: I watched them moving in a lively way. They are said to be newly hatched fish; sometimes they can be seen in clusters, shaped like moons. At night, when the ship is under way and is accompanied by fish, the sea looks like a vast firework show, shining with sparks and silver flashes.

I will let you reflect on the prodigious amount of living beings at home in this element. I will limit myself to some observations on the different species of fish that we found in the open seas.

The *bonnet flamand*, a jellyfish called by the ancients, I believe, the *marine lung*, is a species of animal formed of a gelatinous substance, not unlike a mushroom. Its upper part contracts and dilates by which it moves forward very slowly. I know nothing else about it. This animal is so common that we found the sea covered with it for several days. It varies greatly according to its size and colour, but the shape is always the same. You can find huge ones during the summer on the Normandy coasts.

The *galère* is made of the same substance, but this animal seems gifted with more intelligence and malignity. Its body is a kind of oval bladder, crowned lengthways with a crest or sail that is always out of the water, facing the wind. When a wave overturns it, it rises quickly again and faces the wind with the roundest part of its body. I have seen many together, ranged like a fleet of ships.[24] You might build some sort of sail on this mechanism, along the lines of which a boat would sail against the wind. Underneath hang several blue filaments with which it seizes whatever tries to catch it. These filaments burn you straight away, like the most powerful caustic. One day I saw a young sailor swim out to catch one, and his arms were so burnt that the shock nearly drowned him. This *galère* has beautiful colours while still alive, from sky blues to pinks. The *bonnet flamand* can be found near French waters, the *galère* as you approach the tropics.

In the latitude of the Azores I saw a kind of shellfish floating and living in the sea foam, shaped like the metal of an arrow, or a bird's beak: it is tiny, transparent and easy to break; this is perhaps the same as that found in ambergris. At this same latitude we found blue snails floating on the water's surface, like bladders filled with air. Their shell was very thin and fragile; they were full of a beautiful purplish blue liquor. But this is not the shellfish called "purple" by the ancients.

A much more common shellfish is that which attaches itself to the hull of ships by means of a ligament which it contracts in bad weather. It is white, shaped like an almond and composed of four pieces. It puts out a number of filaments that have a regular motion. They breed in such amounts that the ship's forward movement is retarded by them.[25]

In the tropics the flying fish is very common. It is the same size as a herring, and flies in troops, with a leap as long as that of a partridge. In the sea it is hunted by fish, and in the air by birds. Its destiny appears very wretched as it encounters in the air the danger it flees from under water; but there is a compensation. It often escapes the birds by being a fish and the fish by being a bird. During storms they are chased by frigate birds and tuna fish which leap prodigiously after them.[26]

The *encornet* is a small type of squid that carries out more or less the same actions. It also has the ability to blacken the water by ejecting very dark ink. Perhaps it does not swim as well. It is shaped like a trumpet. These two kinds of fish often fall on to the deck and are tasty to eat.

The tuna of the open seas seemed different when tasted to that of the Mediterranean. It is very dry and has no fat but around the eye. It has small entrails; its flesh is hard against its skin. Eight muscles, four large ones and four little ones, make up its body; a transverse section looks like that of a sawn tree trunk. It is fished at dawn and at sunset when the shadows of the waves disguise the hook in the shape of a flying fish. A school of tuna has been following us for six weeks and is easy to distinguish. One has a red wound on its back after being harpooned two weeks ago. It is not hindered by this.

Can fish live without sleeping and does salt water heal wounds? I read somewhere that M. Chirac cured the Duc d'Orléans' wounded wrist by making him soak it in the waters of Balarue.[27] The flesh of the tuna is healthy, but spoils. I was assured that it was harmful to eat tuna in these latitudes when salted. I saw the results in a sailor who tried it. His skin became red as scarlet and he had a fever for twenty-four hours.[28]

As well as tuna we hooked many bonitos. They are a kind of mackerel and some reach the size of tunas. Inside them I have found soft roe and in their flesh living worms the size of a grain of barley. The fish did not appear to be troubled.

Sharks abound along the Equator. As soon as it is calm, the ship is surrounded by them. This fish swims slowly, without a sound. He is accompanied by several smaller fish called pilots, speckled with black and yellow. If something falls into the sea, in the twinkle of an eye, they come and reconnoitre and then return to the shark which approaches his prey, turns sideways and swallows it. If it's a bird, he won't touch it, but if hungry, the shark will even devour nails. The shark is the tiger of the sea. I have seen some more than ten feet long. Nature has made him very shortsighted. He swims slowly, due to the round shape of his head, which joined to the position of his mouth forces him to turn on his back to swallow, thus preserving most fish from his voracity. He has no bones but cartilage, similar to all voracious sea-fish, like the sea dog, the ray, the cuttlefish. Like the shark they see poorly, are bad swimmers, and have their mouths underneath, and are also viviparous. Thus their gluttony has been mitigated by failings in their speed, their sight, their propagation.

The shark's jaws are armed with five or six rows of teeth above and below. They are flat and cutting on the sides, pointed, and serrated like lances. They have but two rows perpendicularly, the others are hidden and arranged in such a way that they are replaced by an admirable mechanism when they are frequently broken. The shark is baited with a bit of meat fastened on to an iron crook. Before pulling it out of the water, you tie a sliding knot round its tail and when it's on deck and tries to snap at the sailors, they cut it with an axe. Its tail has one fin only, shaped like a sickle. The Chinese value it as an aphrodisiac. Otherwise fishing sharks has no purpose. I have tasted its flesh and it reeks of urine. It is claimed that it induces fever. Sailors only fish sharks to mutilate them. They poke out their eyes, they slit open their bellies, they tie several together by the tail and chuck them overboard again: a spectacle worthy of a sailor. The shark is so vivacious that I saw one move long after its head had been cut off. However, I have seen some drown very quickly after being plunged several times into the sea while still hooked.

You nearly always find a sucking-fish or remora on sharks. It is long like a herring. On its head a slightly concave oval surface is used to attach itself with a vacuum by means of nineteen blades which are displayed like the rods of a screen. I put some living ones in a glass from which I couldn't pull them off. This fish has one striking characteristic: it swims with its belly and gills in the air. Its skin is rough and its mouth is armed with several rows of little teeth. We several times ate these sucking-fish that tasted like fried artichokes. Apart from the pilot fish and the sucking-fish, the shark harbours an insect in its skin, shaped like half a pea, with a long beak. This is a kind of louse.

The porpoise is well-known. I have seen one species with a very pointed snout. Sailors call it the sea-arrow because of its speed. I have seen one swim round the ship while it was travelling at two leagues an hour. They harpoon this animal, which blows out air and seems to complain when hooked; it is a bad fish to catch, its flesh is dark, hard, heavy and oily.

I have also seen a dorado, the fastest of fish, it is claimed. It is erroneously said that this is the dolphin of the ancients, so fully described by Pliny. Whatever may be known, we did not experience its friendship for man. We saw, deep down, its shining golden fins, and its beautiful sky-blue back.

Sometimes about half a league away we saw whales spouting water. They are smaller than those of the North and seem to me, from a distance, like overturned boats.

If these details have annoyed you, think how much I have enjoyed writing them down. There was nothing else to do in an element whose inhabitants have nothing to do with man.

May 1768

On the 1st, at sunrise, the ship we had already seen days before was in our wake, and catching up with us imperceptibly. At ten in the morning she was alongside. We noticed that all her sails were very old and that the crew's chests and beds were on deck. They asked us in English: "What cheer? What's your ship called? Where do you come from? Where are you bound?" We answered in English, and asked the same questions. She had come from London, 64 days before and was bound for China. The wind stopped us hearing more. She had 24 guns and weighed some 500 tons. She wished us a good journey and went on her way.

On the 2nd and 3rd we again saw the English ship followed by the tuna fish which had been following us for so long. We had violent squalls from the west. On the 8th and 9th the wind was ferocious, and the seas very high. The ship tilted to her side and water poured in through the portholes. Towards evening the wind fell, which often happens when the sun sets. We saw many land birds and some gulls, signs that we are near land.

On the 13th calm sea. At nine in the evening as I stood chatting with the captain on the gallery, I saw the horizon light up with luminous fire, running from the east to the north and shooting off red sparks. Violent squalls, with some thunder. Here the southeast winds usually end, but sometimes take you to 28 degrees of latitude. We now sought the westerly winds to help us pass the Cape of Good Hope.

On the 17th, 18th and 19th fine weather with fog. We saw a wave coming from the west, which always precedes wind from that quarter. Last night we saw a second meteor, and in the afternoon, a whale. On the 20th and the 21st it was rainy, with a variable wind. The air was cold. We saw a whale within pistol shot. Some claimed they saw petrels from the Cape. We saw some *taille-vents*. On the 26th a violent wind. Towards evening a storm surprised us in full sail. The boat could not turn, faced the wind and was knocked sideways. You cannot imagine the chaos. At last we were able to manoeuvre ourselves to escape the danger and save our masts. We saw the same birds. Our poor sailors are exhausted: after a storm they are not given anything to eat or drink.

Observations on the Sky, Winds and Birds

On the journey east, stars seem more luminous than those of the west. Apart from the Southern Cross, you can pick out the Magellanic constellation, two clouds formed by thousands of little stars. On one side of this are two spaces than seem darker than the rest of the night sky.

As we approach the Equator, twilight decreases so much that day is completely different to night. Why twilight increases can be easily explained by the refraction of rays towards the poles. In those uninhabited regions light merges with darkness, especially in the Aurora Borealis which is everywhere stronger the lower the sun rises above the horizon. It would have been awkward if night in the tropics had also merged with day for night seems made for the blacks of Africa who wait for the day's end to dance and revel. This is the time when the wild beasts of those parts come to refresh themselves in the rivers, and turtles climb on shore to lay eggs. The torrid zone would have been uninhabitable had there been long periods of twilight. Night in these climates is finer than the day. The rising moon dispels the vapours with which the air is covered. I share with sailors the observation that I have made so often, that the moon swallows up the clouds.

I have often admired the rising and setting of the sun. It is as hard to describe this spectacle as it is to paint it. Imagine on the horizon a beautiful orange colour tinged green that then melts away on the zenith with a lilac hue while the rest of the sky remains magnificently blue. The clouds that float here and there are of a beautiful pearl grey. Sometimes they are shaped into long streaks of crimson or scarlet; all these tints are vivid, distinct and fringed with gold.

One evening the clouds floated to the west in the shape of a vast net, similar to white silk. When the sun passed behind, each mesh of the net looked as if made of gold. The gold then changed into a fiery colour and scarlet, and the depths of the sky turned into light purple, green and celestial blue.

Great varieties of landscapes are frequently formed in the sky, and the most bizarre figures present themselves to the imagination. We picture promontories, steep and rugged rocks, towers and villages over which light diffuses all the colours of the prism. It is perhaps to the richness of these colours that one should attribute the beauty of the peacock and the shellfish which live in or around these seas. I will now describe to you the birds I saw flying past our ship, with the names given them by the sailors. You can guess that my descriptions cannot be very accurate.

In all latitudes the most common bird is a kind of swallow or halcyon called the foul weather bird, or petrel, by the English. It is blackish-brown and skims the water's surface; in bad weather it follows the ship's wake, probably to find shelter from the wind. For the same reason it flies between two waves, skimming the water's surface.

In two and a half degrees of latitude north we saw our first frigate birds. They were thought to have come from Ascension Island. In form and size they are like a stork, black and white, with wings that extend a great way out, and they have a long neck. Under their bills the males have a puff of skin, round as a ball and red. This seabird never rests on the water, yet has been spotted 300 leagues from land.

Larger and more compact is the booby. It is white, mingled with grey, and fishes by diving under water. The frigate bird is at war with the booby. When the booby has filled its beak with fish, the frigate bird attacks it and makes it surrender its spoils, which it catches in the air.

When gulls are found in flocks, it denotes shallow water and means that land is near. They are white and by flight and shape can be mistaken for pigeons.

The *envergure* is larger than a duck. It is white under the belly and greyish brown on the wings and back. Its name comes from the breadth of its wings. The *damiers*, or petrels, are found only near the Cape of Good Hope. They are as big as pigeons, with a black head and tail and a white belly; the back and wings are marked regularly black and white like a draught-board. We next saw the albatross, called *mouton du Cap* in French. It is larger than a goose, has a flesh-coloured beak and huge wings, mixed with grey and white. They are also found around the Cape of Good Hope. I have never seen these birds at rest on the water. Spotting them could indicate latitude.

June 1768

On the 1st westerly winds made us believe that we should soon round the Cape. On the 2nd we took precautions. New rope was tied to the wheel of the rudder and to securing the masts. We put on four new sails. The boats, and everything that was moveable, were tautly lashed.

Every day to the 7th fresh wind. We saw a huge number of gulls, albatrosses and petrels as well as the Cape reed, which looks like those long horns played by shepherds. Sailors make a kind of trumpet from the empty stalks of this seaweed. The sea was covered with mist. Fifteen sailors are ill with scurvy. At midday on the 7th a goose-sized bird, with short tawny brown wings, a head like a hen, and a tail shaped like a trefoil leaf glided above our masts for some time. On the 13th our sounding recorded 95 fathoms, a muddy and greenish bottom. This was a great joy. The sounding indicated that we have miscalculated by about 200 leagues in our logs.

Fresh wind on the 15th. The ship behind us hoisted the English flag and soon passed us. Another ship hoisted the French flag and lowered her sails in order to join us but our captain did not want to come to. The ship was the *Digue*, a man of war which had sailed a month before us.

On the 23rd, half an hour after midnight, a huge wave smashed four of the five windows of the great cabin, even though the shutters were barred with Saint Andrew's crosses. When I heard the din I opened my door and in an instant my room was flooded and my furniture floating about. The water rushed out by the great cabin's door like in a mill's sluice. We called the carpenters and hurried to nail new boards across the windows. We now sailed with the mizzen; the wind and sea terrifying.

Hardly had this emergency been seen to than a large chest used as a table, full of salt and Champagne bottles, broke its lashings. The rolling of the vessel made it slide up and down like a dice. This enormous chest weighed many tons and threatened to crush us in our room. Then it burst open and the bottles rolled out and smashed in utter chaos. The carpenters came back again and fixed it back in place after a good deal of effort.

As the rolling stopped me sleeping, I had thrown myself on to my bed with my boots on and in my dressing gown; my dog seemed seized by panic. As I was busying myself trying to calm it down I saw a flash of lighting through a crack in the porthole and heard thunder. A moment later a second clap of thunder was heard and my dog shuddered and yelped. Then a third flash of lightning, followed by another clap of thunder straight after and I heard someone scream on deck that some ship was in danger. In truth, the din was similar to a cannon being fired close-by. I smelt a strong stink of sulphur and climbing up to the deck immediately felt the extreme cold. There was a strange silence and the night was so dark that I could make out nothing. However, sensing someone next to me, I asked him what was happening. He answered: "We have just carried the quarter-master to his cabin; both he and the first pilot fainted. The thunderbolt fell on to the ship and our great mast cracked." I could then see that the main top-sail had fallen on to the main-top. Neither mast nor rigging could be seen. All the crew had retired to the council room.

We made an inspection around the forecastle. The thunderbolt had gone down the length of the mast as far as there. A woman who had just given birth had seen a globe of fire at the foot of her bed, yet we could find no signs of fire. We all impatiently waited for night to clear.

At daybreak I again climbed up to the deck. We could see some white and some copper-coloured clouds in the sky. The wind blew from the west, where the horizon appeared a flaming red as if the sun had wanted to rise there while the east was still quite black. The sea formed monstrous waves, like pointed mountains surrounded by hills of various heights. On their crests were great streams of foam, coloured like rainbows. The waves were so high from the quarter-deck that they seemed taller than the mast tops. The wind made such a din in the rigging that we could not hear each other speak. We fled with the wind behind us under the mizzen sail. A piece of the topmast hung from the end of the main-mast which was split in eight places to the level of the deck. Five of the six iron rings binding it were melted; the gangways were strewn with debris from the mast. As the sun rose the wind redoubled its fury. Our vessel could no longer be controlled by the rudder and swung sideways. Then the mizzen-sail broke; its flapping was so violent we feared it would smash the mast. In an instant the forecastle was under water with waves breaking over the starboard cat-head so that we lost sight of the bowsprit. Clouds of surf covered everything as high as the poop. The ship could no longer be steered and now lay completely sideways to the waves. With each roll it took in water as far as the foot of the main-mast, and rose upright with the greatest difficulty.

In this moment of danger, the captain shouted to the pilot to put before the wind, but the vessel did not budge or obey the helm. He ordered the sailors to reef the mizzen-sail that the wind was tearing to shreds; these wretched men were terrified and hid under the quarter-deck. I saw some of them weeping, others threw themselves on their knees and prayed. I crept along the starboard by gripping the tackling. A Dominican, who was the ship's chaplain, followed as did Sir André, a passenger. Several members of the crew followed suit and we were able to reef the sail, though more than half had been torn away. They wanted to raise a jib in order to sail before the wind, but it was ripped like a piece of paper.

We remained dry, but rolling about in a terrifying way. Once I let go of the tackle I was holding, and I slipped to the foot of the great mast, up to my knees in water. In the end, next to God, our salvation came from the vessel's solidity, and its three decks. The storm lasted until evening. Our furniture was thrown about and smashed; sometimes I even found myself standing upright on the wainscot of my cabin.

This was the tribute we paid to the straits of Mozambique, more dreaded than rounding the Cape of Good Hope. The officers assured me that they had never seen such a rough sea. All the upper parts of the boat were so loosened that in the joints of the pilasters in my room I could insert mutton bones which were then crushed by the shifting timbers.

On the 24th at four in the morning, the wind died down, although the sea remained very rough. Everybody worked all day to restore the main-mast to its proper place, fastening it with side-pieces. The effects of the thunderbolt defy explanation. The main mast is split in the form of a zig-zag, and five feet under the top is splintered, with more cracks down to the deck. In all these cracks I could detect no sign of blackening and no smell. The wood had kept its natural colour.

We saw some albatrosses. The foul weather had killed off all our livestock and doubled the amount of sailors sick with scurvy. On the 25th we fastened the two side-pieces around the mast. They were two pieces of wood 45 feet long, hollowed in grooves to fit the mast's circumference. Everybody got down to work because the crew was so exhausted. A whale passed within pistol shot; it was about as long as the long boat.

On the 26th the weather became tolerable. We sang the *Te Deum* according to custom to thank God for having survived the Cape and the Mozambique Channel. We spent the whole day fixing the great mast. On the 27th we completed work on the mast that holds the main sail. A man died of scurvy and 21 are now ill and unfit. On the 28th an eight-day infant died of scurvy. There are now 28 sailors sick. To keep watch we have been forced to use the domestic servants on board, as well as passengers not in the great cabin.

Observations of Possible Use for the Better Management of Sailors

To me there did not seem to be proper respect between the officers of the East Indian Company. The superiors are afraid of those below them. As most posts result from favours, no authority can be established in a reasonable ways. This problem seems without a solution.

No ship should be at sea for more than three months without reaching a harbour. Sailors do not have enough water in such hot climates, being reduced to half a pint a day. Sailors are poorly fed. Their biscuits are full of worms; salt beef quickly degenerates into a disagreeable food.

July 1768

On the 3rd fair weather, rough sea. One of the carpenters died of scurvy; forty people now ill with it, and it is making visible progress thanks to the vapours from the hold filled with masts that have been lying in the mud. A sailor on the watch dropped dead on the 9th. We are all faint and weak; some suffer from attacks of vertigo and feel sick in the stomach. Yet we are more than 100 leagues from the nearest land.

On the 11th fair wind. Sixty-six of the men now sick in their beds. Eight more days at sea and we will all die. We buried a young man of 17 at sea. On the 12th fine weather and favourable sea. Now there are only three men to each watch and officers and passengers help man the ship. On the 13th land is sighted. We are so depressed that nobody rejoices. Eighty men are sick with scurvy.

On the 14th, approaching land, many people are ill. I felt uneasy and sweated profusely. We hoisted the colours and fired our guns for help but only one pilot came aboard. He spoke to us about troubles amongst the leaders of the islands about which he guessed we were anxious.[29] On the other hand, we on board thought that our vessel's divisions and miseries would concern the inhabitants on shore.

We passed on our left two small, inhabited islands called Round Island and the Isle of Serpents. We passed then within gunshot of Coin de Mire, another island on the left. We kept a good distance from the shore on account of the reefs at Pointe aux Cannoniers. In the afternoon at half past one we entered the harbour. Two hours later I landed, thanking God for having delivered me from the dangers and exhaustion of so dreadful a voyage.

Four months and 12 days at sea, without touching any port. According to my log, we have sailed about 3,800 marine leagues or about 4,700 ordinary ones, and lost eleven men, including the three washed out to sea, and one who died as he was stepping ashore.

Observations on Scurvy

Scurvy is caused by the poor quality of air and food. The officers, who are better fed and lodged than the sailors, are the last to be attacked by this illness, which spreads even to the animals. My dog was much troubled by it. There is no cure for it other air from land and fresh vegetables. Some palliative may moderate the effects of this illness, like using rice, acid liquors and coffee: and abstaining from all that is salty. Great virtues are attributed to the use of turtle, but that is a prejudice, like many others lightly adopted by sailors. At the Cape of Good Hope, where there are no turtles, those with scurvy, the scorbutic, are cured as quickly as those in the hospital in Mauritius where they are treated with broth made of this creature. On our arrival, nearly everybody was treated this way; but I refused, not being fond of turtle and was the first to be cured because I ate fresh vegetables.[30]

Scurvy begins with a general lassitude; you feel like resting, are depressed, and do not feel like doing anything; daylight is painful, and you are relieved at night only. The disease then erupts as red spots on your legs and chest, and bleeding ulcers in your gums. Sometimes there are no external symptoms, but the slightest wound becomes incurable while still at sea, and then it advances rapidly. I wounded myself slightly on a finger; after three weeks the sore had taken off the skin entirely and it had spread to my hand, despite all the remedies applied. A few days after landing, it cured itself. Before the sick were landed, we were careful to leave them one day on board to breathe little by little the air from land. Despite these precautions, one of the men was unable to bear the change and died.

It is hard to depict the sad state we were in after arriving. Picture the great mast struck by the thunderbolt, a ship with its flag at half mast, firing cannons every minute, with a few sailors like ghosts, sitting on deck; our scuttles all open, out of which wafted a foul vapour; the between-decks full of the dying, the forecastle packed with the sick taking sun and dying even as they spoke to us. I will never forget a young man of 18 to whom the evening before I promised some lemonade. I searched for him on deck among the others; he was pointed out to me on a plank, dead.

It is said that the Abbé de Saint-Pierre, a very fine citizen but, as far as I know, no relation of mine, for originally my ancestors came from Lorraine, attributed all Louis XIV's defects to his education,[31] as I do for our nation's faults. Place two Frenchmen at the ends of the earth, said Montaigne, and they fight. We all speak of freedom and of the Republic, but I have not seen in Paris or elsewhere any society, however small, without its tyrant.

It is far worse on a French ship after a long voyage. When it arrives, everybody gathers around to hear the news. You could bet, without fear of losing, that everybody on board has quarrelled. Many have arranged duels on land but often, thank God, the joy of arrival makes them forget.

I have noted that misfortune makes us wicked, for the unhappy man is wicked if he isn't raised to a state of virtue, that is, to love his neighbours even if they are unjust. Thousands of quarrels are born on board, arising from the simplest of matters. The ignorant do not cause these, but the erroneous; I beg that this word be kept to describe those men struck both by error and by emulation, whose number is infinite among us. I have found nothing so unusual or so lovable as the ignorant, for they seek to listen and learn, but the erroneous want to talk, teach and dogmatize like tyrants. On a ship where men are embittered by the regime, by the food and by irritation with people or by ambition, everything contributes to quarrels. The best thing is to seclude yourself as much as possible.

Besides, much can be done to sweeten the fate of sailors, such indispensable men. The first measure to banish their physical and moral ills would be to abolish corporal punishment, especially with regard to cabin boys and children. Beatings make men cowardly and cruel. They should be punished by depriving them of celebrations and pleasures, stimulating them with prizes, but encouraging them with their duties. They have enough to bear just coping with the elements. It is the tyrant in man who dreamed up beating his fellow men. What would the ship's officers say if they were beaten for their faults? Honour drives them, it is said, and why not let honour lead the sailors? Are they not French, our brothers? We do not beat our grenadiers in their regiments. We do not beat workers in factories who do not carry out their duties, or peasants who do not labour properly. Sailors are rough but it is the way they are treated that has made them so, not the sea. We do not beat fishermen, good sailors, on their boats. Everywhere it's a crime to beat children.

Sailors should be supplied with plenty of fresh vegetables. Potatoes, cabbage and roots like beetroot last a long time at sea. If I was one of the last to be affected by scurvy, I put this down to not having eaten salt beef and that I lived for a long time on beetroots and beans. In the absence of fresh vegetables, one could follow the example of Captain Cook who on his world voyage did not lose one sailor to this cruel disease. His voyage was a model of humanity and precaution. It would make sense to put into port after two months. On the long voyages like those to India you could stop over in Brazil and the Cape of Good Hope. Cursed be the nation that puts mercantile interests above human rights by closing its ports to foreign ships that need to stop there. It is by welcoming foreigners that the Dutch have made the Cape such a place of riches.

At the same time as looking after the physical side, we must provide for the moral angle. We pray together; I would like captains, every Sunday, to read a chapter aloud from the New Testament. This book is ideal for seamen; it was aimed at fishermen, it speaks constantly of union between men. I would, above all, like the evening prayers on Sundays read in French as it seems strange to me that people pray in Latin, a language that they do not understand at all.

They should also be cheered up with celebrations, and games every evening. It was, so they say, Palamedes who invented dice at the siege of Troy to entertain soldiers who lacked bread.[32] Above all it would be good to have music, for music banishes worries. A sailor with some musical talent could earn more. It is incredible how gaiety contributes to health. I have seen one of our foremen who put everybody in high spirits with his good humour, and thus delayed the progress of scurvy. One could, through the consolations of religion and philosophy, come to their help.

I would also like women to be introduced on to merchant ships and, however odd this may seem, I do not think it impossible. One would avoid so much trouble. Tartar and Arab women travelled with their husbands in caravans and long pilgrimages. Many jobs could be given to women like preparing food, washing clothes, putting away sails. Plotting would become harder on a ship than anywhere else as everybody is watching. Married people could have their own quarters. Hard-working women would not excite passions. One could even reward sailors by allowing their wives to accompany them. The chief officers could have the same prerogative. Indeed, some eight to ten women usually travel on a ship to the Indies and, when they are of good education, these are the ships where there is most gaiety, good health, and dare I say, happiness. I have seen women sail on Dutch ships and share the work with their husbands. On long journeys in canoes, savages in the Southern Seas bring women and children. It would be surprising if in states of society that are more civilized that men would be less masters of their passions than in a natural state. The introduction of women on to ships would bring urbanity, and would prevent all kinds of disorder and dissipation typical of sailors on shore.

Letter 5[33]
My Arrival at Mauritius
The ship had its main-mast shattered by lightning and its flag at half-mast, its crew reduced to a handful who wandered about on the bridge, their minds even more sick than their bodies for five or six duels had been arranged on landing at shore. As for me, I was staring at the land and that beautiful dream I had constructed evaporated. All I could see around the harbour was a rugged coast, stripped of trees and covered in yellow grass. The air from the land contrasted with what we had been breathing and made us feel faint. The sick were not allowed to climb to the bridge in case the change of air proved fatal. We learned from the pilot that things on the island were ablaze, with two warring factions headed by the *intendant* and by the governor, and that there was only paper money. The ship entered the harbour, skirting two or three wrecked ships. The captain ordered the hatches to be left open so that air from land could reach the sick. For that reason we couldn't land for

twenty-four hours. We went ashore in the evening. My first task was to locate the chief engineer's house. I found him to be cheerful, gentle but weak. He was called M. du Breteuil. He received me very courteously, although after reading my commission saw that I wasn't from his corps. He offered me a bed and dinner, after which I went to greet the commander to whom M. du Breteuil introduced me. The former was already aware of M. Maudave's enterprise and the arguments I had had with him. He said they desperately needed clever people and that he had heard that I was quick-witted. This exaggerated compliment annoyed me because I realized it had been proffered in order to humiliate my chief with whom he was on bad terms. I returned to du Breteuil's house where we were served sea-cow which I found tough, like beef. I took pleasure in eating salad although I was warned not to have too much, which was odd as there was no fruit for dessert. Eating fruit daily ensured the disappearance of scurvy after three days, while the rest of the crew, eating turtle soup, took several weeks to recover. I am convinced that fresh food like cabbage, chicory and lettuce are more powerful cures for scurvy than animal food. I spent the night on a couch, but longed for the happiness of being free and alone. I was rented a lodging at the edge of the town that they call Port Louis; it was half a ground floor with one large room, its floor partially tiled; its walls were boards plastered with earth and whitewash; there was one single window, without glass but with rattan blinds, following the custom of the island. This lodging cost me ten *écus* a month, without furniture. I was lent a chest, some chairs, and with my cases everything was in the same room. I had no servants. The chief engineer said I could choose one of the King's blacks; the white clerk agreed to choose one for me; he was rather ugly and I realized the next day that he was a scoundrel when he stole a knife. I sacked him without making a fuss and opted for another with frizzy hair whom I had noticed was even-tempered and honest. I was not wrong and have never seen a man of such fine moral qualities.

So I became installed as an engineer during one of the worst squabbles on the island, without money or provisions, reduced from my great speculations about fortune and politics to become a master mason, of which I knew little. But I was consoled by the deep solitude visible through my window where, despite the yellow grass and rocks, my imagination could rest. I recalled the friends I missed, my hopes for great things. All that troubled me, but the melancholic and tranquil view let my soul repose, and the beautiful sky and the murmur of the steady wind threw me into a sweet and restful sadness.

Letter 6
Port Louis, 6 August 1768
Mauritius was discovered by a Portuguese navigator named Mascarenhas, and he called it the Isle Cerné. Then the Dutch claimed the island and named it Mauritius. Admiral Jacques Corneille Necq left Amsterdam with a squadron of eight ships on 1 March 1598.[34] His ships became separated by a storm around the Cape of Good Hope, and five arrived in December 1598 in the harbour in the southeast of Mauritius. They judged that this island was uninhabited: they found, however, on the shore a loaf of wax weighing 300 *livres* marked with Greek writing, some nets and a lever: proof of some shipwreck.[35] It is noticeable that being in the southeastern port, they were in that part of the island where currents bring in many things from the sea.

They remarked on several things not seen since.

On an island to the left of the harbour they found trees which gave them Indian nuts, that is coconut palms; these coconuts had drifted in from the sea. In my time I only saw coconut palms in the southeastern port, which had been planted long before. They also drew some palm trees with round leaves that could shelter a man from rain: I think this was probably a kind of latan palm.

They sowed some orange and lemon seeds: I have only found them in this part of the island. They found a great quantity of very large land tortoises; there were none left in my time. They were brought over from Rodrigues Island. They found extremely odd birds as big as swans, without wings and in their place three or four black feathers. They could not fly. They called them nausea birds partly because they were so tough that they could not be cooked. Bontekoe who put into Mauritius in 1619 found these same birds which he called *drontes* or *dod-aers*. This bird was hideous and travellers described it the same way. It no longer exists on the island. If it is not a misshapen penguin, as it does not seem to be, how did it reach this island as it is not amphibious and could not have come with the currents? It is of note that they were found in that part of the island exposed to Indian Ocean currents.

The Dutch abandoned the island in 1712. The French, who had colonized neighbouring Réunion, only forty leagues distant, established themselves here. In this island there are two harbours; that on the southeast, where the Dutch settled and where the remains of their buildings can still be seen, is called Grand Port. It may be entered before the wind, but is difficult to get out of because the wind is almost always to the southeast.

The second is called Little Port or Port Louis on the northwest coast; ships enter and leave before the wind. This is the island's capital, though situated in the most unpleasant part. The town, also known as the Camp, has scarcely the appearance of a village, is built at the rear of the harbour and at the opening of a valley formed by a chain of high mountains covered with rocks, but without trees or bushes. For six months every year the slopes are covered with burnt grass which makes it all seem black, like a colliery. The highest part terminates in a rock, standing by itself called the Pouce.[36] This part has few trees, but a stream runs down through the town, with water that is not good to drink.

The town or Camp consists of wooden houses one storey high. Each house stands on its own, enclosed within palisades. The streets are regular, but not paved nor planted with trees. The ground is bristling with rocks and it is hard not to trip and break your neck. The town is not walled, nor fortified, except for a kind of mound of stone reaching from the harbour to the mountain. Fort Blanc defends the entrance, with a battery on the other side on the Isle aux Tonnelliers.

By the Abbé de Caille's measurements, Mauritius is 90,668 *toises* in circumference, and its greatest diameter is 31,890 *toises* from north to south.[37] The island is level in the northwest and in the southwest is covered with ridges of mountains. The highest of all stands at the mouth of the Rivière Noire. The most remarkable is called Pieter Both and is topped by an obelisk which is again crowned with a cubical rock which nobody has yet climbed. From a distance this pyramid resembles the statue of a woman.[38]

I cannot give you a more complete account of this place as I have just arrived.

Letter 7
Port Louis, 15 September 1768
Everything here differs from Europe, even the grass. The soil is almost everywhere a reddish colour, mixed with veins of iron, found near the surface in the form of grains the size of peas. In the drier parts the ground is very hard and resembles pipe clay. To make trenches I have seen people cut it with axes. As soon as it rains it becomes soft and sticky, yet they have not made it into good bricks.

There is no real sand here. The sand on the shore is composed of tiny fragments of shells, which become charred when burnt. There are rocks everywhere, from the size of your fist to boulders weighing a ton. They are full of holes at the bottom of which is a further depression shaped like a lentil. Many of the rocks are formed of concentric layers, like an onion. Some are stuck together in large masses, others seem as if broken and re-stuck. The island is paved with these rocks and the mountains formed entirely of such strata. They are an iron-grey colour, and contain a great deal of iron ore. At the foundry I saw some grains of beautiful copper and lead that were extracted from fissures in the rock, but in small amounts. Experiments like these are not encouraged here. The mineral appears too dispersed.

Three species of grass seem natural to the soil. A kind of turf grows along the shore that is thick and elastic. Its leaf is small and so sharp that it can prick you through your clothes. Cattle do not touch it. In fields there is a kind of couch grass that spreads out along the ground, with little branches stemming from its joints. This grass is hard, and cattle like it. The windy side of the island is distinguished by the best grasses, with large green leaves that are tender all year round.

A prickly kind of asparagus grows here, up to twelve feet high, clinging around the trees. I do not know if it is good to eat. I found a species of mallow shrub, with small leaves, which grows along paths. There is also a kind of thistle with yellow flowers whose seeds kill the birds that eat them. At the foot of a nearby mountain I found a sweet basil that smells like clove. It has a healing quality. There are dangerous hedges of prickly pear, with yellow flowers marbled red. The plant is packed with sharp prickles that grow on the leaves and on the fruit. The fruit is not eaten and is sour.

On the sand by the seashore grow *veloutiers*. There is down on this plant's branches, like velvet. The leaves are covered with glittering filaments. It bears white flowers in clusters. This shrub gives off a scent that from afar is pleasant, but as you get near it becomes foul.[39]

There is a plant, half bramble, half shrub, with pods that bristle with prickles and inside smooth, hard nuts of a pearl-grey, the size of a musket pellet. Its kernel is bitter. These nuts are said to be good for venereal diseases. A common shrub with large heart-shaped leaves grows in clearings. Its smell is sweet, like balm, after which it is called. Its only use is in baths.

A herb called pannier grass is found at the edge of woods. People have tried to make thread and cloth from it. Taken as an infusion it relieves chest pains.

A great variety of plants are all called lianas. Some are as thick as a man's leg and curl round trees, making the trunk look like a mast tangled in rigging. They support the trees against the cyclones whose violence I have often seen. When they fell timber in the wood they cut about two hundred trees near the roots and they remain upright thanks to the lianas which sustain them until they are cut down too. When this is done, one whole part of the forest seems to fall at once, with a tremendous din.

Before continuing, please note that I know nothing about botany. I describe things as I see them, but if you can, trust me when I say that everything is inferior to what grows in Europe.

Letter 8
Port Louis, 8 October 1768

I noticed, a few days ago, a large tree among rocks. I approached it and, trying to slice a bit off with my knife, I was surprised at the whole blade sinking in without my using any effort. Its consistency was like that of a turnip, and it had a very disagreeable taste. I tasted it but did not swallow, yet for some hours my throat was inflamed. It was like being pricked by pins. The tree is called a *mapou* and is deemed poisonous.

Most of the trees here take their names from the whims of the local inhabitants. The Watch tree is short, hard and twisted. When it burns it throws off large flames. It is used as a torch, and does not rot.

The *bois-de-canelle*, which is not the real cinnamon tree, is one of the tallest on the island. It is the best wood for carpentry. It resembles the walnut tree by its colour and veins. When it is first used it reeks of excrement, mixed with the blossoms of cinnamon. That is the only resemblance I could find with the spice. Its seed is covered with a red skin which has an acid but rather agreeable taste.

The *bois de natte*, of two species, is tall with small leaves. It is the finest redwood on the island and is used as timber.[40] The olive tree, whose leaf looks somewhat like our olive, is used in building.[41] The apple tree is a redwood of poor quality. I think it is this tree which produces what is called a monkey's apple, of an insipid taste. The jointwell tree, so-called because it joints well, is the most pliable wood around and is used by wheelwrights. It grows very tall and never splits.

The rosin tree, which exudes a resin similar to rosin, is one of the tallest trees of the island. The false *tatamaca* is also used for building. It is very pliable and grows thick. I have seen some 15 feet in circumference. It gives off a glue or resin.[42] The milk tree is so-called because it sweats a milk-like liquid. The stinking tree, excellent for carpentry, gets its name from its smell. The iron tree, whose trunk blends with its roots and shoots up with ribs like boards, deflects the iron of axes.

The *bois de fouge* is a large liana whose bark is very tough. It gives off a milky liquid used to cure wounds. The fig tree is very large, but its leaf does not resemble our fig. The figs look similar to ours and grow in bunches at the tip of a branch. They taste like the monkey apples. Its sweat is milky and when dried produces a glue called "elastic".

The ebony tree, with a white bark, has large, board-like leaves, white underneath and a sombre green above. Only the centre of this tree is black. Its trunk has six inches of wood for two of ebony. When freshly cut, this tree stinks of human excrement, and its flowers of clove. It's the contrary with the cinnamon whose flowers stink but whose bark smells pleasant. The ebony gives fruit like a medlar, full of a viscous, sugary juice with a pleasant taste.

The lemon tree only fruits in cool and damp places; its lemons are small but full of juice. The orange tree grows in the same places; its fruit are bitter. There are many orange trees around Grand Port in the south. I doubt whether these species are native to the island. Sweet oranges are extremely rare, even in gardens.

There is a rare species of sandalwood. I was given a piece that was grey-blue, with a faint scent. The *vacoa* is a kind of small palm tree whose leaves grow spirally round the trunk. It is used to make mats and bags.[43] The *latanier* is a tall palm tree with fan-like leaves at the top, and is used to roof houses. It produces one fan a year.[44]

The palm tree rises above all other trees. At its top it bears a cluster of palms, out of which issues a shoot, the sole part fit to eat. But to get it you have to cut down the tree. This shoot, which is given the name of cabbage, is made of young leaves rolled round each other, and is tender and very tasty.[45]

The mangrove grows directly in the sea. Its branches and roots twist under the sand and are so tangled they cannot be uprooted. Its wood is red and gives off a nasty dye.[46]

I've noticed that the majority of these trees have a very thin bark, some even have nothing but a kind of skin over them, and this makes them very different from trees in the northern hemisphere which nature has preserved from the cold by clothing them in several robes. Most have their roots visible above ground, which allows them to grip rocks. They are not tall, and their tops are hardly full yet very heavy. Tangled in liana, they are thus able to resist the cyclones that would have uprooted our pines and chestnuts.

As for their usefulness, not one can be compared to the durability and solidity of the oak, nor to the pliancy of the elm nor to the lightness of the pine and the chestnut in general. Their foliage has that disagreeable quality of all trees that keep their leaves all year round. Their leaves are hard and of a sombre green. Their wood is heavy, breakable and rots easily. Those that can be used for cabinetwork turn black when exposed to air, which gives the furniture a disagreeable appearance.

Along the streams, in the middle of woods, you come across

profoundly melancholic retreats. Water runs around the rocks, sometimes swirling past in silence, sometimes falling over a ledge with a deafening noise. The sides of these ravines are covered in trees which hang with bunches of scolopendria and clusters of liana, which dangle down. The land around is humped with large black rocks and carpeted by mosses that never see sunlight. Old tree trunks, toppled by time, lie covered with monstrous fungi, striped with various colours. You can find an infinite variety of fern; some, like leaves detached from their stalk, meander around the stones, and gain their subsistence from the rock itself; others rise up like a tree of moss and resemble a plume of silk feathers. The common sort is twice the size of the European one. Instead of reeds bordering the riverbanks, you only find *songes*, which grow profusely. They are a kind of water lily with a large leaf shaped like a heart that floats on the water without getting wet. Raindrops collect there like drops of shining silver. Their root is an onion of malignant quality, divided into white and black ones.[47]

These wild places were never gladdened by bird song or by the mating of peaceful animals. Sometimes your ears are assailed by the croaking of a parrot or by the shrill scream of some malicious monkey. Despite the disorder all around, these rocks could have been made habitable if the Europeans had not brought more evil than is found in nature to the island.

Port Louis, 8 October

When I read this letter to Jean-Jacques Rousseau he said: "But I don't find this place so unpleasant; I could be happy there." To tell the truth, I was too melancholic, my soul was sad and when I observed things my mind experienced all kinds of ills from my past, my present and my future. I was even more like this when I edited these letters in France. Moreover, I knew nothing about plants. I was thus unjust about nature. The *songes*, a type of water lily, prettily border the rivers and although our reeds hold another sort of charm for Europeans, I think that the *songes* are more practical and prevent water evaporation. Anyhow, reeds cannot grow among rocks. As for the roots, it is a fact that runaway blacks live from them and do not get sick: I never tasted them.

Letter 9
Port Louis, 7 December 1768
About Animals Native to Mauritius
Quadrupeds

The Abbé de la Caille said that the Portuguese brought monkeys to Mauritius. I do not agree with him because if they had wanted to settle here, they would not have imported this destructive animal, and if they had wanted to leave it on the island as game, they did not know whether there were fruit that suited it. Anyhow, monkey flesh has a boring taste, and many blacks refuse to touch it. This animal could only have been brought from neighbouring coasts. The monkey of Madagascar, called *maki*, does not resemble it at all, neither does the baboon from the Cape of Good Hope.

The Mauritian monkey is of medium size. It has a thickish reddish-grey fur, with a long tail. This animal lives in groups. I have seen troops of more than sixty together. They often come to pillage the houses. They place sentries on the tops of trees and on rocks. When they spot dogs or hunters, they let out a scream and all decamp. This animal climbs into the most inaccessible mountains. They rest above cliffs on the narrowest ledges. It is the only quadruped of its size that dares to expose itself to danger in that way. So that nature, which has covered even the chinks in rocks with vegetation, has created beings capable of enjoying it.[48]

The rat seems to be the natural inhabitant of the island. There are a prodigious number here. It is claimed that the Dutch abandoned their colony because of this animal. There are some houses where more than 30,000 rats are killed each year. They make large stores for grain and fruit underground; they climb to the tops of trees and eat small birds. They pierce the thickest of beams. At sunset you can see them running all over the place; they can destroy an entire crop in a few nights. I have seen maize fields left without a single ear of corn. They resemble our European rats. Perhaps they were brought here by ships.[49] Mice are very common; the damage done by them is unbelievable.

Birds

It is claimed that in the olden days a great many flamingos could be found on the island. It is a large and beautiful sea bird, of a pink colour.

There are meant to be three left, but I didn't see one. Many *corbigeaux* can be found. It is, they say, the best game on the island. It is very hard to shoot. There are two kinds of *paille-en-queue;* one is white with silver, the other has a red beak, claw and tail. Even though this is a sea bird, it makes its nest in the forests. Its name does little justice to its beauty. The English call it more appropriately the Tropic Bird.

I have seen several species of parrot, but none very beautiful. There is a green one, with a grey head. They are as large as sparrows. You can never tame them. They, too, are enemies of the harvest. They are rather good to eat. You can find blackbirds in the forests, which when called by the hunter come to the tip of his gun. It is easy game. What is called the Dutch pigeon has magnificent colours; another sort has a very pleasant taste, but so dangerous that those who eat it are seized with fits.[50]

There are two kinds of bats here. One looks like ours; the other is as fat as a small cat, with plenty of grease and is eaten by the inhabitants with pleasure. There is a kind of hawk called chicken-eater; they say it also lives off grasshoppers. It remains near the shore. The sight of a man scares it.[51]

Amphibious animals

In the olden days one found many sea turtles on the shore, but today you hardly see any. However, I have seen their traces in the sand, and I have seen them hunting in river mouths. Their flesh resembles beef; their fat is green and very tasty. The seashore is riddled with holes where quantities of *tourlouroux* lodge. They are a kind of amphibious crab that burrows underground like moles. They run fast, and when you try to catch one, they snap their claws and hold them out. They serve no purpose. Another extraordinary amphibious animal is the hermit crab, a kind of lobster whose hind part is without a shell; but nature has given it the sense to lodge in empty shells. You see them running in great numbers, each one carrying its house, which it abandons for a larger one when it becomes too tight.

The most harmful insect on the island is the grasshopper. I have seen them fall on a field like snow, pile up on the ground several inches deep, and devour the greenery in one night. It is agriculture's worst enemy. There are several kinds of caterpillar. Some, like those on lemon trees, are fat and very beautiful. The smaller ones are more dangerous than their butterflies. They devastate vegetable gardens. There is a large night moth bearing the figure of a skull on its body. It is called *haïe* and flies around in rooms. It is claimed that the down from its wings blinds those who are affected by it. Its name comes from the fear its presence inspires.

Houses are infested with ants that plunder all that's good to eat. If the skin of a ripe fruit opens on a tree, it is soon devoured by ants. You can only protect a pantry or food safe by standing their legs in water. The ant's enemy is the *formicaleo*, which burrows into the sand under trees, as in Europe.

Centipedes are frequently found in dark, damp places. Perhaps this insect was destined to drive man from unhealthy places. Its sting is very painful. My dog was bitten on its thigh by one of these animals, which was some six inches long. Its wound turned into an ulcer which took more than three weeks to heal. I had the pleasure of seeing one carried off by a crowd of ants which had seized it by all its legs and dragged it off like a long beam. The scorpion is also very common in houses and can be found in the same places. Its sting is not deadly, but gives a fever. A good treatment is to rub oil in immediately.

The yellow wasp with black rings has a sting that is no less formidable. It builds hives of something like paper in trees and even in houses. They built one in my room; but I soon tired of these dangerous guests. The mason wasp builds a sort of funnel with earth. You could mistake it for a swallow's nest, if there were any on the island. They lodge in rooms that are hardly used, and especially in key-holes which they fill with their works.

In gardens you often find leaves cut into shapes the size of a six-*sol* coin. This is the work of a wasp whose teeth cut out this circular coin with admirable speed and precision. It carries it to its hole, rolls it into the shape of a horn and deposits its eggs inside.

There is a kind of insect similar to the ant, which shows just as much intelligence in making its home. They cause havoc in trees and timber, which they reduce to powder. With this dust they build vaults an inch wide under which they come and go: these tunnels, which are black, run through all the timber in a house. They pierce into trunks and furniture in one night. I have found no remedy so effective as rubbing garlic into the places they frequent. They call these ants *carias*. Many houses have been ruined by them.[52]

There are three species of cockroaches, the dirtiest of all the beetles. One is flat and grey: the most common is the size of a may-bug and is reddish brown. It attacks furniture and especially papers and books. It nearly always lives in corners in the pantry and kitchen. All houses are infected with this insect. When it is rainy, they fly all over the place. Its enemy is a species of beetle or green fly which is very nimble and light. When it locates a cockroach, it touches it and it becomes immobile. Then the beetle looks for a crack to where it drags its prey and pushes it in. It lays an egg in its body and leaves it there. This touch, which some people take for a charm, is the stroke of a sting whose effect is very quick; this insect is hard to kill otherwise. In tree trunks one finds a large worm with legs that gnaws the wood. It is called a *moutouc*. Blacks and even whites eat it with pleasure. Pliny observed that it was served in Rome at the best tables and that it was fattened with flour on purpose. That found in oak trees was the best. It was called *cossus*. Thus have abundance and the worst kind of starvation met in taste, and like all extremes, approach each other.

I have seen our ordinary species of flies, but the gnat is more bothersome than in Europe, especially for those newly arrived whose blood it prefers. Its hum is very loud. This fly is black with white dots. You can hardly protect yourself at night except with curtains of gauze called mosquito nets.

Along streams you find dragonflies of a beautiful violet colour, with heads like a ruby. This insect is carnivorous. I have seen one catch a pretty butterfly in the air.

Rooms, at certain times of the year, are filled with little moths that incinerate themselves in the candle flames. There are so many that one is obliged to put the candles into glass cylinders. They attract a small, extremely pretty lizard, about a finger long, into the house. It has lively eyes. It climbs along the walls and even on glass. It feeds off flies and insects that it watches with extreme patience. It lays little round eggs like peas, having a shell, white and yolk like chicken eggs. I have seen these lizards so tame that they come and take sugar from your hand. Far from being a nuisance, they are very useful. There are some magnificent ones in the forests. They are azure-coloured, with changing greens, marked with crimson on their backs like Arabic script.

The insects' worst enemy is the spider. Some have a belly the size of a walnut with large hairy legs. Their webs are so strong that little birds get caught in them. They destroy wasps, scorpions and centipedes.

Finally, to close my catalogue, I have never seen a country with so many fleas. You find them in the sand all along the coast, right up to the summits of the mountains. It is said that rats brought them here. At certain times of the year if you place a bit of white paper on the ground, you will soon find it covered with these insects.

I will not forget a very unusual louse that I saw attach itself to pigeons. It resembles the tick of our woods, but nature has given it wings. It is well destined for birds. There is a little white louse that attaches itself to fruit trees and kills them, and a bug in the forest whose bite is worse than a scorpion's; it is followed by a tumour the size of a pigeon's egg, which only disappears after five or six days.

You will have noticed that the sweet temperature of this climate, so desired by Europeans, is so favourable to the propagation of insects that in no time at all the fruits are devoured and the island becomes uninhabitable. But the fruits of these meridional countries are wrapped in thick, bitter skins and hard shells and aromatic barks like the orange and lemon trees; thus there are few species where the fly can introduce its worms. Many of these harmful animals fight a perpetual war, like the centipedes and scorpions. The *formicaleo* sets its traps for ants, the green fly pierces the cockroach, the lizard hunts butterflies, the spider sets its webs for anything that flies and the cyclones, which arrive each year, annihilate both a great part of the prey and the predators.

Letter 10
On What Comes from the Sea: Fish, Shells and Coral

I have still to tell you about the sea and its creations, after which you will know as much as the first Portuguese who set foot on the island. If I can add a meteorological journal to this, you will more or less be up-to-date with the whole natural history of this land; we will then move from here to the inhabitants and what they have taken from their soil, where, like all over the world, good is mixed with evil. The worthy Plutarch would have us draw harmony from these contraries; but musical instruments are common and good musicians rare.[53]

Whales are often seen to windward of the island, especially during September when whales couple. I have seen many during this season, holding themselves upright in the water and coming very close to shore. They are smaller than the northern ones. They are not fished; however, the blacks know how to harpoon them. Sometimes manatees are caught. I have eaten their flesh, which tasted like beef, but I have never seen one alive.

The *vieille* is a blackish fish similar to cod by its shape and taste. Sometimes this fish can be poisonous, like other species that I will describe. Those who eat it are seized with fits. I have seen a worker die; his skin fell off in scales. On the island of Rodrigues, not more than one hundred leagues from here, the English lost more than five hundred men during the last war through such incidents and thus could not invade Mauritius.[54] It is thought that the fish become poisonous after eating coral branches. You can tell which fish are poisonous by their black teeth, and if you throw a silver piece into the pan where you are cooking them it turns black. What is odd is that the fish is never dangerous to the windward of the island. Those who blame coral as the cause are wrong for the island is surrounded by coral reefs. I would attribute it rather to unknown fruit from a venomous tree fallen into the water. This is all the more probable because there is only one season, and only gluttonous fish are subject to this danger. Moreover, there is a kind of pigeon, whose flesh occasions fits, which proves that the poison is on the island itself.

Among the number of unidentified fish are several white ones with large bellies and heads, like the captain and the *carangue*. These two have a poor taste. It is believed that those with paved mouths, that is, a rugged bone in their palates, are never dangerous. There are sharks, but they are never eaten. Generally, the smaller the fish, the less poisonous they are. The red mullet is bigger and vastly inferior to the European one. It is considered healthy, and mullets are very common. You can find sardines and mackerel of a mediocre flavour, like all the fish in the sea here. They differ slightly from ours in their shape. The *poule d'eau*, a kind of turbot, is the best to eat. Its fat is green.

There are white rays with a long tail bristling with prickles and others with skin and flesh that are black; *sabres* so-called by their shape; *lunes* variegated with many colours; *ourses* with skin drawn like a network, other fish similar to whitings, but yellow, red and violet; parrot fish are not only green, but have yellow heads, white crooked beaks and live in shoals like birds.

The devil-fish is small and odd shaped. Its head is like a pike's. On its back it has seven points as long as its body. Its prick is extremely poisonous. They are linked together by membranes similar to a bat's wing. It is streaked with brown and white bands which begin at its muzzle, just like the Cape zebra. One fish is square like a trunk, from which it gets its name, and is armed with two horns like a bull. There are several species, and it does not grow to be large. The *porc-épic* bristles with long pricks; the octopus which climbs into pools of water with its seven arms armed with suckers, changes colour, vomits out water and tries to catch whatever tries to catch it. All these species are so strange in shape and can be found in the reefs, but are not great to eat.

Saltwater fish are inferior in taste to European ones; on the other hand, the freshwater ones are better than ours. They seem to be the same species as the saltwater ones. You can pick out the *lubine*, the mullet and the carp which differ from those in our rivers; the *cabot* that lives in torrents among the rocks to which it attaches itself with a concave membrane, and shrimps that are enormous and tasty. The eels are leathery, a kind of conger. They reach seven or eight feet long, as fat as a leg. They hide in holes in the rivers, and sometimes devour those who are stupid enough to bathe there.

There are lobsters and crawfish of monstrous size. Their claws are not large. They are blue, marbled with white. I saw a small species of lobster with a charming shape: it was sky-blue and had two claws divided into two articulations a bit like a knife whose blade folds into the handle. It seizes its prey as if it was one-armed.

There is a great variety of crabs. Here are those which struck me as remarkable. One species is rugged with tubers and points like a piece of coral; another carries on its back the imprint of five seals; there is one with something shaped like a horse-shoe at the tip of its claws; another is covered in hairs, has no pincers and sticks to the bottoms of boats;

there is a crab marbled with grey whose smooth shell is very uneven. You notice countless uneven and bizarre shapes which are, however, constantly the same on each crab; take the one with eyes at the end of two long pipes like telescopes; when not using them, it hides them in grooves along its shell; or the sea spider, a crab whose claws are red with one far larger than the other; or a little crab whose shell is three times larger than it is, covered like a great shield; you hardly see its legs when it walks.

In several places along the shore some feet from the water, you can find large, living creatures like *boudins* [blood sausages], red and black. Pulled out of the water, they release a thick white slime that at once changes into a number of small and glutinous threads. I believe that this animal is an enemy to crabs, among which it can often be seen. Its viscous mucus is apt to entangle their claws, which anyhow could not grab the elastic hide and cylindrical form. Sailors give them such a foul name that I will render it in Latin as *Mentula monachi*.[55] The Chinese make a great fuss about them and regard them as a powerful aphrodisiac.

I think that we can place among the shellfish a shapeless, soft and membraneous mass in the middle of which you find one single flat bone that is slightly arched. In this species the usual order seems reversed; the animal is on the outside and the shell on the inside.

There are several kinds of sea urchin. The ones that I have seen fished are: a violet-coloured sea urchin with very long spikes: under water its eyes glint like two lapis lazuli seeds. I have been painfully pricked by one of these. A grey sea urchin with round, fluted spines; a sea urchin with blunted spikes, veined in white and violet. That species is very beautiful; there is also a grey one. The sea urchin looking like an artichoke without spikes is rare. The common sea urchin with small spikes looks like a chestnut in its shell. These animals are found in holes in rocks and coral where they are protected from bad weather.

I now enter a subject of such abundance that it is very hard to find some order. Argenville's system does not please me because many species are in the wrong place.[56] The same thing happens with all classification in natural history. The families that mix with each other ceaselessly create confusion in our minds. All methods are defective; so I would rather imagine one for the following genres that could be applied to others.

I place in the middle the most elementary living being and from there I draw spokes on which I order the beings that are composed from it. Thus the limpet, a creature that is but a tiny funnel that sticks to rocks, is at the centre of my spherical order. On one of the spokes coming out from it I place the sea-ear, which already forms a kind of pad on one of its sides; then the shells where the whorl is completely finished; in laying out all the tiny differences of this family, no individual escapes me.

I deduce that the limpet ends in a long pyramid, which is in fact the case. I draw another spoke along which I dispose the vermicular species: the vermicules that turn in spiral shapes like the nautilus or Ammon's horns, etc. Small limpets can be found that reveal the beginning of a spiral inside: I would have another line for different species of whelks [*tonnes*] or periwinkles. There are limpets with a small stud at their opening: I deduce from this the origin of the simplest bivalves.

If I find species that do not belong to one spoke or another, I draw a string between analogous individuals: this string becomes the diameter of a new sphere, and my new shell becomes its centre.

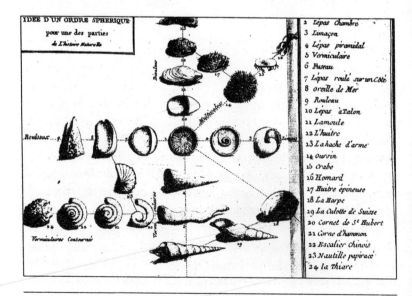

One could extend this system, it seems to me, to all the animal kingdom, and if our natural history cabinets do not provide us with species to fill out the spokes and strings linking the spokes, we could find out perhaps which families are missing, for I believe that nature has done all it can, not only in the chain of beings glimpsed by naturalists, but in an infinity of others that cross into each other. As a result, all is linked in every sense, and each species forms great spokes in the universal sphere, while being at the same time the centre of a particular sphere.

Back to our shells. You find a levelled and flattened limpet-shell in Mauritius; as well as a star-like one, and one from the rivers, which like all river shells is covered with a black skin; the sea-ear shell has a mother-of-pearl interior; also a kind of white shell in which the edges are even more convoluted.

We note something, in fact, that is very unusual; all univalves are turned from the left to the right when one observes the shell lying on its mouth, its point turning towards one's self. There are few exceptions to this rule. What law has determined that they begin their convolutions on the same side? Could it be the same one that makes the earth turn from West to East? In this case the sun could well be the cause, as it is of all colours that become more beautiful the closer you approach the Equator.

I have read all that has been written on the formation of shells and do not understand anything. For example, the scorpion-shell, which ends in very long hooks, expands its shell every year. The old hooks become useless, and new ones are made. What has it done with the others? In the same way, the cowrie-shell has a thick mouth and is carved in such a way that it cannot increase its convolutions without destroying the shell at its opening. I suspect that these animals have their own liquid that dissolves the walls of the shell they are expanding; and if this dissolvent exists, it seems that one could use it against stones that form in the bladder, made of glutinous humours like the prime matter of shells.[57]

Among the bivalves are: the common oyster that sticks to rocks, in a shape so baroque that it can only be broken open with a hammer; it is good to eat. Also, a species called the leaf because of its shape; an oyster that is no different to the European one; a grey oyster that sticks to the keels of boats and whose shell is thin and elastic; it is rare. The pearl oyster is white, flat, thick and very large; it is found far from land; it is the same as the one that gives pearls; another pearl oyster is flatter, of a dark violet colour; it attaches itself with strings like the mussel and is common around the southeast port; it is found in river mouths, and its pearls are violet.

An oyster called the *tile* is common here, of the same kind as those used as holy water founts in the St. Sulpice church. It is perhaps the largest of the seashells; some found in the Maldive Islands can hardly be dragged by two oxen. It is very strange that this oyster can be found as a fossil on the Normandy coasts, where I have seen it.

There is another grey and thin oyster species, which resembles the Mediterranean snail in its shape and lodges in holes within corals; a white mussel with an elastic shell which is found inside sponges; this one is an intermediary shell between two species. If I ever make a cabinet, it would easily find its right place thanks to my method.

It appears that shellfish do not live in any more peace than other animals. You find many of them smashed on the shore. Those that are found whole are always pierced. I recall finding a snail armed with a pointed tooth which it used to pierce the shells of mussels. It was found in the Magellan Straits and was called an armed *burgau* or land-snail.

To gather beautiful shells you must fish them alive. Some clean-shelled species bury themselves in the sand during storms, the others stick to rocks. Mussels find niches in the branches of the madrepores where they barely multiply. If they spawned freely on the rocks as in Europe, the cyclones would destroy them.

There is plenty of ingenuity and variety in the hinges of shells. Our arts could benefit from this. Oysters have little skin, but they are like an integral part of the rocks; mussels have a tough elastic skin, the razor-shell but one fold; the heart-shells, if they are regular, have little teeth in their hinges which fold one into the other. One sees an admirable geometry in their curves.

Mauritius is completely surrounded with corals. They are a stone-like vegetation in the shape of plants and bushes. They are so abundant that whole reefs are made up of them. I distinguish those that are not tied to the ground from those that are attached. Of the first are: the

Mushroom, which appears to be made of leaves; the Plume, which is the same species; the Plume with three or four branches; Neptune's brain.

Of those that carpet the sea bed and appear to attach roots, are: the Cauliflower; the Cabbage, whose appearance and look are very like that plant; it is of the large sort like another madrepore whose stages form a kind of spiral; it is very brittle. Another resembles a tree with its tall stem and the mass of its branches; a very pretty kind that I call the Sheaf seems made of several bunches of ears of wheat; and the Paint-brush or Pink-flower, where at the centre of each opening one notices a little green. A common kind can be gathered in handfuls like a mignonette with its cones of flowers; a very pretty madrepore grows in the shape of an island with its shores and mountains; another's leaves have fingers like a hand; there is the Stag-wood with horns that are detached and fragile. The Beehive is a large shapeless mass with regular holes over its surface; a pale-blue coral is rare for in the inside it is of a darker blue; a coral hinged in white and black contains some red coral that hasn't been found here yet. There is coral vegetation in blues, white, yellows, reds, all so fragile and pierced that nothing can be sent to Europe.

Among the lithophytes is a plant similar to a long straw without leaves, knots or buds; a sort of vegetation like a small forest of trees: its roots are very interwoven, each one has a little bunch of leaves. The substance of this lithophyte is of the nature of wood and burns in a fire: it is nevertheless classed among the madrepores.

I have seen three kinds of starfish, which are not very remarkable. Formerly, grey ambergris was found on the shore: there is even a small island downwind called by this name.[58] It is sometimes brought from Madagascar.

Today no one doubts that madrepores are the work of an infinity of tiny animals, although they are just like plants in their appearance, their stems, their branches, their shapes and even in their colourful flowers. I accept this finding with joy for I love to see the universe populated. Moreover, I conceive that so regular a work must have been made by some agency with its share of order and intelligence. These sorts of vegetation really do resemble ours, their matter apart, so much so that I could be persuaded to think that all our plants are the fruit of the work of a multitude of animals living together. I prefer to think that a tree is a Republic, rather than a dead machine, obeying God knows what hydraulic laws.[59] I could defend this opinion with plenty of curious observations. Perhaps one day I'll have the leisure to do it. These researches could be useful: but when not employed to good purpose, they divert our eager curiosity to know and judge, which throws itself, lacking nourishment, on to all that surrounds us, and becomes the prime cause of our disputes. Our histories are often nothing but calumnies, our moral treatises are but satires, and our societies and academies but places for slander and epigrammatic wit. After that, we complain that friendship and confidence no longer exist, as if they could among people who wear a shield over their hearts and a dagger under their cloaks. Let us either chatter less, or let us construct systems. *Tradidis mundum disputationibus.* Let us dispute then, without getting angry.

Port Louis, 12 January 1769

Meteorological Journal
July 1768
During this month the winds rule from the southeast, as they blow nearly all year from there. The breeze is strong during the day and drops at night. Although this is the dry season, it often rains. There are violent squalls that do not last long. The air is very fresh. You cannot do without clothes of proper cloth.

August
It rains nearly every day. The mountain summits are covered with smoke-like vapours which drift down to the plain accompanied by gusts of wind. These rains often create rainbows over the mountainsides, which remain none the less black.

September
Same kind of weather and wind. It is harvest time. If heat and humidity are the sole causes of vegetation growth, why are there no young shoots at this time of year? It is no less hot than in May in France. Can there be some spirit of life accompanying the return of the sun? The Romans paid tribute to the west wind and fixed its arrival on 8 February. They

called it *favonius*, that is, nurturing. It is the same as the Greeks' Zephyr. Pliny said that it "served as husband to everything that grows from the earth." They were perhaps as ignorant as we are, but their philosophy seems more touching to me, and they did not get angry when you did not share their view.

October

Same temperature, the air a little warmer, but it is always cool inland. At the end of this month they sow the land with wheat and harvest in four months; then they sow maize, which ripens in September. There are two crops in the same field; but this is not too much given the plagues that desolate this land.

November

The heat begins to be felt, the winds are variable and sometimes come from the northwest. Rain storms. No ship from France, no letter. It is sad to expect a portion of our happiness to come from Europe.

December

The heat is tiring, the sun is at its highest, but the air is tempered by abundant rain. It feels as if I have experienced greater heat during some summer days in St. Petersburg. At the start of the month I heard thunder for the first time since my arrival.

Cyclone

On the morning of the 23rd the winds came from the southeast, and seemed to announce a storm. Clouds gathered round the mountain peaks. They were of an olive and copper colour. One could see a long range of them, higher than the rest and motionless. Clouds lower down were blowing rapidly past. The sea smashed against the reef with a din. Many seabirds flew inland for shelter. Domestic animals seemed uneasy. The air was heavy and hot, even though the wind had not fallen.

With these signs promising a cyclone, everybody rushed to prop up their houses with poles and close all their doors and windows.

At about ten o'clock at night the cyclone arrived. There were terrifying squalls, followed by alarming moments of calm as if the wind was building up its strength. It became fiercer and fiercer all night. My hut was shattered; I spent the night elsewhere. My hostess broke down in tears, fearing to see her home destroyed. Nobody went to bed. Towards morning the wind redoubled and I realized that one side of our palisade fence was about to fall and that part of our roof was pushed up at one corner; with some planks and rope I prevented further damage. While crossing the yard to give some orders, I thought several times that the wind would blow me over. In the distance I saw walls collapse, and thatch roofs fly like a pack of cards.

Rain fell by eight in the morning, but the wind never ceased. It blew horizontally and with such violence that it penetrated the house like a fountain through the openings. It spoilt some of my papers.

At eleven the rain fell from the sky in torrents. The wind died down a little, and the ravines in the mountains turned into prodigious cascades. Large rocks broke off with a noise similar to cannon shots. As they rolled down the hills they made large holes in the forests. The streams flooded in the plain that became a sea. You could no longer see banks nor bridges.

By one o'clock the wind veered to the northwest and drove the surf from the sea in large clouds along the land. The ships in the harbour were driven ashore, and kept firing guns as signals of distress, but pointlessly, for no help could be given them. With repeated gusts, the buildings were pushed from the other side, with equal violence. About midday, the wind shifted to the east and then the west. Thus it went around the circle of the horizon in 24 hours, as is usual; after which there was a perfect calm.

Everywhere trees were blown down and bridges carried away. Not a single leaf remained in our gardens. Even the hardiest herbs were cut to the very ground.

While the cyclone raged, a worthy man whose name is Leroux, a joiner, sent his blacks and workers to help those who wanted assistance, and all this without charging. Good actions should not be forgotten, especially in this place.

At four minutes past five on the 23rd there was an eclipse, but the bad weather prevented it from being observed.

Such terrible squalls, it seems, come regularly every year in December, and sometimes in March. As the winds circle the horizon there is not a cave on the island that is not filled with rain, which drowns thousands of rats, grasshoppers and ants and they are not seen again for some time. The ravages made by this dreadful visitation are more to be feared than all the calamities of winter. That of 1760 will be long remembered. A shutter was seen lifted into the sky, and then flew like an arrow to a roof some distance away. The lower masts of a sixty-four-gun ship were twisted and snapped off. No tree in Europe could withstand the force of these whirlwinds.[60]

January 1769

A great deal of rain, the weather hot and humid; great storms but little thunder. Gales blow hard in this season and all shipping is at a standstill from December to April.

All the meadows on the island recover their greenness, and the earth presents a delightful picture, but the sky remains covered.

February

Still much stormy weather, and violent gusts of wind. Both *L'Heureux*, a passage-boat on its way to Madagascar, and the *Favori* from the Cape, were lost.

Clouds gathered on the 25th, with a northwesterly wind, into a long range from Pavillon Mountain to the Isle des Tonneliers. It is motionless; claps of thunder come from it. The storm lasted from six in the morning to midday, and lightning struck, killing a grenadier, a negress, and an ox on Tonneliers island. A gun in an officer's house was melted. People claim that lightning never strikes in the capital, but the thunder was so loud that it sounded like a bombardment. I think that if they had fired one cannon the explosion would have dispelled the motionless clouds.

March

The rains have abated, the air is clearer and winds blow always from the southwest. The heat is bearable.

April

An attractive time of year. The grass is so dry that should it catch fire, the countryside would be black for seven months.

May

The wind, as is usual, turns at the end of this month to the west and northwest. We are now in the dry season. I went to Plaine de Willhems where I found the air and temperature pleasant and refreshing.

June

The winds are steady from the southeast. Small rainstorms begin again.

There is no special disease related to this country; and one dies of the same ones as in Europe. I have seen people die of apoplexy, of smallpox, of pleurisy, and of blockages in the liver, which come more from grief than from the quality of the water, as is claimed. I have seen a stone larger than an egg pulled out from a black man in the countryside. I have seen paralytics and people tormented with gout, and epileptics in fits. Children and blacks are very susceptible to worms. Venereal diseases produce crabs in the latter: there are painful cracks on the sole of their feet. The air is good as in Europe, but has no special medicinal quality and I would not even advise gout sufferers to come here as I have seen them stay in bed for more than six months.

People's temperaments are visibly altered by the changes in the seasons. You are subject to bilious fevers and heat leads to breakdowns in health, but temperance and bathing will keep you well. However, I have observed that one enjoys better health in cooler countries and a more vigorous mind: it is even very odd that history does not speak of one famous man born in the tropics, except Mahomet.

Letter 11

Port Louis, 10 February 1769

Morals and Habits of the White Inhabitants

Mauritius was deserted when Mascarenhas discovered it. The first French people who established themselves were farmers from the nearby island of Réunion. They brought with them simplicity of manners, good faith, love of hospitality and even an indifference to riches. M. de La Bourdonnais who is, in a way, the founder of that colony, brought over his workers, good, honest men, and some evil types sent over by their relatives, but he forced them to be useful.[61]

After he had transformed this island by his works, and after it was seen as a business and warehousing venture on the India route, all kinds of people arrived.

First the employees of the East India Company.[62] The main jobs on the island were held by them, so they lived there rather like nobles in Venice. To their aristocratic manners they added that financier's spirit which scared off the impetus to carry out agricultural work. Every appointment was in their hands. They ran the police, the administration and the shops. Some of them cleared the land and built, and resold the results at high prices to those who came out to settle. People cried out against them, but they were all-powerful.

Sailors from the Company were settled there, who have long been unable to conceive that all the dangers and fatigue of the Indies trade are their lot, while the honours and profits are for others. This settlement, so near to the Indies, raised great expectations after their arrival. But they were unhappy before really establishing themselves, and remained thus for a long time.

The Company sent army officers out to the island. They were gallant men, many of noble birth. They could not even imagine that an officer could sink so low as to accept orders from a man who had once been a merchant's office boy, except to receive their pay. They did not like the sailors, who were too blunt: in becoming settlers, they could not change their attitudes, and so did not make any money.

Some of the royal regiments touched land and even stayed. Their officers, seduced by the beauty of the sky and by a love of idleness, remained for good. Everything was subject to the Company. There were none of those garrison distinctions that so flatter subaltern officers: each one had his pretensions; they were looked on really as aliens. They complained loudly in the King's name.

Missionaries of St. Lazarus arrived there, who peacefully looked after the upright men who first settled on the island; but when they saw that as society increased it divided further, they kept to their pastoral functions and to some of the better families and forgot the rest. Then some merchants with money arrived. In an island without trade, they added to the abuses of speculation that they found already established, and introduced further little monopolies. They quickly became loathed by the different classes of men, who could not bear each other. They were designated as "Banians", which would be like calling them Jews in

France.[63] On the other hand, they also claimed to scorn the distinctions of rank, engaging each person who had crossed the Equator as if they were all equal.

Finally, the recent war in India threw there, like a tide, bankrupt men, ruined libertines, thieves, and scoundrels of every sort who, chased out of Europe for their crimes, and out of Asia by bad luck, tried to re-establish their fortunes on the public's ruin. On their arrival, general and particular complaints increased; reputations were stained with an Asiatic ingenuity unknown to our slanderers. There were no longer any chaste women, nor any honest men; all trust was extinguished, all honour sullied. By vilifying everybody, they had reduced everybody to their level.[64]

All their hopes were pinned on a change of administration and they succeeded in displeasing the Company, which in 1765 yielded their stormy colony to the King. This time it was believed that peace and order would be restored in the island. But in fact, new yeast was thrown into the ferment. A great number of favourites from Paris disembarked to make their fortunes on an island without culture or trade, where the only money was pieces of paper. These were disgruntled people of another kind.

A segment of the inhabitants, who remained attached to the Company out of gratitude, viewed the new Royal administration with grief. The rest, who had counted on the favours of the new government, and seeing that it was concerned solely with economic plans, were all the more embittered by having hoped for so much.

To these new divisions can be added those among several bodies of men who, even in France, cannot make peace with each other, from the King's navy, to the pen and the sword. In short, the mind of every member of the military and of the administration, being neither dissipated with pleasures or by business as in Europe, became isolated and fed off its own worries.

Discord reigns in all the classes and has banished from this island all love for society that should prevail amongst Frenchmen exiled in an ocean at the end of the world. Everybody bears a grudge, all want to get rich and leave quickly. To overhear them, you would think that everybody wants to leave next year. Some have been talking like this for over thirty years.

The officer who arrives from Europe soon loses here his competitive military sense. In general, he has little money and lacks everything. His hut has no furniture; his rations are extremely expensive and he finds himself the sole consumer between the landowners and the merchants, who outdo each other to get rich at his expense. He wages a defensive war against them; he buys wholesale; he dreams of seizing the opportunity of making a profit because the merchants double their prices when the ships leave. He tries every means to buy things cheap. When he begins to enjoy the fruits of his thrift, he thinks that he is an exile from his native land, for a limitless time, in a poor country. Idleness, the lack of society and the bait of trade continue to engage him now out of self-interest rather than out of necessity. There are doubtless exceptions and I would willingly name them if they weren't so numerous. M. de Steenhovre, the commanding officer, is a model of virtue.[65]

Soldiers supply many workers, for the heat allows whites to work outdoors. We have not made sufficient use of them for the good of the colony. Often among the recruits from Europe you can find villains capable of any kind of crime. I cannot imagine the policy that decrees that those who commit crimes in the old society can contribute to a new one. Despair often seizes these wretches and they kill each other with their bayonets.

Although sailors do but come and go, they too have a strong influence on the manners of this society. Their policy is to complain about the place they have just left and then about the one they have just reached. To hear them, you would think that good times are over, that they are ruined. They buy things expensively and sell cheaply. The truth is that no bargain is a good one unless they have made 150 per cent profit. A barrel of Bordeaux wine costs 500 *livres*, and everything else in proportion to that. One would never believe that European goods were more expensive than in India, and those from India more than in Europe. The sailors are highly regarded by the inhabitants because they could not exist without them. Their gossip, the continuous arrivals and departures, give the island the manners of an inn.

From so many emigrants from such disparate conditions emerges a people made up of differing nations who cordially hate each other. Only falsity is honoured. To point out a man of wit, one says he is cunning. It is the kind of praise due to a fox. Cunning is a vice and bad luck to that society where such a quality is esteemed. On the other hand, suspicious people are much disliked. This may appear contradictory, but there is nothing to gain from people who are on their guard. The suspicious man disconcerts the rogues and rejects them. People gather around this cunning man and help him dupe the ignorant.

Here everybody is completely insensitive to all that constitutes the happiness of generous minds. No taste for the arts or for literature. Natural feelings are perverted. People miss their homeland; they miss the Opera and the women. Everything is dull here. I went to the funeral of a highly-considered merchant where not one person showed any emotion. I overheard his brother-in-law remark that the tomb was not deep enough.

This indifference spreads to everything that surrounds them. The streets and courtyards are not paved nor planted with trees; houses are mere cabins of wood that could be carted anywhere on wheels. They have neither windows, nor glass nor curtains, and but little, miserable furniture.

Idle people meet in the public square at noon and in the evening. Here they speculate, slander and talk scandal. Few people are married in this town. Those who are not rich blame their mediocre financial circumstances on not having married; the rest, they tell us, prefer to wait and establish themselves back in France. But the real reason for not marrying is the ease with which they find black mistresses. Moreover, there are few good matches for men; it is rare to find a girl with a dowry of ten thousand francs.

Most married people live on their plantations. The women hardly ever come to town except for balls or for Easter celebrations. They love dancing, with a passion. No sooner is a ball announced than they arrive in crowds, in carriages or in litters perched on four long bamboo poles and supported on the shoulders of four black slaves. Four more slaves follow as a relay. The more children they have, the more litters with eight slaves. Prudent husbands oppose these journeys as they upset plantation work, but the roads are so bad that wheeled carriages cannot operate.

Women remain pale with good figures, and most are pretty. They are naturally witty and if their formal education had not been so neglected, they would be great company, but I met few who could read. Any one of them could gather around a great number of men in town if they so wished, but these mistresses of plantation houses care little about seeing each other outside the ball season. When they do all meet together they hardly utter a word to each other. Each woman brings some secret pretension which comes from their fortune, their jobs or the birth of their husbands. Others count on their beauty or on their youth; a European woman feels superior to a Creole, whilst a Creole finds the European a simple adventuress.

Whatever scandalmongers might say, I believe that these women are more virtuous than the men, who usually neglect them in favour of their black slave mistresses. Those who do show some kind of morality are all the more praiseworthy as they do not owe it to their education. They have to struggle with the heat and sometimes the indifference of their husbands and often are pursued by big-spending, amorous sailors. If the state of marriage leads to infidelities, the fault is ours, we who have brought our French morals to an African sky.

Otherwise they possess very valuable domestic qualities: they are extremely sober and usually only drink water. They are very clean in their clothes. They dress in muslin trimmed with rose-coloured taffeta. They adore their children. No sooner are they born than they run naked through the house; never wear underclothes; are often washed; and eat fruit as they think fit; they live without care, without schooling and quickly grow up strong and robust. Puberty arrives early with both sexes; I have seen daughters married at eleven years old.

This education, which resembles nature's, leaves them completely ignorant; but the vices of the black women, which they suck in with their milk, and the whims which they inflict tyrannically on the poor slaves, are added to all society's depravity. To remedy this evil, the wealthy send their children at an early age to France, from where they return home with more amiable vices, and more dangerous ones.

There are hardly more than 400 planters on the island. There are around one hundred women of quality and only about ten of them live in town. Towards evening you can go and visit them in their houses; you gamble or you get bored. When the cannon fires at eight o'clock we all get up and leave to have dinner at home.

Some Famous Men I Met in Mauritius

Just as in a forest one notices that certain trees stand out by their bearing, their leaves, or fruit, so certain famous men that I met in Mauritius stand out, made celebrated by intrinsic values or great moral qualities. One should honour virtue wherever it is found.

First I met two officers in the King's navy who became famous at the start of the American war. The first was called M. de la Clocheterie: he was a young man, with a dashing figure, very modest, who hardly spoke and was devoted to his duties. His comrades held him in the highest opinion. I did not strike up a friendship with him, but did with the chevalier Grenier, his comrade and friend, and I knew his brother who was a Navy guard. It was the elder brother, M. de la Clocheterie, who has since commanded the frigate *Belle Poule,* who was the first to hold up the French flag in our war against the English for the liberation of America.

The second was also an officer in the Royal Marine, the famous Du Couedic, who eventually, after a famous battle, died of his wounds after sinking his enemy's vessel. He had just wed a widow far older than himself who brought with her a dowry of a fine plantation. As he lived next to one of my former comrades, I was able to meet him and sometimes dine with him. He was a serious man, ceaselessly attentive to the honours of his house. It was perpetually crowded with Breton volunteers who found an open table at all hours. This gave him a double pleasure, that of saving his poor compatriots money and that of amusing his aged and ill wife. I did not notice, as was said during his life, that he had anything to do with literature, but his pleasure was to force the fortune that came to him through marriage on those who were more needy. His wife died soon after and I went to the burial. Since I left the island I have been told that he remarried a young woman, that he had children and that he sought glory in the American War.

There was another famous sailor on the island called M. Marion, who had been for ages with the East India Company and was a knight of St. Louis. On seeing his heavy and swaying gait, you could have mistaken him for a peasant. However, he was one of the most famous sailors with the Company. He carried the claimant to the throne of England to France, which earned him the St. Louis cross. Something else that made him famous on Mauritius was that his vessel sank to the bottom during a cyclone at the entrance to Port Louis harbour, and was covered by the waves. When the storm was over, the vessel's keel was smashed, and it was decided that its cargo was lost and that the ship was beyond repair. M. Marion alone managed to unload the boat of its cargo of wine, drag it off the reef, rebuild its keel and bring it back to France. When I knew him he owned a beautiful farm in France and a rich plantation on Mauritius, and was extremely old. The means to live happily and quietly did not tempt him as much as the sea, with its mixed pleasures and adventures, picked up from his childhood.

On this small island I also met M. de Bougainville on his voyage round the world, and the Prince of Nassau who was on board and since famous for scattering the Turkish fleet.[66] There was M. Magon who had been *intendant* at Saint- Denis and governor of Mauritius, with a round head and inset eyes.[67] M. Poivre had been a missionary and had lost an arm in a sea-battle which forced him to leave the clergy; he had been working with the Company and so impressed the governor with his knowledge of India that he was chosen to be *intendant* of Mauritius, where he planned to steal spice plants from the Dutch in the Moluccas and naturalize them on Mauritius. He was tall and always good-tempered. I have met few men as attractive as he. He knew everything about natural history. It was thanks to him that I developed a taste for this kind of study, convinced, with reason, that he found his main happiness there. He had created a small garden with banana trees among the rocks in front of the *intendant's* house. However, despite these qualities, he made many enemies, which I put down to the ease with which he promised things and the taste he had for mocking everything and for politicking, which spoils the best natures. He might have had his complaints about me, but I was genuinely attached to him. His defects were all to do with politics, but I miss him and regarded him as a true philosopher and a man who could have created happiness in the colonies if he had not suffered the passions brewing against him on the island.[68]

Goodbye my friend; in speaking of men I am angry with myself for only producing satires.

Letter 12
Port Louis, 25 April 1769
On Blacks

The rest of the island's population is made up of Indians and Negroes. The first are the Malabars. They are a very gentle people. They come from Pondicherry where they lease themselves for several years.[69] They are nearly all workers; they live in a neighbourhood called the Camp of the Blacks. These people are darker than the Madagascar islanders who are proper Negroes; but their traits are regular like those of Europeans, and they do not have frizzy hair. They are sober, thrifty and adore women. On their heads they wear turbans and dress in long muslin gowns, with large gold rings in their ears and silver bracelets on their wrists. Some of them lease themselves to rich or titled people as *pions*. This is a kind of servant who carries out the work of our footmen, except that he executes every commission with the utmost seriousness. As a sign of dignity he carries a cane in his hand, and a dagger in his belt. It would be desirable to have a great number of Malabars established on

J.M. Moreau le J.ne inv. 1772.   D. Née Sculp.

this island, especially the worker caste; but I have seen few who like working in the fields.

It is to Madagascar that one goes to find blacks to work the land. You can buy a man for a barrel of gunpowder, linen and especially *piastres*. The most expensive cost less than fifty *écus*.

These people do not have a nose as squashed nor the skin as black as Negroes from Guinea. Some are even brown; and some, like the Balambous, have long hair. I have even seen fair-haired and redheaded ones. They are skillful, intelligent and sensitive in matters of honour and gratitude. The greatest insult you can shout at a black is to curse his family: he hardly reacts to any other kind of insult. In their own country they make countless small objects with great art. Their assegai or half pike is well forged though they use only stones for both anvil and hammer. Their cloths, woven by the women, are very fine, with lovely dyes. They wrap them round themselves gracefully. Their hair is made up of regular curls in rows and braided artfully, again done by the women. Their instruments are the tam-tam, a kind of bow with a gourd fitted to it. They extract from it a sweet sound that accompanies the songs they invent: love is the perennial subject. Girls dance to their lovers' songs; spectators beat time and applaud.

They are very hospitable. A travelling black enters into the nearest hut without being known; those he finds inside share their food with him; they do not inquire where he comes from or where he is going; that is their custom.

They arrive in Mauritius with these arts and habits. They land from the ship naked, with a cloth around their waist. Men are placed on one side, and women on another, with their little children clinging to them in panic. The slave buyer examines them all over and buys those he finds suitable. Brothers, sisters, friends, lovers are separated; they say goodbye in tears and leave for their plantations. Sometimes they give into despair; they imagine that whites are going to eat them, will make red wine out of their blood, and gunpowder out of their bones.

Here is how we treat them. At dawn, three cracks of a whip are the signal to call them to work. Each one turns up with his spade for work, almost naked, in the sun's heat. For food they are given crushed maize boiled in water and manioc bread; for clothes a single piece of cloth. On making the slightest mistake they are tied hand and foot to a ladder; the overseer, with his carriage driver's whip, gives them fifty to a hundred lashes on their naked behinds. Each lash rips off skin. Then the wretch, covered in blood, is untied and has an iron collar with three spikes fixed around his neck and is sent back to work. Some have to wait for more than a month before they can sit down again. Women are punished in the same way.

In the evening, on the way back to their shacks, they are forced to pray for the prosperity of their masters. Before going to bed, they have to wish them a good night.

There is a law passed for their benefit, called the Black Code.[70] This favourable law ordains that blacks should not receive more than thirty lashes for any one offence; that they should not work on Sundays; that they be given meat once a week, and clothes for all year round. But nobody follows it here. Sometimes when they are old, they are dismissed and have to fend for themselves. Once, I saw a black slave, who was but skin and bone, cut meat off a dead horse in order to eat; he was a skeleton devouring another skeleton.

When Europeans react with distress, the plantation owners say they know nothing about blacks. They are accused of being greedy, of sneaking out at night to steal food from neighbouring houses; of being so lazy that they pay no attention to their master's business, and that their women prefer to abort rather than give birth, so miserable are they when they become mothers.

By temperament, Negroes are naturally playful, but after some time as slaves they turn melancholic. Only love seems to still conjure away their sorrows. They will do anything to get hold of a woman. If they can choose, they prefer women who have passed the prime of youth; they say "they make better soup." They give them everything they own. If their lover belongs to another master, they will travel overnight three or four leagues across rough terrain, just to be with her. When they love, they do not fear fatigue or punishments. Sometimes they arrange to meet in the middle of the night and dance behind some boulders to the sad music of a gourd filled with died peas. But if they spy a white or hear a dog bark, they scatter immediately.

They also have dogs. Everybody knows that these animals recognize perfectly not only whites, but the dogs of the whites, in the dark. They have nothing but fear and hatred for these whites; they howl when they approach. The dogs of the blacks only love the blacks and their friends, whom they never betray. White men's dogs, on the other hand, have adopted the feelings of their masters and at the slightest signal leap furiously on to the slaves.

Indeed, when blacks can no longer put up with their lot, they give in to despair: some hang or poison themselves; others climb into a pirogue without sails, provisions or compass and risk the journey of 200 leagues to return to Madagascar. If they are caught boarding, they are returned to their masters.

Usually they hide in the forest, where they are hunted by parties of soldiers, Negroes and dogs, with some of the local plantation owners joining in for the fun. They are dragged back like savage beasts. When they cannot be caught, they are shot by rifle, their heads are severed and carried back in triumph to town on the end of sticks. That is what I have seen every week.

When runaway blacks are caught, they have an ear sliced off and are whipped. A second time, they are whipped, their hamstrings are cut and they are put in chains. A third time, they are hanged, but not publicly accused as their masters fear losing their money.

I have seen them hanged and their bones broken while still alive; they went to their execution joyfully, and suffered without a sound. I saw a woman throw herself from the top of the ladder. They believe that in the next world they will find a happier life and that the Father of men will not treat them unjustly.

It is not that religion does not try to console them. From time to time they are baptized. They are told that they have become brothers to the whites and that they will ascend to paradise. But they can hardly believe that Europeans will lead them to heaven, for on earth they are the cause of all their misery. They say that before Europeans landed on their island, they fought each other with iron-tipped sticks; that we taught them how to shoot each other from far off with bullets; that we stirred them up to fight wars and sowed discord in order to get cheap slaves; that they used to follow fearlessly their natural instincts and that we have poisoned them with terrible diseases, that we have often left them without clothes or provisions and that we beat them cruelly, without giving any reason. I have seen all this more than once. An almost-white female slave came one day and threw herself at my feet; her mistress made her get up at dawn and go to bed late at night and when she was finally asleep rubbed her lips with dung. If she did not lick her lips, she was whipped. She begged me to plead for her, which I did. Often the masters listen to such pleading, but two days later, they double the punishment. It is what I saw at the property of a counsellor whose blacks complained to the governor: this same man assured me that he would flay them the next day, from head to toe.

Day in and day out I have seen men and women whipped for breaking some piece of pottery, or for having forgotten to close a door; I have seen them covered in blood, rubbed in vinegar and salt to heal them. I have seen them at the harbour, overcome with pain, unable to scream; I have seen others bite the cannon to which they are tied... My pen is weary of writing down these horrors; my eyes are tired of seeing and my ears of hearing them. How happy you are over there! When the evils of town wound you, you can flee to the country. You can see beautiful plains, hills, villages, harvests and people who dance and sing, the very image of happiness, but here I see poor Negresses bent over their spades, with their naked children stuck to their backs; I see blacks who pass in front of me trembling; sometimes I hear their drums in the distance, but more often I hear the snap of whips like pistol shots in the air and screams that pierce my heart... "Mercy, master, mercy..." If I wander deep into the country I find myself in a barren landscape, bristling with rocks and mountains with inaccessible peaks under cloud and streams crashing down into abysses. Winds that howl in these wild valleys, the deafening sound of the waves crashing on the reefs, that vast sea which stretches out to regions unknown to man: all this casts me into melancholy and fills my head with ideas about exile and abandonment.

PS

I do not know if coffee and sugar are necessary for happiness in Europe, but I do know that these two plants have led to misery in two parts of the world. We have depopulated America in order to clear land to plant them and we are depopulating Africa to find workers to harvest them.

It is claimed that it is in our interests to plant foodstuffs which have become essential for us, rather than buying them from our neighbours. But since carpenters, bricklayers, masons and other European workmen can work out of doors, why are there no white workmen here? What would happen to the current landowners? They could live in ease with twenty farmers, and are poor with eighty slaves. There are some 20,000 slaves here and an eighteenth part of these have to be replaced every year. Thus this colony, left to its own devices, will destroy itself within eighteen years. The truth is that people cannot live without freedom and property, and that injustice is a poor housekeeper.

It is said that the Black Code was passed to protect them. So be it, but the harshness of their masters exceeds the permitted punishments, and their meanness robs them of the food, rest and rewards due to them. If these wretches wanted to complain, to whom could they? To judges who are often their very tyrants.

But they claim that one can only contain this race of slaves with great severity; you must impose torture, the iron collar with three spikes, whips, fetters for their legs and chains for their necks; you must treat them like animals so that whites can live like humans... Ah, I well know that once one has accepted an extremely unjust principle like slavery, one can only expect very inhumane consequences.

It was not enough for these wretches to be bound to the meanness and cruelty of depraved landowners, but they also had to be the toys of their sophistry.

Theologians assure us that slaves in this life will find some kind of spiritual freedom. But most are bought at an age when they cannot learn French and missionaries do not learn their language. Anyhow, those who are baptized are treated like all the others.

They add that they deserve punishment in heaven by selling themselves to others. Should we thus be their executioners? We might as well leave the killing of kites to vultures.

Politicians have excused slavery by saying that war justified it. But blacks do not do it to us. I agree that human laws allow it; at the least we should ensure that its prescribed limits are respected.

I am annoyed that philosophers who fight abuse so courageously mention the slavery of blacks as the subject of jokes. They avoid the problem by looking into the past and speak of the St. Bartholomew massacre, of the destruction of the Mexicans by the Spaniards, as if the crime did not exist today and as if more than half of Europe was not taking part. Is it worse, then, to suddenly kill people who do not share our opinions than to torment a nation to whom we owe our pleasures? Those beautiful pink and flame colours in which our ladies dress themselves, the sugar, coffee, chocolate they eat for lunch, the rouge used to counteract their pallor: all this has been prepared by the hands of miserable black slaves for our women. Women of sensibility, you weep at tragedies in theatres, but what constitutes your pleasures is soaked in the tears and stained with the blood of blacks!

Letter 13
Port Louis, 29 May 1769
Agriculture, Herbs, Vegetables and Flowers Brought to the Island
The government had the majority of plants, trees and animals that I am about to describe for you brought over here. Some of the inhabitants have also contributed, including M. de Cossigny, Poivre, Hermans and Le Juge.[71] I would like to have known the names of the others in order to give them the respect due to them. The gift of a useful plant seems to me to be more precious than the discovery of a gold mine and a monument more lasting than a pyramid.[72]

Here is the order I will place them in: 1. Plants that reproduce themselves, and are as if naturalized in the countryside; 2. Those that are cultivated in the countryside; 3. Herbs from kitchen gardens; 4. Those from flower gardens. I will follow the same plan with shrubs and trees. I will not omit one of those known to me. One should not scorn the description of any plant that nature did not scorn creating.

One finds in some of the plains near to the town a kind of indigo which I believe is foreign to the island. It is of no use. Purslane grows in sandy places and is probably natural to the island. I think this way because it belongs to the family of thick-leaved plants. Nature seems to have destined this class, which grows in arid places, to help other vegetation grow.

Watercress is found in all the streams. It was brought here ten years ago. Dandelion and wormwood grow easily in scrub-land or recently ploughed land; and everywhere the mullein spreads its large, downy leaves and raises its cluster of yellow flowers to a surprising height.

Bulrush (which is not the Chinese plant with the same name) is a grass about the height of the best rye. It spreads each day more, choking other weeds. Its defect is to be tough when dried. It should be cut early. It is green for five months of the year, then it is set on fire, despite it being forbidden. These fires burn and dry the forest edges.

White grass (thus named from the colour of its flower) was brought here as good fodder. No animals eat it. Its seed looks like that of chervil. It multiplies so fast that it has become an agricultural pest.

Brède, whose name in the Indian language means a leaf that is good to eat, is a kind of nightshade. There are two kinds: one called Madagascan *brède*. Its leaf is prickly, but sweet tasting; it is a purgative. The other is more common and is served at table like spinach. It is the only vegetable freely available to blacks: it grows everywhere. The water in which this leaf is boiled is very bitter. The blacks soak their cassava in it, mixing it with their tears.

Manioc grows in the driest soil. Its juice has lost its poisonous quality. It is a sort of shrub whose leaf is webbed like hemp. Its root is as thick and long as an arm; you grate it and without pressing it you can make very heavy cakes. It is given three times a day to blacks as their sole food. This vegetable spreads easily. M. de Labourdonnais had it brought over from the Americas. It is a very useful plant in that it can be protected from cyclones, and ensures subsistence food for Negroes. Dogs refuse to touch it.

Maize or Turkish corn grows extremely well. It is a precious grain and has a high yield but will not keep for more than a year as the mites get into it. In Europe we should encourage the cultivation of this kind of wheat which cannot be stored. It feeds the blacks, chickens and animals. Note that some inhabitants speak highly of maize and manioc, but do not touch them. I have seen maize served in the form of little cakes as a dessert. When mixed with plenty of sugar, wheat-flour and egg yolk, it is quite tasty.

Wheat grows well but not very high. It is planted as single seed by hand because of the amount of rocks, is cut with a knife and tressed with sticks. It does not store for more than two years. According to Pliny, in

North Africa and Spain the whole head of wheat was buried in a hole in the ground, being careful to let in some air. Varro says that it could be stored for fifty years that way, and millet for a century.[73] Pompey found some broad beans preserved that way in Ambratia from the time of Pyrrhus, some 120 years before.[74] But Pliny did not like the soil being worked by prisoners or by slaves who can do nothing, he wrote, worthwhile. Although wheat flour in Mauritius never comes out white, I prefer bread made with it than that made with European flour, which always ferments during voyages.

Rice, the best and perhaps healthiest of foods, thrives here. It can be stored for longer than wheat and yields more. It prefers wet places. There are more than seven kinds of rice in Asia, of which one grows in dry places; it would be good if it could be grown in Europe, due to its fertility.

Small millet yields a prodigious amount. It is seldom given to anyone other than blacks and animals. Oats thrive but are not cultivated. All that is useful to the well-being of slaves and animals is completely ignored. Tobacco is of poor quality. Only Negresses cultivate it for themselves.

Fataque is a long-leafed grass, like a small reed. It makes fine artificial meadows. It comes from Madagascar. The colonists have tried unsuccessfully to grow sainfoin, clover, hemp, flax and hops.

Concerning vegetables I will begin with: 1. Those which are useful in terms of their fruit; 2. Those useful in terms of their leaves or stems; 3. Those useful for their roots or bulbs. You will notice that most of our vegetables degenerate, and every year those who want to have some good ones, have seed sent from Europe, or from the Cape of Good Hope. Peas are tough and not sweet; beans are hard; there is a kind that is larger and more tender called the Cape pea; it is worth introducing in France. Another kind of bean is stored in barrels: you chop the husks to pieces and dress them as peas. The marsh broad beans grow well.

Artichokes grow huge leaves and small fruits. The cardoon thistle is very tough; they make hedges with it, as it is very prickly and grows tall.

The *giromon* is a pumpkin less large than ours, and I think, if that's possible, even more tasteless. The cucumber is smaller and not so plentiful as in Europe. The melon is good for nothing, although much praised because it is rare; the watermelon is a little better. The climate suits them, but the soil does not. Gourds grow to enormous sizes and are useful as the blacks make utensils out of them.

There are two kinds of aubergine: one has a small round and yellow fruit; its stem is extremely prickly. It comes from Madagascar. The other, which is known in Paris, is a violet fruit, the size of a large fig. When this fruit is well seasoned and grilled, it is not bad.

There are two sorts of pepper, the one known in Europe, and another one native to the island; it is a shrub whose fruit is tiny and shines like coral seeds on leaves of a most beautiful green. The Creoles use it in all their stews. There is no pepper more strong: it burns your lips like a caustic. It is called mad pepper.

The pineapple, the most beautiful of fruit due to the chain-mail of its suit of armour, its purple crest and its scent of violets, never ripens perfectly. Its juice is very cold and dangerous for the stomach.[75] Its skin has a strong taste of pepper and burns, perhaps as a corrective to the juice. Nature has often created opposites in the same species; the skin of a lemon heats while its juice cools; the leather of a pomegranate is astringent while its seeds are laxative etc.

Strawberries are beginning to thrive in cool places. They are less perfumed and sugary than ours: they produce few fruits, as with raspberries whose fruit has degenerated. There is a fine variety from China, with fruit the size of cherries and abundant but without taste or scent.

Spinach is rare; garden cress, sorrel, chervil, parsley, fennel and celery have stringy stems and do not grow well. Leeks, lettuce, chicory, cauliflower are smaller and less tender than ours; the cabbage, the most useful of vegetables, grows everywhere and well. Burnet, purslane and sage grow in abundance, but above all, nasturtium, which grows on large espaliers, is a lively plant.

Asparagus is as thin as string: it has degenerated in its stem and taste, as have carrots, parsnips, turnips, and radishes, which are too spicy. There is, however, a species of radish from China that grows well. Beetroot grows beautifully, but very ligneous. The potato, *solanum americanum*, is not larger than a walnut. Those from the West Indies that are named *cambar* weigh more than a pound. Its skin is a fine violet colour; inside it is very white and tasteless: it is given as food to the blacks. They multiply plentifully, as do the sweet potatoes, some of whose varieties are better than our chestnuts. Saffron is a root that colours stews yellow, as do the stamens used in Europe. Ginger is less hot than the Indian type. The peanut, which is not the fruit of the pistachio tree, is a little almond that grows under the earth in a wrinkled shell. It is rather good when roasted, but is indigestible. It is grown to extract oil for burning. This plant is a sort of phenomenon in botany, for it is rare that vegetables give oily fruit underground.

In the plants that bring us pleasure, I shall speak of ours, then those from Asia and Africa.

Reseda, tuberose, larksfoot, the great daisy of China, and small pinks grow as well as in Europe; the large pinks and lilies bear a number of leaves, but rarely flower. Anemones, daisies, large pinks and the Indian rose grow poorly, as do July-flowers and poppies. I have seen no other flowering plants from Europe grown by inquisitive gardeners. Many have struggled pointlessly to try and grow thyme, lavender, field daisy and the simple, beautiful violets and bluebells that glitter in the gold of our harvests. Lucky French people! A corner of your field is more magnificent than the most beautiful of our gardens.

As for flowering plants from Africa, I know only the beautiful immortelles from the Cape, whose seeds are as large and red as strawberries and grow in clusters at the tip of a stem whose leaves look like strips of grey sheet: another immortelle has purple flowers and grows everywhere. A reed the size of a horsehair with white and violet flowers can be seen from far off; it comes from the Cape, as does a kind of tulip which has two leaves stuck to the ground. A plant from China seeds itself, with little flowers like roses; each stalk gives five or six, in different colours from blood red to brick red. None of these flowers has a scent; even flowers brought from Europe lose their scent.

The aloes do well here. Much could be made from their leaves, whose sap gives a medicinal gum and whose threads are good enough to make cloth. They grow on rocks and places scorched by the sun. Some have strong, thick leaves the size of a man, armed with long darts: from its centre grows a stem as tall as a tree, covered in flowers from which the aloes drop. Other kinds are straight as tall candles covered in very sharp prickles; these are marbled and look like snakes crawling on the ground.

It seems that nature has treated Africans and Asians as barbarians to whom she has given magnificent and monstrous vegetables while she acts with us as if with sensitive friends. Oh, when will I be able to breathe in the scent of honeysuckle, and stretch out in a field of milkweed, saffron crocuses and purple clover on which our happy flocks feed and hear the songs of the workers who salute dawn with happy hearts and free hands!

Letter 14
Port Louis, 10 July 1769
Shrubs and Trees Brought to the Island
We have the rosebush here that thrives so well that hedges are made of them. Its flower is not as tufted, nor scented as ours; there are several varieties, among them a small species from China which flowers all year round. Jasmines from France and Spain are well naturalized; I will speak of the Asian ones in their place. There are pomegranate-trees with double flowers and fruit, but they yield little. The myrtle does not grow as well as it does in Provence.

So much for the shrubs from Europe. Those from Asia and Africa and America are: the acacia [*cassis*] with a jagged leaf which does not resemble ours at all; it is a large shrub, covered in yellow, scented flowers, like small tassels. They yield a bean whose seeds are used as a black dye. As it is prickly, it makes good hedges.

The *foulsapatte*, an Indian word that means shoemaker's flower, has a flower that when rubbed on leather dyes it black. This shrub has pretty green leaves larger than those of the hornbeam, in the middle of which shine flowers similar to large dark-red pinks; there are several varieties.[76]
The *poinciana*, originally from America, is a kind of bramble that has clusters of yellow and red flowers from which emerge flame-coloured tufts. This flower is very beautiful, but fades quickly; it gives beans. Its leaf is divided like all leguminous shrubs. The jalap gives crimson-red flowers in the shape of a funnel, which open only at night. They have a scent like that of the tuberose; I have seen two species.

The Madagascan vine is a liana from which cradles are made: it gives yellow flowers. Its downy leaf seems covered in flour. There are several flowering lianas in the gardens, but I do not know their names. The frangipane is a jasmine of another kind.[77] This shrub grows in the form of stag-wood; from the tips of its horns sprout bunches of long leaves in whose middle can be found large white flowers in funnel-shapes, of a charming scent.

Indian lilac grows and soon dies: the leaf is jagged and a beautiful green. It is loaded with clusters of flowers that have a pleasant scent and then turn to seed. This shrub rises to the height of a tree and looks good. Its green is prettier than ours, but it flowers less. The cotton tree grows in dry places like a shrub. It has a pretty yellow flower, soon followed by a pod which contains the flock. This flock is not harvested, for lack of mills to turn it into cloth. There is no profit in it. Its seed is good for encouraging milk in wet-nurses.

We have a species of sugarcane that ripens to perfection. The inhabitants make a poor liquor from it which they call *flangourin*. There is but one sugar-mill on the whole island.[78]

The coffee-bush is by far the most useful bush on the island. It is a kind of jasmine. Its flower is whiter, its leaves a fine green, shaped like laurel leaves. Its fruit is a red olive, like a cherry, which separates into two beans. They are planted seven and a half feet apart and are cropped when six feet tall. They last seven years: after three years they bear their berries. The annual produce of each tree is a pound of seed. A black can attend to one thousand feet of these a year, irrespective of the seeds he needs for himself. The island does not produce enough coffee for its own consumption. The locals claim it is as good as Mocha coffee in quality.[79]

The bamboo resembles, at a distance, our willows. It is a reed that grows as high as the tallest trees and shoots out branches with leaves like those of an olive; pretty avenues are made with these, with the wind ceaselessly murmuring among them. It grows quickly and its cane can be used for the same purposes as willow. There are many Indian pictures where this bamboo is poorly represented.

The fruit trees here are: the *attier* whose triangular flower, formed of a solid substance, tastes of pistachio; it is a fruit that looks like a pine-cone. When ripe it is packed with a white, sugary cream and smells of orange blossom. It is full of black pips. The *attier* is very tasty, but you quickly tire of it. It is rich and gives you a sore throat.

The mango is a very beautiful tree: the Indians represent it often on their silk cloth. It is covered with superb clusters of flowers, like the horse chestnut. They are followed by quantities of fruits shaped like large fat plums, covered with a skin that smells of turpentine. This fruit has a vinous and agreeable taste, and apart from its smell, it could compete with the best fruit from Europe. It never makes you sick. It would make a healthy and tasty juice. The sole inconvenience is that this tree is heavy with fruit during the cyclone season when most are blown down.

The banana-tree grows everywhere. It has no wood, being only a tuft of leaves that rise in columns and spread out at the top in large bands of a beautiful satin green. After a year, a long stem, bristling with fruit, emerges from the top, shaped like a cucumber. Two of these stems are a load for a black. This fruit is doughy and agreeably tasty and very healthy. The blacks love it. They are given bananas on New Year's day as a gift; and they count their sad years by the number of banana feasts.[80] Cloth could be made from banana leaves, which are shaped like silk belts. The length of the fruit bunch hangs down to a man's height, with a violet tip resembling a snake's head, which could have led to its name of Adam's fig tree. The fruit lasts all year. There are several species, from the size of a plum to others as long as an arm.

The guava tree resembles the medlar; its flower is white and its fruit always retains its smell of bugs. It is astringent, the only fruit on the island in which I found worms. The jama-rose affords plenty of shade. It is not tall and its fruit smells like rosebuds, and its nut tastes rather too sugary and insipid. The paw-paw is a kind of fig tree with branches. It grows quickly and rises like a column with a capital of large leaves. From its trunk shoot out the fruit, similar to small melons, of poor taste: their seeds taste of watercress. The trunk of this tree feels like a turnip. The female paw-paw only gives flowers; they have the shape and scent of honeysuckle.[81]

The *badamier* [82] seems to have been made to give shade. It rises like a beautiful pyramid, made of several well-separated levels. One could build charming cabinets between each floor; the leaves are beautiful. It gives almonds that taste rather good. The avocado is a beautiful tree. It gives a pear that contains a large seed. The flesh of this fruit is similar to butter. When you season it with sugar and lemon juice, it is not bad and is rich.

The *jaca* is a tree with sweet foliage that gives a monstrous fruit. It is as big as a long pumpkin; its peel is a pretty green and grained all over. It is packed with seeds whose covering, like a sticky, sweet, white skin, is eaten. It stinks like rotten cheese. This fruit is an aphrodisiac. I have seen women who loved it with passion.

There are several kinds of orange tree, among them one that gives an orange called a mandarin, as big as a lady's apple. A large kind is the grapefruit, with red flesh but a middling taste. A lemon tree bears huge fruit with little juice.

Coconut palms thrive in the sand. It is one of the most useful of trees in the India trade; however, it gives hardly anything other than a bad oil and poor ropes. It is claimed that in Pondicherry each coconut palm is worth one *pistole* a year. Travellers have greatly praised its produce, but our flax will always give better cloths than the coconut's hairs, our wines will always be preferred to its liquor, and our simple hazelnuts to its gross nut.

The coconut palm prospers near salt water, and salt is placed in the hole when it is planted to facilitate its growth. Coconuts seem designed to float in the sea with their coarse hairs that give them their ability to remain floating and by the hardness of their shells, resistant to water. It does not open by a joint, as with our nuts. Instead, the seedling's roots emerge through three little holes which nature has contrived at its ends after covering the nut with thick hairs. Coconut palms have been found at the sea's edge, on desert islands and even on sand shoals. This palm tree is the tree of Southern riverbanks, like the pine is the tree of the North while the date palm is the tree of the scorched mountains of Palestine.

I do not think that I am wrong in saying that the coconut was made to float, and then germinates in the sand; each seed has its own manner of reseeding itself that is unique; but that kind of study would lead me too far off. Perhaps I will take it up one day and that would give me great pleasure. The study of nature makes amends for that of mankind, and makes us see everywhere an intelligence in harmony with goodness. But if it were possible to be misled by this study, if everything surrounding mankind was made to confound him, at least let us choose our mistakes, and let us prefer those that can console us.[83]

As for those who believe that nature, in raising the heavy fruit of the coconut palm so high up, has deviated from the law which decrees that the pumpkin should creep along the ground, they have not paid attention to the fact that the coconut palm has only a small crown that hardly gives any shade. There is no way that you can seek shade and freshness, as under an oak. Why not rather note that in India as well as in Europe fruit trees which bear soft fruit are of a mediocre height so that they can fall to the ground without smashing, while those that have hard fruit, like the coconut, the chestnut, the acorn and walnut are very tall so that when their fruit falls it is not damaged. Moreover, the leafy trees in India give, as in Europe, a shade without danger. Some yield large fruit like the *jaca*, but carry them close to the trunk, within reach of the hand. Thus nature, which man accuses of imprudence, has contrived both shelter and food.

A crab that lives at the foot of coconut palms has recently been discovered. Nature has given it a long claw with a nail at the end. It uses it to extract the pulp of the coconut through its holes. It does not have large pincers like other crabs; it would have no use for them. This animal can be found on Palm Island to the north of Madagascar, discovered in 1769 when the ship *L'Heureux* sank on its way to Bengal.

Just discovered on the island of Seychelles is a tree bearing double coconuts, some of which weigh up to forty pounds. Indians attribute great virtues to it. They believe it grows from the sea because currents have thrown them up on the Malabar coast. It is called the sea coconut. This fruit represents a naked woman's buttocks and pubic hair, and has leaves as large as a house, shaped like a fan.[84] Order can be observed everywhere in nature. The tree that yields this enormous nut bears three or four at a time, while the common coconut bears bunches of thirty or more. I have tasted both and think that their flavour is very similar. This sea coconut has just been planted in Mauritius and has begun to grow rapidly.

There are other trees which are but objects of curiosity, like the date-palm, which rarely bears fruit; the palm known as the arak, and the palm that produces sago.[85] The *caneficier* and the mahogany give flowers without fruit. The cinnamon tree, of which I have seen whole avenues, looks like a big pear tree. Its small flower-clusters smell of excrement. Its cinnamon is poorly aromatic. There is only kind of one cacao tree on the island; its fruit never ripens. The nutmeg and the clove have to be imported. Time will decide how successful these trees will be when transplanted from the Equator to about 20 degrees latitude.

This little note has made me notable enemies: many people are ignorant of the fact that there is as much difference in latitude between the Equator and the tropic as there is between the tropic and the Arctic Circle. One is tempted to think that all the trees that grow in the tropics could grow equally anywhere, but those who have eaten bananas from India know that this fruit is far tastier there than in Mauritius. Each degree of the globe has its vegetation that grows to perfection there, but when grown some 15 to 20 degrees further north or south, it degenerates. Thus the vine which gives such good fruit in Spain and which gives such good wine degenerates in Berlin, where it only gives verjuice. The same happens in the tropics with the perfumed Mocha coffee which degenerates on the Equator, and the coffee that the Dutch have planted in Java, much further to the south, cannot be compared to it. In short, the pine from the north cannot grow among tropical palm trees. With this the case, it is not amazing that the clove and nutmeg did not succeed in Mauritius. These spices grew but did not produce anything for trade, as I had predicted.

While I was there, 22,000 germinating nutmeg trees and cloves were brought in; each plantation was given between twelve and twenty-four. Each one planted them with the utmost care, lured by the idea of making a fortune: some even promised freedom to the blacks in charge of them if it succeeded. It was like a collective fever. Everybody was infatuated with the idea; I thought, however, to myself that if the 22,000 nuts brought to the island grew successfully, it was obvious that the island would produce 12 million pounds weight a year, which was more than all the nutmegs the French eat. A single man cannot go against popular opinion. I dreamt myself of benefiting from this blessing: I obtained a nutmeg from the *intendant* and, as I did not have a square inch of land, I filled a bucket with earth and planted it, happy that I would soon have a thousand *écus* of income on my window sill. I watched over it with my eyes. At the end of six weeks I noticed that nothing had sprouted. I cleaned away the earth around the top of the seed and saw a small canker. I cleaned it as carefully as I would have cleaned my eye and found that the canker was formed by tiny white worms, like hairs. I warned M. Poivre, the *intendant*, who said: "Your nutmeg isn't growing because you keep touching it too much." I told him about the worms, which he rejected out of hand. In the end, after two months, I impatiently lifted it out and under its thin skin I noticed that these white worms had gnawed it everywhere.

I do not meant to imply that it was wrong to seek nutmegs in the Moluccas, to recompense those who had gone to the colonies in danger of their lives, or for plantation owners to earn a good income caring for them. I think, in terms of natural rights, that it is not fair that the Dutch forbid the export of these plants to Mauritius. A plant belongs to mankind, as do the earth, the sun and the elements.

Long ago, some *ravinesara*, a species of Madagascan nutmeg, was planted here, as were mangosteens and lychees, which bear, so people say, the best fruits in the world.[86]

The temperature of this island seems too cold for Asian trees and too hot for European ones. Pliny noted that the influence of the sky is more important than that of the earth for the growth of plants. He said that in his day you saw pepper and cinnamon trees in Italy and incense trees in Libya, but that they merely vegetated. But I think that you could naturalize the coffee bush, which likes a cool and temperate region, in southern France. These expensive experiments can only be carried out by princes; but the acquisition of a new plant is also a sweet and human conquest from which the whole nation benefits. What have we gained from so many wars at home and abroad? What do we care that Mithridates was beaten by the Romans and Moctezuma by the Spaniards? Without certain fruit, Europe would just be weeping over useless trophies. But whole people live in Germany on the potatoes brought over from America, and our beautiful women eat cherries that they owe to Lucullus.[87] Dessert has cost us dearly, but our fathers paid for it. Let us be wiser, let us gather the good things that nature has dispersed and let us begin with ours.

If I ever work for my own happiness, I would make a garden like the

Chinese. They chose a terrain by the banks of a stream; they prefer an irregular piece of land with old trees, boulders, small hills. They surround it with a boundary of rough rocks, with holes and sharp points. These rocks are placed one on the other, so that their junctures cannot be seen. On them they grow clumps of moss and tendrils with blue and purple flowers, and ferns of all kinds. A stream of water meanders through the plants, from where it escapes in cascades. Life and freshness are disseminated over this spot which with us is nothing more than an arid wall.

If there is some dip in the terrain, they make a pond and put fish in and border it with grass or trees. They are particularly careful not to level or align; no apparent masonry; the hand of man corrupts nature's simplicity.

The plain is intermingled with tufts of flowers, and edged with fields, in which some fruit trees grow. Hillsides are carpeted with clumps of shrubs, some with fruit, some with flowers and the heights are crowned with bushy trees under which can be found the master's roof.

There are no straight alleys that reveal every object at once, but pleasing paths which show them in succession. There are no statues or useless vases, but a vine loaded with beautiful grapes or rose bushes. Sometimes one can read some pleasing poem written on the bark of an orange-tree, or a philosophical aphorism on an old rock.

This garden is not an orchard, nor a park, nor a lawn but a blending, similar to the countryside, of plains, woods, and hills where objects have value by contrast with each other. A Chinaman has no more idea of a regular garden than he has of a square tree. Travellers assure us that one leaves these charming retreats with regret; for myself, I would still prefer a loving female companion and, close by, a friend like you.

Letter 15
Port Louis, 15 July 1769
Animals Brought to Mauritius
Exotic fish have been brought here; the *gourami* comes from Batavia, a fresh-water fish that passes as the best in India. It is similar to a salmon, but more delicate. You find goldfish from China which lose their beauty as they get bigger. These two species multiply in the ponds. Unsuccessful

attempts have been made to import frogs to eat the mosquito eggs deposited in stagnant puddles.

A very useful bird has been imported from the Cape. The Dutch call it the gardener's friend. It is brown and about the size of a big sparrow. It lives off worms, snails and small snakes. Not only does it eat them, but it also makes an ample store of them by hanging them from prickles in the hedges.

The martin is a bird that has multiplied prodigiously in the island. It is a kind of Indian starling, with yellow beak and claws. It only differs from ours by its plumage, which is less spotted. But it has the same chirping, aptitude for talking and mimicking ways; it counterfeits other birds. It approaches other animals in a familiar manner to pick them off; it particularly devours grasshoppers. Martins always live in couples. They meet in the evenings at sunset in their thousands on trees which they come back to. After a general chirping, the whole republic of birds falls asleep and at dawn disperses in couples to different areas of the island. This bird is not worth eating at all; even so, it is shot, despite it being banned.[88] Plutarch relates that the lark was worshipped at Lemnos because it lived off grasshopper eggs, but we are not in Greece.

Many crows were left in the woods to destroy mice and rats. Three males remain. Locals have accused them of eating their chickens and in this quarrel, they are judge and executioners.

There is no way of hiding the damage that the Cape bird carries out, a kind of small finch, the only forest bird that I have heard sing. They were brought out as curiosities, but escaped to the forest where they multiplied and live at the expense of the harvests. The government has placed a price on their heads.

There is a beautiful tit with white specks on its wing; and the cardinal which during a part of the year has its head, neck and chest a lively red: the rest of its plumage is a fine pearl-grey; these birds come from Bengal. There are three kinds of partridge, smaller than ours. The male's cry resembles that of a slightly hoarse rooster: they perch at night in trees, doubtless scared of the rats.

Some Guinea fowl and recently the beautiful Chinese pheasant have been let loose in the forest. Geese and wild ducks have been released on some ponds; there are also tame ducks, like the Manila duck, which is very pretty. There are chickens from Europe and one from Africa whose skin, flesh and bones are black. The cocks of a small species from China are very brave and fight the Indian cocks. One day I saw one attack a big Manila duck; the duck seized this tiny champion with its beak and smothered it under its belly and long feet. Although the cock was pulled out half dead, it returned to the charge with renewed fury. Some locals make a lot of money from their chickens because of the scarcity of other kinds of meat. Pigeons survive well, and are the best birds of flight on the island. Two kinds of turtledove and hares have been released on the island.

In the woods are wild goats, wild pigs and, above all, deer which have really multiplied; whole squadrons have been supplied with them for their provisions. Their flesh is excellent, especially from April to August. Some have been kept tame, but do not breed.

Among the domestic quadrupeds there are sheep that get thin and lose their wool, goats that thrive, and oxen of a Madagascan breed that have a great lump on their neck; their cows bear little milk; European ones give more, but their calves degenerate. I have seen two bulls and two cows no bigger than an ass, coming from Bengal. This little breed did not succeed.

We can seldom get butcher's meat here. Pork is the staple and is better than the European sort. However, it does not salt well on account of the salt here being too sharp. The female pig is liable to produce monsters on this island. I have seen a little pig preserved in spirits with a snout stretched out like an elephant's trunk.

Horses are not attractive and are very expensive: an ordinary horse costs 100 *pistoles*. They are worn out very quickly in Port Louis, due to the heat. They are never shod, although the island is littered with rocks. Mules are rare, asses are small and there are few of them. The ass could be the most useful animal on the island and could relieve the blacks in their work. Every load is carried on the heads of the slaves, who end up exhausted. A little while ago, two fine wild asses were brought from the Cape, a male and a female, the size of mules with stripes on their shoulders like zebras. These animals, though young, could not be tamed.

Cats do not thrive here; most are skinny, and rats are not scared of them. Dogs are far better rat-catchers: my "Favori" has often distinguished himself. I have seen him strangle the largest rat in the Southern Hemisphere. In the long run, dogs lose their skin and sense of smell. They claim there is no rabies here.

Letter 16
Port Louis, 15 August 1769
A Tour Around the Island

Two men interested in natural history, M. de Chazal, Counsellor, and M. the Marquis d'Albergaty, Captain of the Legion, offered to take me, some time back, to see a large and noteworthy cave some one and a half leagues away, and I accepted. We went first to Grande Rivière. This large river, like all those on the island, is but a big stream that no sloop could navigate beyond a rifle shot from its mouth. There is a small settlement there, consisting of a hospital and some stores and it is here also that the aqueduct that brings water to town begins. You can see a fort defending the bay on a little hill shaped like a sugar loaf.

After crossing the Grande Rivière, we took the local carpenter as a guide. We walked for about three-quarters of an hour westwards through a wood. As we were on a plain, I thought the cave, whose mouth I expected to be an opening in a cliff, was far off, when we came across it without thinking, at our feet. It seemed like the hole of a cave whose vault had collapsed. Several roots from a *mapou* hung down and blocked the entrance. The head of an ox was nailed on the arch.

Before descending into this abyss, we had breakfast. After which we lit a candle and torches and furnished ourselves with tinderboxes to strike fire.

We climbed down some dozen steps on the rocks that block the cave's mouth and I found myself in the vastest cave I had ever seen in my life. Its vault is formed with black rock, it is about thirty feet long and twenty high. The very level ground is also rock and covered with fine earth that rainwater has deposited. On each side of the cave, at about breast-height, a large line is drawn around the rock. I think this to be the work of the waters that drip down in the rainy season to different levels. I could confirm this observation by several land and river shells that I saw there. However, the country people believe that it is the ancient crater of a volcano. It seems to me to be more like an ancient underground river. The roof is vaulted and covered with a shining, dry, varnish, a kind of stony concretion that extends to the walls and even down to the ground. There are ferruginous stalactites that broke under foot as if we were walking on a crust of ice. We walked for quite a while on perfectly dry soil, except for some three hundred paces from the entrance where a part of the vault had collapsed. Rainwater seeped through the earth and left a few puddles.

The vault became lower and lower. We were forced to crawl on hands and knees; the heat was stifling. I did not wish to go further. My companions were more nimble and lightly dressed and so continued.

On turning back, I found a root as thick as my finger, attached to the vault by tiny filaments. It was more than ten feet long, without branches or leaves and seeming never to have had them. I think it is a special species. It was filled with a milky sap.

I came back to the grotto entrance where I sat to breathe some fresh air. After some time I heard a dull humming and in the light of the torches carried by the blacks I saw our travellers in their caps, shirts and pants so dirty and red that they could have been taken for characters in an English tragedy. They were bathed in sweat and smeared with red earth along which they had dragged themselves on their bellies until they could go no further.

It seems to me that one could turn the cave into a fine store by cutting walls to prevent water entering. The Marquis took measurements and in the evening we returned to town.[89]

This excursion gave me a taste for further ones. I had long been invited by an inhabitant of Rivière Noire called M. de Messin to visit him: he lived seven leagues from Port Louis. I took the opportunity of going in his pirogue, which came to the harbour once a week. A pirogue is a kind of boat cut from a single trunk with oars or sails. We were nine people aboard.

We left the harbour at half past midnight by rowing. The sea was very rough and smashed on to the reefs. We often passed over the foam created by the reefs without realizing it, for the night was very dark. The master said that he could not continue his journey until the day broke, and that he would put in to land.

We had travelled about a league and a half; he moored a little beyond Petite Rivière. The blacks carried me to the shore on their shoulders, after which they took two pieces of wood, one from the *veloutier* tree and the other a bamboo, and they lit a fire by rubbing them together. This is a very ancient method: it was employed by the Romans. Pliny says that there is nothing better than ivy-wood rubbed against laurel wood.[90]

Our men sat around the fire, smoking their pipe. A kind of crucible at the tip of a long reed, they pass it round. I shared out some brandy and went to sleep on the sand, wrapped in my coat.

I was woken up at five to board again. Day seemed about to break, I saw the mountain peaks covered in clouds moving past fast: the wind chased away the mist in the valleys; the sea was white with foam and the pirogue with both its sails travelled quickly.

When we reached a place on the coast called Flic en Flac, about half a league from land, we encountered choppy waves, with several squalls that forced us to lower our sails. The master said to me in his rudimentary patois: "This no good, mister." I asked him if we were in danger. He answered me twice: "If no mishap, that good." At last he told me that a fortnight before in the same place the pirogue had turned over and one of his comrades had drowned.

We had the wind gusting against the shore, which was rocky and impossible to land on; blown by the wind, we would pass beyond the island and would not be able to tack back; it had to be just right. We had to use oars, as we could not rely on the sail. The sky was more and more uncertain, we had to hurry. I gave more brandy to the rowers, after which, by rowing hard and risking being submerged twenty times, we left the waves and were out of the wind, coasting between the reefs and the shore.

During this emergency the blacks were as relaxed as they are on land. They believe in fatality. They have an indifference to life that is worth all our philosophy.

I disembarked at the mouth of the Rivière Noire at around nine in the morning. The master of the plantation did not expect his pirogue to be back that day: I was showered with expressions of friendship. His land covers the whole river valley. It is poorly described in the Abbé de Caille's map: he has omitted a branch of the mountain on the right bank which runs to the Tamarin Morne. Moreover, the river does not flow in a straight line; near its mouth it turns left. This learned astronomer only really drew the outline of the island. I have made a few additions to his map, thanks to my excursions.

There is abundance at Rivière Noire: game, venison, fresh and saltwater fish. One day at table we were told that some manatees had been seen in the bay, and we immediately ran to see. Nets were cast at the entrance and after pulling the two ends together we saw rays, *carangues*, swordfish and two sea turtles, but the manatees had escaped.

There is a great sense of order on this plantation, as there is in all those I visited. The huts of the blacks were lined like tents in a military camp. Each one has his small garden where he grows tobacco and squashes. Many chickens and sheep are bred on the plantation. The grasshoppers do great damage to the harvests. The crops are transported to town with difficulty because the land roads are impassable and the sea wind blows against those returning to Port Louis.

After resting for a few days, I decided to return to town by making a tour through the Plaine de Willhems. The master of the house lent me a guide and some pistols, in case of runaway slaves.

I left at two in the afternoon to spend the night at Palma, M. de Cossigny's plantation, about three leagues away. There are only paths through the rocks; you have to walk. When I had climbed up and come down from the Rivière Noire mountains, I found myself in a large forest with no clearings. The path led to an isolated plantation, the only one around here, and passed close to it. The master stood in his door, with his legs naked, his sleeves rolled up, in a shirt and socks. He was amusing himself rubbing a monkey with ripe red berries from Madagascar; he was smeared in the same red juice. This man was a European and had enjoyed a considerable fortune in France and squandered it. He led a sad and poor life in the forest, with a few blacks, and on land that was not his.

From there, after half an hour's walk, I reached the banks of the Rivière du Tamarin whose waters flowed with a loud noise over a bed of stones. My black found a ford and carried me over on his shoulders. I saw before me the high mountain called the Trois Mamelles, and the plantation called Palma was on the other side.[91] My guide made me skirt around the side of the mountain, assuring me that we would soon find the paths that led to the summit. We got round it after walking for an hour: I then saw my man puzzled and retraced my steps, reaching the foot of the mountain as the sun was about to set. I was exhausted and thirsty; had I had water, I would have spent the night there.

But I made a decision. I decided to climb up through the forest, although I could find no path. I clambered over rocks, sometimes gripping trees, sometimes supported by my black who was walking behind me. I had been walking for half an hour when night fell. Then my sole guide was the slope of the mountain itself. There was no wind, the air was hot and I cannot tell you how I suffered from thirst and fatigue. Several times I lay down, set on staying there. At last, after incredible exertions, I realized that I was not climbing any more: soon after I felt a fresh southeasterly breeze on my face and I saw lights in the distance in the countryside. What lay behind me was covered in deep darkness.

I climbed down, often letting myself slip, inadvertently. The sound of a stream guided me and I reached the bottom bruised all over.

Although sweating, I drank carefully, and having felt leaves under my hands, had the good luck to find watercress which I ate by the handful. I continued walking towards the light I had glimpsed, taking care to carry my pistols loaded and fearing I might find a group of runaway slaves: it was a clearing with several tree trunks on fire. There was nobody about. In vain I listened and shouted in the hope that some dog would bark; I only heard the distant noise of the stream and the dull murmur of the wind in the trees.

My black and my guide picked up some burning twigs and with their feeble light we walked through the ashes of this cleared plot towards another distant light. We found three blacks guarding a flock of sheep. They belonged to one of M. de Cossigny's neighbours. One of them accompanied me to Palma. It was midnight, everybody was asleep, the master was absent. But the black in charge saw to it that I had all I wanted. I left early in the morning to walk the two leagues to the property of M. Jacob, a landowner on the high grounds of the Plaine de Willhems; I found good open roads everywhere. I walked alongside the Corps de Garde mountain, which is very steep, and arrived early, upon which my host received me with the utmost hospitality.[92]

The air in this part of the island is much cooler than in town and in the place I had left. I happily sat by a fire. It is one of the best-cultivated areas of the island. It is watered by several streams, some of which, like the one called Rivière Profonde, rush down ravines of a frightening depth. On my way back to town, the path passed very close to its edge: I worked out that I was 300 feet above the riverbed. The sides are covered with five or six tiers of large trees: the view made me giddy.

As I walked down to town I felt the heat return and I saw the greenery fade until I reached the port, which was completely dry.

Letter 17
Journey on Foot Around the Island

An officer had offered to take me on a tour around the island on foot, but just before we were due to leave, he cried off. I decided to go alone.

I could count on Côte, one of the King's blacks who had already accompanied me; he was small, following the meaning of his name,[93] but very strong. He was a man of a proven fidelity, of few words, was sober and shocked by nothing.

I had recently bought a slave, to whom I gave your name, as a good omen for him. He was well built, with an alert expression, but of delicate complexion and not speaking a word of French. I could still count on my dog to guard us at night, and look out for game by day.

As I knew that I would often be alone, without a place to stay in over night, I supplied myself with all I thought necessary for myself and my party. I had set aside a cooking pot, some plates, 18 pounds of rice, 12 pounds of biscuits, the same amount of maize, 12 bottles of wine, six bottles of eau-de-vie, butter, sugar, lemons, salt, tobacco, a small cotton hammock, some linen, a map of the island rolled inside a hollow bamboo, some books, a sabre and a cloak; all weighing two hundred pounds. I spread all this into four baskets: two weighed sixty pounds and two forty. I had them tied to two strong reeds. Côte was in charge of the heavier weight, Duval took the other. As for myself, I wore my waistcoat, carried a double-barrelled shotgun, a pair of pocket pistols, and my hunting knife.

I decided to start my trip in that part of the island that was in the lee of the wind. I had chosen to follow the seashore, so as to get an idea as to how the island might be best defended, and incidentally, to make some natural history observations. M. de Chazal offered to accompany me as far as his plantation, some five leagues from town in the Plaine Saint-Pierre. Monsieur the Marquis d'Albergaty joined our group.

We left early on 26 August 1769 along the shore. From Fort-Blanc, to the left of the harbour, the sea stretches over this sandy shore, which is not steep, as far as the point called the Pointe aux Sables. There the Paulmy battery has been built. Landing would be impossible on this beach because of a bank of reefs, at a two-musket shots distance, which makes a natural defence. From the Paulmy battery, the shore falls down steeply and the sea breaks so roughly that nobody could approach. As for the plain, the prodigious amount of rocks scattered about would make it impractical for cavalry and artillery. There are no trees: you only see some *mapous* and *veloutiers*. The steep shore ends at the Petite Rivière bay, where there is a small battery.

We found there a man, M. de Séligny, of singular merit and not sufficiently employed, with whom we dined. He showed us the plans of a machine with which he traced a route to the ship *Neptune*, run aground during the cyclone in 1760. It consisted of two iron rakes, set in motion by two large wheels supported on barges: these wheels increased their effect by using levers on rafts.

He also showed us a cotton mill of his own invention: the water made it turn. It was made of many little cylinders of metal placed in parallel. Children place the cotton on to two of these cylinders, the cotton passes through and the seeds remain. This same mill was used to blow wind in a forge, to grind meal and to make oil. He told us that he had found a vein of coal, some iron ore, earth suitable for making crucibles, and that the ashes of *songes*, a kind of water lily, when burnt with coal, produced glasses of different colours. In the afternoon we left this useful and unrequited citizen.[94]

We followed a path that left the shore, about a rifle shot from the sea. We forded the Rivière Belle Isle, whose mouth is boxed-in. A quarter of a league from there one enters a wood leading to M. de Chazal's plantation. This land, called Plaine Saint-Pierre, is more littered with rocks than the rest of the route. Several times our blacks were forced to put their loads down and help us climb. Half an hour before arriving, Duval, no longer able to stand his load, put it down. We were very disconcerted because it was dark and the other blacks had gone on ahead. How would we find him in the middle of the wood and undergrowth? I struck a light with my gun, and kindled a fire with some straw and dry sticks; after which we left Duval there, and when we arrived at the house, we sent some blacks with baskets to find him.

The whole coast is very steep from the Petite Rivière to the Plaine Saint-Pierre. My curious companions had found in the rocks the purple-fish of Panama, the silver-mouth, sea urchins and other shells. On the beach we only found the debris of coral, shells and sea grapes.

We had walked for five hours in the morning and four after noon.

27 August 1769
We rested all day. All this stony land is good for cotton growing, but the yield is small. The coffee is of a good quality, but yields little as is usual in dry places.

28 August
My companions wanted to accompany me until dinner; we set off at

eight in the morning. We first passed the Rivière du Dragon by ford, then the Galet river in the same way. The coastline ceases being steep and we had the pleasure of walking on sand along the sea in a great plain that leads as far as the Anse [bay] du Tamarin; it could be a quarter of a league wide and at least a league long. In many places hardly anything grew at all. Coconut palms could be planted here as they like sand. To the right is a stream of bad water flowing through woods.

We found beds of fossil madrepores in areas no longer covered by the sea, which proves that the sea once washed this coast. We dined on the right-hand bank of the bay, then separated after embracing each other and I was wished a good journey. We had found debris of seashells in the sand.

There was but a short league to cover before reaching Rivière Noire and spending the night with M. de Messin. I first forded the back of the Bay of Tamarin and from there followed the seashore, exhausted; it is sheer as far as the Rivière Noire. Along the sea rocks I found many kinds of crab, and that sort of *boudin* [blood sausage] I have already mentioned.

The bay is sandy and a landing could be made here if the positions on the sides of the bay did not expose one to crossfire. A battery on the sandy headland on the right-hand bank of the Rivière Noire would be very useful. I had walked three hours in the morning and three after noon.

29 & 30 August

At low tide I strolled along the seashore; I found the great conch and a fish called the false admiral.

31 August

I left at six in the morning. I forded the first stream of the Rivière Noire, near to the house, then having cut across a kind of island covered in trees and stones, I became lost in the long grass and with difficulty found the path again. It led me to the shore I was following, as the tide was out. All along this beach there are oysters stuck to rocks; Duval, my new black, cut his foot badly walking on shells: it was at one of the two mouths of the smaller stream of the Rivière Noire. We stopped there at eight in the morning and I washed his wound, and made him drink some brandy, as I did Côte. As they carried heavy loads, I decided to halt twice a day, which divided my morning and evening journeys, and to give them some refreshments. This slight indulgence gave them strength and spirits: they would have willingly followed me to the end of the earth.

Between the two mouths of the Rivière Noire, a stag chased by dogs and hunters ran straight towards me. It was crying and bellowing: unable to save it and not wanting to kill it, I fired some shots into the air. It threw itself into the water where the dogs killed it off. Pliny observed that this animal, when cornered by a pack of hounds, throws itself at the mercy of man. I halted at the first stream we came across after the two parts of the Rivière Noire: it rushes into the sea near the little island called the Ilot du Tamarin, which is not on the map. You can reach it by foot at low tide, as well as the Ilot du Morne, where sometimes ships are left in quarantine.

I had all I needed for dinner, except good cheer. I saw a pirogue sail along the coast, packed with Malabar fishermen. I asked them if they had any fish: they sent me a beautiful mullet, for which they did not want any money. I erected my kitchen at the foot of a *tatamaque* tree: I lit a fire after one of my blacks had fetched some wood and the other some water, as the water nearby was brackish. I dined very well on my fish and gave all my people some.

I noticed blocks of ferruginous rock, abounding in minerals. A band of reefs stretches from the Rivière Noire to the Morne Brabant, the most leeward part of the island. There is only one place to land behind the Tamarin island.

At two in the afternoon I left, taking care how I walked. I was going to cross more than twenty leagues of the island that were deserted, with only two plantations. This is where the runaway slaves hide. I forbade my men to disperse; even my dog which always went ahead, had to follow a few paces behind me; at the slightest sound he would lift his ears and stop: he could smell if there were men about. We walked thus in good order following the shore, which forms many pretty bays. On the left we skirted woods where the most profound solitude reigns. They back on to a low chain of mountains whose summit we could see: this land is not very good. We saw *polché* trees, imported from India, and further evidence that man had settled here before. I had taken the precaution of bringing some bottles of water and I was right, as all the streams here had dried out.

I was worried about my black's wound, which bled profusely; I walked slowly, and we stopped at four o'clock. As night was approaching, I did not want to walk round the Morne, so I took a short cut through a wood across the isthmus joining the two mountains. This isthmus is nothing more than a small hill. Standing on this hillock, I met a black belonging to M. Le Normand, whose house I was on my way down to, and which was about a quarter of a league away. This man went ahead while I stopped and looked with delight at the prospect of the two seas. A house built in this place would be in a charming situation; but there is no water. As I walked down the hill, a black ran up to me with a jug of cool fresh water and announced that I was awaited at the house. I arrived. It was a long hut in the form of a palisade, covered with *latan* leaves. The whole plantation consisted of eight slaves, with nine members of the family: master and mistress, five children, a young cousin and a friend. The husband was away. That is what I learned as I entered.

The whole house was a single room; in the middle, a kitchen; at one end, the stores and the bedding of the servants; at the other end, the matrimonial bed, covered with a bedspread on which a hen was brooding its eggs; under the bed, ducks; pigeons in the leaves of the roof, and three huge dogs at the door. On the wall all the instruments used in the home and in the fields were hanging on hooks. I was truly shocked to find a very pretty woman in this miserable dwelling. She was French, born into a good family, as was her husband. They had come here several years before, to seek their fortune; they had abandoned their relations, their friends, their country to spend their days in a wild place, where one saw only the sea and the frightening cliffs of the Morne Brabant.[95] But the air of contentment and the good nature of this young mother of a family seemed to make all who got close to her happy. She was breast-feeding one of her infants; the four others stood round her, playful and content.

When night fell, we were served all that this house could offer in the most proper way possible. Dinner was extremely agreeable. I did not tire of watching the pigeons flying around the table, the goats playing with the children and so many animals mingling around this charming family. Their peaceful games, the seclusion of the place, the noise of the sea, gave me an image of the early times when Noah's children, on first touching new land, could still share their roof, table and bed with the gentle and affectionate animals.

After dinner I was led to bed in a wooden hut that had just been built some two hundred paces away. The door had still not been hung and I closed the gap with recently cut planks. I loaded my weapons, as this place is surrounded by runaway blacks. A few years back, forty maroons escaped to the Morne where they planted their food. They were attacked and rather than surrender threw themselves into the sea.

1 September
The master of the house returned in the night and persuaded me to postpone my departure until the afternoon. He wanted to accompany me a part of the way. There were only three short leagues to Belle Ombre, the last plantation house in which I could sleep. As my black slave was injured, the young woman wanted to prepare herself a cure for his wound. She brewed a kind of Samaritan's balsam over the fire, with turpentine, sugar, wine, and oil. After dressing his wound, I sent him ahead with his comrade. At three o'clock, after lunch, I took my leave of this hospitable home, and of this amiable and virtuous woman. Her husband and I then set off. He was a very robust man; his face, arms and legs were burnt by the sun. He himself worked in the fields, felling and carting off trees. But he only complained about the work his wife had in bringing up the children; she had just taken in an orphan. He only told me about his worries, as he saw that I felt how happy he was.

We passed a stream near his house and we walked on grass until reaching Pointe du Corail. Here the sea runs inland, between two outcrops of sheer rock: you have to follow this chain of rocks, walking along broken paths, gripping the rock face. The hardest part was the far side of the bay, turning what is called the Cape. I watched some black slaves pass by sticking close to the rock cliff; one false step and they would fall into the sea. In bad weather this path is impassable; the sea crashes and breaks against it. In calm weather small boats enter the bay and load with wood. Luckily for us, the King's ship the *Désir* was there and we borrowed her boat to cross the straits. M. Le Normand led me to the other side, and then said goodbye as we heartily hugged each other.

After three hours walking on grass, I reached Pointe Saint-Martin. Often I walked on sand and sometimes on delicate grass that grows in thick tufts like moss. Here I found a pirogue where M. Etienne, partner in the Belle Ombre estate, awaited me. We were soon at his house, situated at the mouth of the Rivière des Citroniers. On the left bank, a two-hundred-ton ship was being built.

From M. Le Normand's house to here, everything is fresh and charmingly green, beautiful grasslands without rocks, lying between the sea and the forest.

Before passing the Cape, I noticed a huge coral reef some fifteen feet high, seemingly abandoned by the sea. It looms over a large pond of water, which could be turned into a basin for small ships. From the Morne Brabant to here runs a belt of coral reef where the ocean breaks, with no entrance for ships except where rivers run out to sea.

2 September

The remedy applied to my black's wound had almost cured him so I arranged to leave in the afternoon. During the morning I took a ride in a pirogue between the reefs and the coast. The water was extremely clear to the bottom: I could see forests of madrepores rising five to six feet up, like trees. Some even had flowers. Different species of fish of every imaginable colour swam among their branches: I could see beautiful shells and fish meandering about, especially a magnificent tuna fish that hid under a coral tuft scared by the motion of my pirogue. I could have made a beautiful collection but I did not have a diver or proper iron pincers to pull up the plants of this sea-garden, or to uproot these stone flowers. I did bring with me rocks called Midas' ear, Golden Cloth and some large roller-shaped creatures covered in hairy skin.

We had dinner on board the *Désir* with two officers, who, with M. Etienne, wanted to accompany me to the sound at Savanne, three leagues away. Nobody lives there, but there are some straw huts. In the morning we sent all the blacks ahead: in the afternoon I set off ahead alone. I reached the Poste Jacotet, a place where the sea runs into the land forming a round bay. In the middle you can see a small triangular island: this bay is surrounded by a hill that shuts it off, like a dock.[96] It is only open at the entrance where the sea enters, and at the end of the bay is a beautiful beach with streams running out from a freshwater lake, full of fish. Around this lake are several little hills rising one above the other in the form of an amphitheatre. They were crowned with clumps of trees, some pyramid-shaped like yews, others like umbrellas. Behind them towered palm trees with branches like arrows with feathers. All this mass of greenery, rising up from the grass, joins the forest and a branch of the mountain leading to the Rivière Noire. The murmuring of the springs, the beautiful green of the sea waves, the steady breeze, the scent of the *veloutier* trees, the harmonious plain, and the shaded hills seemed to spread happiness and peace around me. I regretted being alone; I invented plans, but from the rest of the world I would have only wanted some beloved objects to spend my life here.

I left this beautiful place in sorrow. I had hardly taken two hundred paces when I bumped into a troop of blacks armed with rifles. I walked towards them and recognized them as a detachment, a sort of island police force. They halted when they came up to me. One of them carried two small puppies in a gourd; another one dragged a woman with rope made of rushes tied around her neck. This was the booty that had been taken from a camp of black maroons that they had just routed. They had killed one, whose *gris-gris*, a kind of talisman made like a rosary, they showed me. This black woman seemed overwhelmed with grief. I asked her some questions, which she refused to answer. On her back she carried a bag made from the vacoas tree. I opened it and was appalled, alas, to find a man's head inside! The beautiful scenery vanished, and I was faced with a land of abominations.

My companions caught up with me as I was descending a difficult slope near the sound at Savanne. It became dark, so we sat under some trees at the end of the bay and lit torches and ate dinner.

We spoke about runaway slaves, because they too had met the detachment with the wretched woman who was perhaps carrying her lover's head! M. Etienne told us that there were troops of two to three hundred fugitive blacks around Belle Ombre and that they elected a chief whom they obeyed under punishment of death. They are forbidden to steal anything from neighbouring plantations, or to go along the banks of rivers looking for fish or *songe*. At night they go down to the sea and fish; in the daylight they drive deer deep into the forest with well-trained dogs. When there is only one woman in the troop, she belongs to the chief. If there are many women, they belong to everybody. They kill all the children born there, so they say, in case their bawling betrays the hideout. They spend all morning casting lots to predict the outcome of the ensuing day.

He told us that while out hunting the year before, he had bumped into a runaway slave, and began to chase him with his loaded rifle, but missed him three times. He was going to knock him down with his rifle butt when two black women emerged from the forest, and ran to throw themselves at his feet, sobbing. The slave seized his chance and escaped. He brought these two generous creatures back home and one morning pointed one of them out to us.

We spent the night under a straw shelter.

I had observed that we could convert the Poste Jacotet, that attractive place, into an excellent harbour for small boats by clearing the coral beds from underwater. The Savanne sound would also serve to load barges.[97] This is by far the most beautiful part of the island. However, it remains uncultivated and out of reach from Port Louis because of the inland mountains and the difficulty of sailing against the wind round the Morne Brabant.

3 September

M. Etienne and M. de Clezemure, captain of the *Désir*, accompanied me as far as the left bank of the Savanne river, which is even steeper than the right bank: in this place their dogs cornered a stag.[98] I took my leave from them to cover the remaining twelve leagues through uninhabited countryside.

I noticed as I was walking that the meadows became larger, the woods thicker and better grown. The mountains are pushed far inland and you can only see their peaks in the distance.

Every now and then I came across a ravine. During a two-hour walk I waded across three rivers. The second is called the Rivière des Anguilles and was hard to cross; its bed is full of rocks and its current fast. It flows from springs of ferruginous water, covering the surface with an oil the colour of a pigeon's throat.

On my way I saw one of those hawks called chicken-eaters. It was perched on a branch of a *latan* tree. I aimed at it with my gun, lit both my primes, but no shot sounded. The bird remained calmly on the branch and I left it there. That little adventure reminded me to keep my weapons in a better state in case of attack by runaway slaves.

I halted on the right bank of the third river, near the sea on a level part of the rocks, shaded by a *veloutier* tree. My blacks made a kind of tent for me by throwing my jacket over some branches. They cooked dinner and fished some conch shells and Midas' ears.

Two hours after dinner, I was on my way again, my rifle cleaned and my men in good order. Surprises were not to be feared. The plain was open and the forest far off. The path was beautiful and sandy. To walk more comfortably and so as not to take my shoes off each time we reached a river, I decided to walk barefoot like early morning hunters. This way of walking is not only more natural, but safer: your foot knows the angles of rocks as if it was a hand. Blacks are so expert with their feet that they use them to pick up a pin on the ground. It is not in vain that nature has divided this part of our body into toes, and toes into articulations.

After thinking this out, I pulled my shoes off and waded across the first river. But in coming out of the water my legs were terribly burnt by the sun and became red and swollen. Crossing the second river, I cut my heel and my little toe. In putting my bare foot into the water one of my cuts hurt me incredibly. So I renounced my intention, annoyed at having lost one of the advantages of our human constitution through lack of practice.

I reached the Rivière du Poste, crossing on the back of my black, a cannon shot from its mouth. The river crashes noisily over rocks. Its waters are so transparent that I could pick out black snails on the bed. I experienced a kind of horror during this crossing. The sun was close to setting and I did not want to go any further. I walked on the stones of the left bank to find the straw shed I had seen on one of the spits in the river's mouth, but it was impossible to reach it over the blocks of rocks.

I retraced my steps, and took the path that led back to the top of the ravine where down below the river flowed. On the left hand side, in a recess, I saw a little clump of bushes, trees and lianas, into which nobody could enter. It occurred to me to cut open a passage with my axe and live there as in a nest. This resting-place seemed safe to me, but as raindrops started falling, I thought it wiser to spend the night under a poor roof. I climbed down the recess until I reached sea level and was overjoyed to find the straw shack that I had glimpsed from the other side. It was a roof made of *latan* leaves built against a rock; on the right was the path I had tried to take, on the left the path I had come down. Facing me was the sea. Everything combined to make me feel safe and comfortable: a bed of dried leaves was prepared for me and I lay down to sleep. I had my baskets hanging on their sticks on the left and right of my bed, like barriers and one of my blacks at each entrance, with my pistols under my pillow, my rifle next to me and my dogs at my feet.

I had hardly finished organizing everything when I was seized with shivers. It is the aftermath of sunstroke, which nearly always leads to fever. My legs were painful and swollen. They made some lemonade for me and lit a candle while I busied myself writing down what I had noticed during my trip, and corrected mistakes on my map.

The entire coast after the Savanne river is steep and inaccessible. The rivers that rush down there have steep banks. It would be impossible to make this journey on horseback. The march of an enemy could be easily halted, each river being a ditch of a frightening depth. As for the countryside, it seemed to me to be the most beautiful on the island.

By midnight my fever died down and I fell asleep. At half past three in the morning my dog woke me and rushed out of the improvised shelter, barking wildly. I called Côte and told him to get up. I went out with my weapons but I only saw the sky thick with stars. My black returned moments later and said he had heard somebody whistle twice near the wood. I had the fire re-lit, ordered my men to keep watch and placed Côte as sentry with my sabre.

The ocean waves smashed against the rocks, almost reaching my hut. This din, added to the darkness, rocked me to sleep; but I was not without worries. I was five leagues from any house, and if the fever should flare up again, I did not know where to find help. The black runaway slaves did not scare me; my two blacks seemed resolute men, and I was in a place where I could last out a siege. After all, I congratulated myself on not having camped in the woods.

As soon as I could make out objects, I gave my blacks a glass of *eau-de-vie* each and set off. They were less weighed down, as our provisions were decreasing day by day.

4 September

I left at half past five in the morning, resolving to make an effort to reach the nearest house without stopping. After an hour's walk the fine grass that starts at the Morne Brabant ends and you enter a terrain covered with rocks, like everywhere else on the island. But the grass is greener, with larger leaves, ideal for pasture.

I waded over the Chalan inlet across a sandbank. It is badly depicted on the map. The sea runs deep inland through a narrow passage that could, I believe, be blocked with nets to make a fine reservoir for fish.[99] On the left-hand bank I found a hut where I rested.

Half a league from there the path divides into two; I took the left one which passes through a wood and which led me along a wide road marked with wheel tracks. The sight of the ruts suggested that an important establishment was close at hand, and that pleased me. I preferred to see horse tracks to man's footprints. We reached a plantation house whose owner was away and so had to turn back and follow the path through the wood, which took us to a house inhabited by a M. Delaunay. I arrived just in time as I could hardly stand up on my legs. He lent me a horse to take me the two leagues to a plantation inhabited by priests.

I crossed successively the River Chaux, which is extremely enclosed, and the Créoles river.[100] At three-quarters of a league from the last river I crossed one of the bays of the southeast in a pirogue.

The shores are covered in mangroves. All the landscape is very agreeable; it is cut with hills covered with plantations. From time to time we crossed small woods of orange trees. At six in the evening I arrived at the priest's house. My legs were bathed in elder flower water and I rested in great comfort.

5 September

It is no more than one league from there to Grand Port. One of the priests lent me a horse and I reached the village as it struck ten. The most remarkable buildings are a ruined mill and the governor's house in equal disrepair. Behind the town rises a great mountain and in front is the sea, forming here a wide bay two leagues out, including the reefs at its entrance, and four leagues wide from the Isle des Deux Cocos to the Pointe du Diable.

I returned to the curate's house.

6, 7 & 8 September

I was delighted with my host and with the landscape I had seen, but you should not trust places where the orange blossoms. The priest drank only water, as did his parishioners. It often takes a month to travel here by sea from Port Louis, and the locals are often liable to lack anything that comes from Europe. I gave some of my provisions to M. Delfolie, the missionary, who was a good, honest man.

The Port was first inhabited by the Dutch. You can still see one of their ancient buildings, which is used as a chapel. You enter the port through two passes, one at Pointe du Diable for smaller vessels; the other, wider, by an island in the middle. There are two batteries on those places and a third called the Queen's battery at the bottom of the bay.[101]

Had I not been feeling ill, I would have examined the strange creatures that the sea throws on to the reef to gain some notion about the windward part of the island. But I could hardly stand up, and the skin on my legs peeled off completely.

Here is all that I could pick up:

Whales sometimes enter the Port where they are easily harpooned. The coastal sea is full of fish, and it is the best place on the island to find beautiful shells. I was shown some violet-coloured oysters from the mouth of the Chaux river and a kind of crystallization that can be found on the bed of the River Sorbès, next to it.

Three nights running I saw a comet which first appeared two weeks ago. Its nucleus was pale and nebulous, its tail white and very long, its rays hardly diverging. I sketched its position in the sky, just above the Three Kings. It was travelling eastwards and its tail pointed to the west.

At half past two on the morning of the 6th it seemed to be about 50 degrees above the horizon. I could not make a more precise measurement for I lacked the instruments.

Here the air was agreeably cool, the country beautiful and fertile: but the village so deserted that in one day I only saw two blacks in the public square.

I had recovered sufficient strength to continue my journey through more inhabited parts. I decided to halt four leagues from the mouth of Grande Rivière, which is a bit bigger than the river with the same name at Port Louis.

We left at six in the morning, following a shoreline cut by bays with mangrove swamps. It is likely that the sea has brought seed from land upwind. We went along the side of a range of high mountains covered in forest. The countryside is divided by small hills covered with fresh grass. This part of the country where cattle breed is agreeable to the eyes, but tiring to walk over.

After walking two leagues, we saw a fine stone house on a hill. I stopped there to rest: it belongs to a rich landowner called V... who was away. His wife was a large, gaunt Creole who walked about barefoot, as was the custom of the country. When I entered her room, I found her surrounded by five or six daughters and as many mastiffs which nearly strangled my dog. They were kicked out of doors and Mme. de la V... posted a naked black woman, clothed only in a ragged petticoat, to keep watch on them. After some small talk, one of the dogs found a way to get back into the room and the uproar began again. Mme. de la V... held an electric ray's prickly tail in her hand and whipped the slave's naked shoulder with it, leaving a long weal, and then gave a backward swipe at the dog which ran out howling.

This lady told me that she had narrowly escaped drowning when she went out in a pirogue to harpoon a turtle on the reef. She would also go off into the forest to hunt runaway slaves: she was proud of herself, but told me that the governor had reproached her for hunting deer, which is forbidden. This reproach outraged her: "I would rather that he had stabbed me with a dagger in the heart," she said.

At four in the afternoon, I left this War Goddess Bellona who hunted men. We took a short cut across La Pointe du Diable, so called because the first navigators, so they say, saw their compass vary without explanation. In a canoe we crossed the mouth of the Grande Rivière, which is just navigable because of a sandbank in the middle and a waterfall some quarter of a league away.

On the left-hand bank a redoubt had been built at the start of the road to Flacq: we took the road because the coast was broken by rocks and impossible to follow. Here one enters a beautiful forest, with countless orange trees. After a quarter of a league I found a house whose owner was away: I halted there.

I had walked for two hours in the morning and the same in the afternoon.

10 September

We followed the main route to Flacq as far as a quarter league from the Sèche river, which we waded across like the others: then took a path on the right and reached the sea at the Eau Douce bay where there was a military post of thirty men.

We took to walking along the shore again. I was carried on Côte's back over an inlet that was quite deep. From time to time the sand is covered in boulders, up to a long prairie carpeted with the same dog's tooth grass as at Belle Ombre. All this part is dry and arid; the forest is low and feeble, and stretches to the mountains in the distance. This plain, which has three good roads, is not of great use: it extends to a plantation called Quatre Cocos. There is no water except from a brackish well dug in rocks veined with iron ore.

After dining, a path on the left led us through a wood which was very stony. We reached the bank of the Flacq river, near its mouth, which we crossed on planks. We followed the riverbank passing several plantations and came down to a store on the left bank. There was a military post commanded by a captain of the Legion called M. Gautier, who offered to put me up for the night.

I rested. This area called Flacq is one of the best cultivated on the island: much rice is grown. There is a gap in the reef that allows barges to dock at shore.

My host wanted to accompany me part of the way: we went in a pirogue as far as the Fayette post. Nearly all the coast is covered with broken boulders and mangrove swamps. Near the landing place we saw turtle traces in the sand. So we landed but could only find a nest. We waded through the Anse aux Aigrettes, a wide bay. I was on my black's shoulders. In the middle of the crossing the sea rose and nearly knocked him over; water rose up to his neck and I was soaked. Nearby, we came across another bay called Requins or Sharks Bay. I noticed a large shelf of rock, pierced by round holes about a foot wide: some were as deep as my walking stick. I presumed that in the remote past some volcano's lava had flowed over a forest and had burnt the tree trunks, but left their imprint.

From Poste de Lafayette to the Rivière du Rempart, the prairie continues. This area is still well cultivated. We dined. I crossed the river and continued alone to beyond the Rivière des Citronniers. The sun was dipping below the horizon when I found a gentleman who very kindly invited me to his house. This good man's name was M. Gole.

In the morning he lent me his horse to go to town, which was about five leagues away. I would have loved to complete my tour of the island, but there were four leagues of uninhabited land without water. Besides, I already knew the coast from Pointe aux Cannoniers right down to Port Louis.

I accepted my host's offer. I left the area known as Poudre d'Or, so called, it is said, because of the golden sand which to me seemed as white as anywhere else. I crossed the river that bears the same name as the whole area. I entered a large forest, where the soil is good but there is no water. I reached Pamplemousses: the land seemed exhausted because it has been cultivated for over thirty years without ever having been manured. I waded across the Sèche and Lataniers rivers and reached Port Louis.

I had found all the lands seen during my tour to be covered in stones, except some at Pamplemousses.

During my journey I did not see one interesting monument. There are three churches on the island: the first at Port Louis, the second at South-East Port and the third, which is the most appropriate, at Pamplemousses. The first two resemble little village churches. They had built one at Port Louis with an attractive design, but the roof was too raised and the cyclones had cracked the supporting walls. It is used

sometimes as a store, as these are rare on the island. Most are built in wood; it is a material which should not be used for public buildings, especially here where beams do not last longer than forty years, if worms do not destroy them before. Moreover, stones can be found everywhere, and the island is surrounded by coral from which lime is made. The greatest difficulty concerns the foundations as one is always obliged to blow up the rocks with gunpowder: yet, all things considered, I do not think building in stone costs a third more than building with wood. It is true that wooden buildings are soon ready, but they decay quickly. People in a hurry to enjoy themselves never properly enjoy anything.

It is reckoned that the island is about 45 leagues in circumference. It is watered by many streams in deep ravines: they rise in the island's centre and run out to sea. Though we were in the dry season, I crossed more than 24 streams filled with healthy, fresh water. I guess that half the island lies fallow, a quarter is under cultivation, and another quarter is pasture ground, both good and bad.

Besides, I noticed many essential things about tides while touring Mauritius. I had really taken this trip to lighten both the confusion in my head and my worries about my lack of fortune. I had already asked to be sent back to Europe, victim of the Engineer Corps' persecutions. My mind was not free enough to really study nature. Nature distracted rather than occupied me. I should have made notes on these effects of the sea out of which I have later drawn conclusions that are important to physics. All I could bring back was what the Abbé de Caille had already said, but having later collected all that travellers have written, I have based my theory of the tides on the alternate melting of the polar ice caps.[102]

Letter 18
On Commerce, Agriculture and the Island's Defence

One letter is insufficient to go into details concerning these three subjects, which are enormous. To begin with the first, I do not known any corner of the earth that extends its needs so far. This colony obtains its dishes and plates from China, its linen and clothes from India, its slaves and cattle from Madagascar, a part of its provisions from the Cape of Good Hope, its money from Cadiz and its administration from France. M. de la Bourdonnais wanted to turn it into the warehouse for all trade with India, a second Batavia. With the opinions of a great genius, he had his human weaknesses: place him on a point and he will make it the centre of everything.

This country, which only produces a little coffee, should only busy itself with its own needs; and it should buy its supplies itself in France, to be useful through what it consumes to the metropolis, to which it will never give anything back. Our foodstuff, our cloths, our linen, what we manufacture, should be enough, and Normandy cotton is far better than the Bengal cloth given to slaves. Only our money should circulate. A paper currency has been invented in which nobody has any confidence. At the best rate of exchange it loses 33 per cent and often 50 per cent. It is impossible for this paper money to lose less: it is payable in France six months after sight; it takes six months to travel there and six to return; thus 18 months. Ready money is reckoned here to produce 33 per cent in 18 months when placed in the maritime trade. Whoever receives paper money for *piastres* looks at it as a deal that runs more than one risk.[103]

The King pays for all that he buys at a third, at least, above its value;

the grain of the farmers, the buildings, stores and expeditions of all kinds. A settler would build a store for 20,000 francs cash; if you pay him in paper, that's 10,000 *écus*; over that there is no dispute.

But that is the only money anybody is paid in. It had been thought that it would never leave the island; not only does it leave, but the *piastres* too, never to return: if not, the colony would be in want for everything.

Of all the foreign places the island trades with, the only one indispensable to its present constitution is Madagascar, for slaves and cattle. Those islanders were happy with our poor rifles before, but now they want *piastres*, and those edged-rolled. All the world is bettering itself.

Also, if one thinks that the day will come when there will be a surplus to make trade flourish, then they must hurry to clean up the harbour. There are seven or eight wrecked ships that are becoming islands with coral growth making them larger and larger.

Nobody should be allowed to own land that is easy to clear and near the town, without having it valued. Nobody should be allowed to grant himself large, beautiful plantations to resell to others. Laws prohibit this abuse; but nobody follows laws.

I found that it was a catastrophe to cut down the trees indiscriminately everywhere. We have strayed from the physical and moral laws of nature. First, we should never have divided the land into plots of 200 acres. We should imitate nature and limit ourselves to its divisions. We want to reduce everything to our set-squares. Nature has grander plans. Two things are necessary for plantations at the start: mountains and water. Mountains nourish trees and through them attract clouds that furnish water for streams; running water makes machines work and is useful for watering fields and animals, factories and navigation. Mountains and water should belong to all. So the island should be divided into natural divisions from the mountains down, following the streams to the sea.

As for trees on the summits, it was crucial to leave them with their natural trees. First, they attract and fix the clouds and summits are the source of eternal streams and springs. As I have shown in my studies, one of the causes why so many rivers are drying up on our continent is that their summits are stripped of woods.

Even more, narrow mountain peaks crowned with trees serve to embellish the landscape, and nature enjoys allowing strange plants to grow there, with wild animals and birds contrasting with domesticated trees and animals in the valleys and plains. There is nothing more entrancing than human cultivation mixed with nature's. All the countries rich in wheat like Flanders are sad to look at, and though rich are only so in appearance, for that country has to sacrifice a part of its wheat to buy whatever wood is necessary.

Beasts of burden should be bred, especially donkeys, so useful in a mountainous country; a donkey carries twice the load of a slave. The slave may cost a little more, but the donkey is stronger and happier.

Many laws relating to what should be planted have been made. Nobody knows better than the planter of this island what is in his own interest and what is best suited to the soil. It would be better to find the means of tying the farmer to land that he now farms reluctantly, for judges' orders cannot overcome feelings.

There are many useless soldiers, to whom agricultural land could be given through assisting them in clearing it: and they could be married off with free black women. If my plan was followed, within ten years the whole island would make a profit: it would be a nursery producing Indian sailors and soldiers. This idea is so simple that I am not surprised it has been scorned.

As for means one might propose to alleviate the lot of the black slaves, I will leave it to others; there are abuses that should never be tolerated.

If you ask a naval officer about the island's defence, he will say that one squadron is enough; an engineer will propose fortifications; an infantry brigadier is convinced that you need regiments and the colonists believe that the island defends itself. The first three of these approaches depend on the administration and are costly, though partially necessary. I will stop at the last point, so as to convey some money-saving views.

I observed while making a tour of the island that it is largely surrounded by a belt of reefs, some distance from shore, and that where the belt is not continuous, the coast is made of inaccessible boulders.

This formation astonished me, but it is a fact. The island would be inaccessible but for some breaks in the reef. I counted eleven; they are formed by currents from rivers, always close by.

The outer defence of the island would consist, then, of blocking these entry points. Some could be closed with floating chains, others could be defended by gun batteries on shore. As one can sail in a boat between the reefs and the coast, small, armed sloops could be used to good effect when the pass is not within cannon shot of the coast.

Inside the reef, the shore is very easy to jump on to, as the sand is flat. You could make these areas impracticable as they have become in the bays of South-East Port. You have merely to plant mangroves, the same kind of trees that once grew in the sea, forming impenetrable forests. Where along the coast there are any flat rocks of easy access, such places are not large and could be defended by raising a dry wall, by keeping *cheveux de frise*[104] ready to throw into the water, and by planting cacti in the drier places. But if there is any sand underfoot, mangroves will grow; their branches and roots tangle up so much that no boat could land. Natural means of defence, such as trees, thorny bushes etc., are all too often overlooked. They have this advantage: that they cost little and that time, which destroys other means, increases and strengthens these. So much for maritime defence.

I view the island as a circle, with each river coming from the centre, like so many radii of this circle. The shores could be cleared and planted with cacti and bamboo on the parts near the town, and the bank opposite cleared for three hundred *toises*. Thus all land between two streams would become fortified space, and the stream itself a dangerous ditch. All the directions in which an enemy would want to cross would be open, defended by colonists behind lines of protection. The enemy would only reach the town through a thousand obstacles: this system of defence could be applied to all small islands where water runs from a centre to a circumference.[105]

Two wings of mountain embrace the town and the harbour, leaving little need to defend it except for the part looking out to sea. On the Ile des Tonneliers a fort should be built, with gun batteries placed in a sort of covered path to open fire at ground level. There should be many mortars, so terrifying to ships. To the left and the right as far as the ends of the promontories, land should be seized to make respectable lines of fortification. Nature has already borne a part of the costs of defence on the right; the Lataniers river protects the front.

At the back of the town is a deep valley formed by mountains, which encompasses a vast area of land where all the island's inhabitants and their blacks could be assembled. The other side of these mountains is inaccessible, or could be made so at little expense.

There is even a peculiar advantage: at the back of the valley in the highest part of the mountain, in the place called Le Pouce, is a large piece of land planted with tall trees with two or three streams of very healthy water. You can climb up from town along a difficult path. A large path was attempted, using mines, to link this place with the interior part of the island, but the other flank of the mountain is terrifyingly scarily steep; only blacks and monkeys can climb up here. Four hundred men in this post with provisions could never be dislodged; the whole garrison could retreat here.

To these natural means of defence, one could add those that depend on the administration, a squadron and troops. Here are the obstacles an enemy would have to overcome.

1. He would have to fight at sea.

2. Supposing our squadron was defeated, it could delay the victor's disembarkation by making him drift to the windward of the island.

3. Then the difficulties of disembarking would have to be overcome. He could only attack the coast at particular points and never straight ahead.

4. Each riverbed would cost him a disadvantageous battle, if he were forced to stay out in the open.

5. The enemy would be forced to lay siege to the town from a narrow strip of land, under fire from the hills overlooking it, and to dig trenches in rock.

6. The garrison, if forced to abandon the town, would find a safe redoubt high in the mountain, provided with water, where it could even be reinforced from inland.

This would be the place to talk to you about defending the neighbouring island of Réunion (Bourbon), but I do not know it. I only know that a landing there is impracticable, that it is well peopled, and that more corn grows there than they can use. However, I hear everybody say that the fate of Bourbon is tied to that of Mauritius. Is it because the military chest is kept here?

Preamble to the End of the First Volume

On Whites and Blacks

Although we Europeans boast about being particularly favoured by God in many ways, it is a fact that we commit crimes in three parts of the world. We have destroyed the people of America, we have reduced the Africans to slavery, and today we are looting the Asians. For us, history has always been a constant succession of discord, offering more wars, atrocities, trials, quarrels, duels and theft than all the rest of the world put together. These thoughts are useful to make us doubt the kindness of our institutions because when all is said and done we are responsible for mankind's misery. We must thus be those most remote from nature, whose only aim is man's happiness. This European trait has existed for a long time, because it was that of the ancient Greeks and the so vaunted Romans. The first conquered Asia, India under Alexander, and lived in continuous strife; as for the Romans, they spread to Africa and Asia and they, like us, caused suffering for other people and for themselves. And seeking the cause of such a denatured character, I have found it in ambition. This vice, the greatest of all, source of all crime, has become so familiar to us that far from calling it a vice, we have made it the prime virtue. We honour it, we preach it, we sanctify it. We call it during infancy, emulation, men of letters call it glory, nobles and military call it honour, the merchant, credit. Today it is money, because money leads to everything.

From infancy a European is everywhere a man who wants to be preeminent, whether in a physical or moral sense, or in the name of God or of the King. Wherever he goes he makes slaves, and finding resistance, he wages perpetual war with others and with himself, never realizing that he carries inside him the source of so much evil which is ambition, inspired from childhood by an education that teaches him that he must be first.

Seneca advises us to read stories of shipwrecks and misfortunes to endure the evils to which human life is liable.[106] For myself, bearing in mind the blacks, I can think of nothing worse than slavery. I have sometimes stopped to ponder this unfortunate human condition to find my own more bearable. They are first deprived of their homeland, then of their family, and denied the sweetness of married love, most plantations not having enough women, which does not bother the landowners, even though they cost less because they are less robust. There it is whips, starvation, endless work for somebody else's benefit. We preach a religion that enslaves them to these duties and privations and which scares them with terrible threats in the afterlife if they fail to submit themselves during their lives.

All the ills of the blacks come from the ambition of the Europeans. It is not because they are black that we reduce them to slavery, as we would enslave our fellows if we could; one part of Europe still treats another in that way.

I have often been amazed that black slaves can resist so many ills, but nature has given them a very excitable imagination. Provided that their physical needs are satisfied, love consoles them; they go off at night to their lovers; only for a brief moment do they believe the religion that we preach and only adopt what suits their superstition. They are indifferent to moral scruples and nature has come to their aid; as we must die and nature has given them as many reasons to love death as life, they quit it without fuss.

On the other hand, I have never known men so wretched in terms of morality as the landowners, for they constantly mistrust their blacks and live among them as if surrounded by the enemy, their hate always leading them to cruel punishments and injustice. From this, few landowners stick to their principles in their actions, and it is remarkable how vanity and ambition make them depraved. They laugh far less than do their slaves. And you notice immediately that they are usually sombre, hard and sad.

It is impossible for these men to have any feeling for the divine, and although we have arranged for religion to accommodate the barbarity of the *Code Noir*, and although secular politics have used its laws to justify slavery (in other words, a crime), that crime is so opposed to natural law that it is hopeless integrating it with a feeling for God, the father of all men, nor to the Gospel which forbids us in the second commandment to do to others what we would not do to ourselves. There is no sophistry that could link the Gospel with slavery, nor any ritual that could mix them together.

Priests favour slavery; they bless the ships that trade in slaves; they bless the flags that soldiers hang in their temples, houses of peace.

Letter 19[107]

Departure for France, Arrival at Réunion, Cyclone

After receiving permission to return to France, I prepared to embark on board the *Indien*, a ship of 64 guns.

I freed Duval, the slave with your name; I gave him in trust to an honest man on the island, until he could pay off the small sum of money he owed to the Administration. If he could have spoken French, I would have brought him with me. His tears were witness to his sadness on seeing me leave. He was more affected by this than by my freeing him. I proposed to Côte to buy his freedom if he would follow me. He confessed that had a mistress on the island whom he could not abandon. The fate of the King's slaves is bearable: he was happy and that was more than I could promise. I would have been very pleased to bring Favori back to his homeland, but a few months before my departure he was stolen. I lost a faithful friend and often miss him.

A few days before leaving for France, I again saw Autourou, the islander from Tahiti, who was being brought home after having been introduced to French customs. On his way out to France, I had found him to be frank, jolly and a little bit the libertine; on his way back I saw him reserved, polite and affected. He was enchanted with the opera in Paris, and imitated its songs and dances. He owned a watch and recognized the hours by the activities he associated with them; he showed the hour when he got up, ate, went to the opera, and took a stroll. He expressed what he wanted through signs.[108] Although men from Tahiti pass off as not having had any communication with other nations until M. de Bougainville arrived, I observed, nevertheless, a word in their language and a custom that was common to many different people. *Matté* in the Tahitian language means to kill. *Matar* in Spanish and *mat* in Persian mean the same. They also draw on their skin, like many people of the Old and New World. They knew about iron, which they did not have, calling it *aurou* and begging for it; they also had venereal diseases that come, so they say, from the New World. But all these analogies are not enough to go back to the origin of a nation. The follies, the needs, the evils of mankind seem naturalized in all people. A better way to distinguish them would be by studying their languages. All European nations eat bread, but the Russians call it *gleba*, the Germans *broth*, in Latin it is *panis*, in Breton *bara*. An Encyclopedic Dictionary of Languages would be philosophically extremely worthwhile.

Autourou was very bored while on Mauritius; he walked about alone. One day I found him deep in thought: he was staring at a black slave, by the prison gate, round whose neck they were rivetting a large chain. It was a strange sight for him that a man of his colour could be so treated by whites, who had loaded him with presents while in Paris; but he was unaware of those passions that drive men overseas and that morality, which checks these passions in Europe, does not apply in the tropics.

When I embarked on 9 November 1770 several Malabar Indians accompanied me to the quayside; they wished me a speedy return, and wept. These good people never lose hope of seeing again those who have helped them in some way or other. Among them I recognized a master carpenter who had bought my geometry books, even though he could not read; he was the sole person on the island who would have them.

A calm forced us to remain there in the roadstead for eleven days. On the evening of the 20th we set sail and on the 21st at three in the afternoon we anchored off Réunion, outside the port of Saint-Denis.

This island lies forty leagues to the leeward of Mauritius. You need but one day to reach Réunion and often a month to return. From far off, it looks like part of a sphere. Its mountains are very high. Land is cultivated up to a height of 1,600 *toises*, as far as the summit of the three Salasses, three inaccessible peaks.

Its shores are very steep; the sea rolls with a great surf which allows pirogues alone to land without being smashed. At Saint-Denis they have built a drawbridge held by iron chains to unload the sloops. It juts out over the sea by more than eighty feet. At the end of this bridge is a rope ladder which those who want to land must climb. Around the rest of the island you can only land by jumping into the water.

As the *Indien* had to remain three weeks at anchor to load coffee, several passengers decided to spend some days on the island and even to go and wait at Saint-Paul, seven leagues to leeward, for our ship to come and complete its loading. I decided to follow them, given the lack of provisions on board and the example set by the captain and several officers from other ships.

In the afternoon of the 25th I embarked alone on a small yawl and, despite the violent breeze, I kept the boat's head against the breakers and landed at the drawbridge. It took an hour and a half to make the crossing, which was not more than half a league. I went to salute the Commanding Officer. He informed me that there was no inn at Saint-Denis, nor anywhere else on the island, and that strangers usually lodged with those inhabitants with whom they were doing business. Night approached, and having nothing to do there, I was preparing to return to my ship when this officer offered me a bed.

I then went to pay my respects to M. Cremon, the commissioner, who offered me his house for as long as I wished to stay on land. This suited me better, as I wanted to see the Réunion volcano and I knew that M. Cremon had climbed it. But I never had a chance to go there, as the path is very difficult, few inhabitants knew it, and you needed to be away from Saint-Denis for six or seven days.

From the 25th to the 30th the swell was so great that few sloops could land. Our captain took advantage of a favourable moment and got on board his ship to attend to his affairs, but bad weather stopped him returning to land. The wind, coming from the southeast, rises at six in the morning and falls at ten in the evening. At this time of year, it blows all day and night, with a steady violence. On 1 December, the wind dropped, but a monstrous wave rose from the open sea and broke with such force on the shore that the sentry on the drawbridge was forced to quit his post.

The mountain peaks were covered with thick clouds, which did not move away. The wind was still blowing from the southeast, but the sea ran from the west. We saw three huge waves following each other, approaching the coast like three long hills. Geysers broke off from their crests, forming a kind of mane. They rushed towards the shore, forming a vault rolling on itself, billowing foam more than fifty feet into the air. We could hardly breathe, the air was so heavy, the sky so dark, as clouds of sea birds sought refuge on the coast. Land birds and animals seemed disturbed. People, too, felt a secret dread at the sight of a terrifying storm in the midst of a calm.

On the morning of the 2nd the wind fell suddenly and the sea became rougher; waves were more numerous and came from further out. The shore, battered by waves, was covered with white foam, like snow, which piled up like cotton bales. The ships at anchor pulled at their cables. There was no longer any doubt about it being a cyclone. The pirogues on the pebbles were hauled high up on land and everybody rushed to secure their houses with rope and cord. At anchor were the *Indien*, the *Penthièvre*, the *Amitié*, the *Alliance*, the *Grand Bourbon*, the *Gérion*, a sloop and a small boat. The coast was crowded with people drawn to the spectacle of the ocean, and the danger faced by the ships.

At midday the sky became overcast and the wind began to freshen from the southeast. It was feared that it would blow from the west and run all the vessels ashore. From the battery, the signal was given to leave by hoisting a flag and firing two cannons with shot. Immediately they cut their cables and set sail. The *Penthièvre* abandoned its sloop, which it could not lift on board. The *Indien*, anchored further out, sailed with the wind in her four main sails. The rest followed. Some blacks in a sloop took refuge on board the *Amitié*. The little boats were already in the waves and vanished every now and then: they seemed to fear putting out to sea but at last set sail, drawing all the spectators' worries and prayers to them. After two hours the whole fleet had disappeared towards the northwest and a black horizon.

At three in the afternoon, the cyclone made its presence felt with a terrifying din; the wind blew from all quarters. The sea, beaten and churned up in every direction, threw clouds of foam, shells, sand and stones on to the land. Sloops being refitted on land were buried under the surge; the wind carried away a sheet from the roof of the church and a colonnade from the governor's house. The cyclone lasted all night and only ceased at three in the morning.

On the 6th the two small boats returned to anchorage with a letter from the *Penthièvre* saying it had lost its top-gallant-mast. They had not suffered too much. Often those lowest down are the happiest. On the 8th the *Gérion* appeared. She had put into Mauritius and informed us that the *Garonne*, the King's pink, had sunk while anchored.

By the 19th we had had news of all the boats except the *Amitié* and the *Indien*. The power and size of the *Indien* had seemed to place it beyond any damage and we did not doubt that it had continued on its way to take in provisions at the Cape of Good Hope and from there gone on to France. I knew that was the captain's plan.

On the morning of the 19th a signal was made that a ship had been sighted; it was the *Normande*, the King's pink; it sailed past Saint-Denis and anchored at Saint-Paul. It had come from Mauritius and was fetching provisions from the Cape. This opportunity seemed too favourable to ignore and another officer and myself took it up. M. and Mme. Cremon provided us with beds and linen for on board, and we got hold of horses and guides to take us to Saint-Paul. One of their relations accompanied us.

I had come ashore with just one change of clothes; all my luggage was on the *Indien*.

We left on the 20th at eleven in the morning. There were seven leagues to cover. The pink was to leave in the evening; there was no time to lose. We bade our hosts farewell. Our horses climbed the Saint-Denis mountain up a zig-zagging path, littered with sharp stones. They were strong and their step was sure, although they were not shod, as is the custom of the island.

Two and a half leagues out from Saint-Denis we rested by a stream, in the shade of a lemon tree, and ate a dinner that Mme. Cremon had prepared. After eating we rode downhill and then climbed the Grande Chaloupe, a gloomy valley formed by two parallel and very steep mountains: we had to walk part of the way because rain had made the path dangerous. We found ourselves at the bottom between the two mountains in one of the weirdest and loneliest places I have ever been in; we were as if between two walls, the sky above us and the sea on our right. We crossed the stream and came to the bank opposite the Chaloupe: an eternal silence reigns in this abyss, although the wind blew hard up on the mountain.[109]

Two leagues from Saint-Paul we entered a vast sandy plain that stretched to the town. It was built just like Saint-Denis. There are large sites in rows, surrounded by hedges with a house for the family in the middle. These towns have the air of large villages. Saint-Paul is situated by a fresh-water lake where a port could perhaps be made.

It was night by the time we arrived; we were exhausted and did not know where to find lodging, or even find some bread to eat as there was no baker in Saint-Paul. My first concern was to speak to the *Normande's* captain whom I luckily found on shore. He told me that he could not be responsible for taking us on board without an order from the governor in Mauritius, who was at the time at Saint-Denis; he was not to sail until the following day.

I wrote to the governor and to Mme. Cremon on the spot. I gave my two letters to a black, promising him a reward if he could return the next day by eight in the morning. It was six in the evening and he had fourteen leagues to cover. He set off on foot.

I went to find my comrades who were supping at the storekeeper's. We were lodged in a house belonging to the King. The only furniture consisted of chairs, which we arranged into beds; at dawn we were up on our feet. At nine we saw a black arrive with answers to my letters whom my messenger had sent in his place. I paid him well and went to find the captain to give him the letter from the governor. You cannot imagine our shock when we learnt that the governor had left the matter to his discretion! At last, after much bargaining and having given bills of payment for our passage, he agreed to take us on board. Departure was postponed until the next day.

Here is what I could learn about Réunion. We know that the first inhabitants were pirates who lived with black women from Madagascar. They settled here around 1657. The East India Company also had at

Réunion a warehouse and a governor who lived with the pirates in great circumspection. One day the Viceroy of Goa anchored near Saint-Denis and ate with the governor. Hardly had he set foot on land when a fifty-cannon pirate ship anchored next to his and captured it. The captain landed immediately and demanded to dine with the governor. He sat at table between him and the Portuguese gentleman, whom he said was now his prisoner. When the wine and good cheer had put the pirate into a jovial mood, M. Desforges, the governor, asked him how much the viceroy's ransom was to be. A thousand *piastres* said the pirate. "That's too little," answered M. Desforges, "for a brave fellow like you and a great lord like him. Ask for a lot or for nothing." "Ah, well, I'll free him then, said the generous pirate. The viceroy returned to his ship straightaway, and lifted anchor, very happy to have escaped so cheaply. The governor's action was later rewarded by the Portuguese Court who sent the Order of Christ for his son. The pirate then settled on the island and was hanged long after the amnesty was passed in favour of pirates because he had forgotten to include himself. This injustice was committed by a judge who wanted to appropriate his spoils for himself; but this last villain, not long after, came to an end almost as miserable, although the justice of men had nothing to do with it. It is not long ago that one of these pirates, called Adam, was still alive. He died at the age of 104.

When more peaceful work softened their habits, all that remained was a certain spirit of independence and freedom, which was softened by the arrival of many worthy people who had come to Réunion to work the land. The population consists of 60,000 blacks and 5,000 colonists. The island has three times more people than Mauritius, on which it depends for its exports. It is also better cultivated. That year it had produced twenty thousand quintals of wheat, and a similar amount of coffee, besides the rice and other provisions consumed. Herds of oxen are not scarce. The King pays the colonists well.

The main place on Réunion is Saint-Denis, where the governor and the Council reside. The only noteworthy building is a closed redoubt built of stone, but situated too far from the sea, a battery in front of Government House and the drawbridge already mentioned. Behind the town is a large plain called the *Champ de Lorraine.*

The soil seems more sandy on Réunion than at Mauritius: far inland it is mixed with the same round pebbles found on the seashore; which proves that the sea has withdrawn or that the island has risen, which seems feasible to judge by the cracked and broken mountains in the interior. When speculating about nature, contrary opinions always present themselves with equal probability. Often the same effects arise from different causes. This insight could be extended a long way and should make us very modest in our judgments.

An old man of more than eighty years took possession of Mauritius when the Dutch abandoned it. Twelve Frenchmen were detached for that purpose, and landed in the morning. In the afternoon of that same day, an English vessel anchored with the same intention.

The manners of the early settlers on Réunion were very simple; most houses were not locked. A lock was a curiosity. Some placed their money in a tortoise shell above their door. They walked about barefoot, dressed in blue cloth and lived on rice and coffee; they needed nothing from Europe, happy to live without luxuries as long as they lived without want. To this moderation they added virtues which emanated from it; good faith in trade and nobility in going about it. As soon as a stranger appeared, the inhabitants offered him their home, without knowing him.

The last war in India has slightly changed their customs. The volunteers from Réunion distinguished themselves by their bravery; but fabrics from Asia and military distinctions from France have entered their island. The children who are richer than their parents want to be treated with more consideration. They have not been content to enjoy a quiet and obscure happiness. They go to Europe to find pleasures and honours in place of close family relations and a quiet country life. As the attention of fathers falls primarily on sons, they send them to France from where they seldom return. From this one can count 500 young girls who age without marrying.

We embarked on the *Normande* on the 21st in the evening. We found a case of wine, liquors and coffee that M. and Mme. Cremon had sent on board for our use. In their house we had encountered the hospitality of the oldest inhabitants of the island, and the politeness of Parisians.

I am etc.

On Réunion, this 21 December 1770

Letter 20

Leaving Réunion, Arrival at the Cape

We left the bay of Saint-Paul at ten in the evening. The sea is calmer here and the anchorage safer than at Saint-Denis, which is spoilt by so many abandoned anchors. Their cables are easily cut; however, sailors prefer Saint-Denis. When there is a gust of wind blowing straight in, you cannot leave Saint-Paul's bay, and if a vessel was thrown on shore, all the crew would perish as the sea breaks on a very high sand.

On the 23rd we lost Réunion from sight. The attention we had received from M. and Mme. Cremon during our stay, the favourable winds, the good food and the company of an honest captain, M. de Rosbos, led us to believe we would find the *Indien* again. We pitied the passengers on board, who had had to put up with bad weather and a lack of provisions.

There are about 900 leagues between Réunion and the Cape. On the morning of 6 January 1771 we saw Point Natal, ten leagues ahead of us. We were estimating three days before we could board the *Indien* again. The wind had been behind us up to here. In the evening it calmed down, and the heat was stifling. At midnight the sky was ablaze with lightning and the horizon covered with heavy, black clouds. The sea sparkled with fish leaping around our boat.

At three in the morning a contrary wind rose from the west with such violence that it forced us to make for the Cape under our mizzen. The storm drove a small bird on board, similar to a titmouse. It was a little thicker, with a flat arched beak. I fed it for two days with mashed sea biscuit but it died on the third day. The arrival of land birds on vessels is always a sign of very bad weather, for it is proof that the violence of the storm is strong on land.

On the third day of the storm we noticed that our mizzen-mast was damaged four feet above the yard; we reefed the sail and bound the mast with rope and bits of wood and made for the Cape with the mainsail. The sea was monstrous and blocked the horizon. We were extremely surprised to see, within cannon-shot, a Dutch vessel steering as we did. It was impossible to hail it. On the fifth day, the wind died down. We examined the mizzen-mast which had completely snapped. This accident redoubled our wish to reach the Cape.

The foul weather had made us lose time and then the calm made us even slower. On the 12th we again saw the Dutch vessel and we spoke to her. She took the precaution of lighting her wicks and running her guns out as we approached. She came from Batavia and was going to the Cape.

On 16 January, in the afternoon, we caught sight of the Cape. We tacked about all night. On the morning of the 17th a violent wind arose, and the sky was covered with a thick mist which completely hid the land from us. We were about to miss the entry into the bay when we saw the Table Mountain in a flash of lightning. Then we tacked hard and towards midday found ourselves near the coast, which is very high. It is completely stripped of trees; its upper part is very steep, comprised of layers of parallel rocks. It resembles ancient fortifications, with a ramp.

We skirted the land. At midday we found ourselves behind Lion Mountain, which from a distance looks like a lion at rest. Its head is detached and formed by a great rock whose ridges look like its mane. From the Lion's head a flag signals to vessels.

There is no wind in the lee of Lion Mountain: to get into the bay, we had to pass between Robben Island visible on our left and a neck of land called Hanged Man's Point, at the foot of the Lion. We were within two cannon shots and our impatience redoubled. It is from here that you can see the vessels in the road, and the *Indien* would not be the least conspicuous among them. The tide lifted us in bit by bit, and from the tops we saw twelve vessels appear successively at anchor, but not one of them flew a French flag: it was the Dutch fleet. We dropped anchor at the bay's entrance. At three in the afternoon, the harbour master came on board and assured us that the *Indien* had never turned up.

We could see the Table Mountain at the end of the bay, the highest land in the entire stretch of coast. Its upper part is flat and steep on all sides, like an altar. The city lies at its foot, on the bay's edge. A thick, white, piled-up fog often gathers on the Table. The Dutch say that the tablecloth is laid. The commander of the road hoists his flag as a signal for all vessels to be on guard, and forbids sloops to put out to sea. From the mountain's tablecloth a wind mixed with mist blows down, looking like long strands of wool. The earth is darkened by clouds of sand, and often the vessels are forced to set sail. At this time of year, this breeze only rises at ten in the morning and lasts until the evening. Sailors like the Cape, but fear the road, which is even more dangerous from April to September.

In 1722 the whole Indies fleet sank at anchor, with the exception of two vessels. Since then, all Dutch ships had been forbidden to anchor after 6 March. They go to False Bay where they are sheltered. They tried to link Hanged Man's point with Robben Island to turn the road into a harbour with but one opening, but it was useless work.

I intended to land that same evening, but the wind prevented me. In the early morning the *Normande* anchored nearer the town. It is made up of white houses in rows, which look like little card castles. At dawn, three prettily painted sloops boarded us. They were sent by townspeople who invited us to lodge with them. I climbed down into the sloop of a German, who assured me that for my money I would be very comfortable with M. Nedling, the townspeople's aide-de-camp.

Crossing the bay, I thought about the awkward situation I would find myself in, without clothes, without money, without acquaintances, but with the Dutch, at the tip of Africa. But I was distracted from these thoughts by the novelty of the view. We passed close by a number of sea calves, lying without a care on masses of floating-seaweed, like the long horns with which shepherds call their flocks. Penguins swam quietly around our oars, sea birds settled on the sloops, and I even saw, as I jumped on to the sand, two pelicans playing with a large mastiff, taking his head in their beaks.

I developed a good opinion of a land whose shore was so friendly, even to animals.

Cape of Good Hope, this 10 January 1771

Letter 21

About the Cape. Journey to Constantia and Table Mountain

The streets in the Cape are well laid out. Some are watered by canals and most are planted with chestnut trees. It was very pleasing to see them covered with leaves in January. The facades of the houses were shaded by their leaves and the sides of the doors were bordered with brick or turf seats where ruddy, fresh-faced ladies sat. I was overjoyed at seeing European faces and buildings at last.

With my guide I crossed the square and went into Mme. Nedling's house. She was a cheerful, fat Dutch woman drinking tea, surrounded by seven or eight officers of the fleet who were smoking their pipes. She showed me round a very clean room and assured me that everything in her house was at my service.

When you have seen one Dutch village, you have seen them all; the order in one house is the same in all the others. Here is how she kept hers. There was always company in the drawing-room, and a table covered with peaches, melons, apricots, grapes, pears, cheese, fresh butter, wine, tobacco and pipes. This table was set for anybody who arrived, whether of the house or strangers. At eight tea and coffee were served; at midday plenty of game and fish; at four tea and coffee and at eight, a supper like lunch. These good people eat all day.

The price for full board used to be half a *piastre*, but French sailors, to distinguish themselves from other nations, raised the price to one *piastre*, and that today for them is the ordinary price. This price is excessive, given the abundance of provisions, even if it is true that these places are far more honest than our best taverns. The servants are at your disposition, you can invite to dinner whomsoever you wish; you can spend some days in the country with your host, use his carriage, and all that without paying more.

After dinner I went to see Governor M. de Tolbac, an eighty-year-old man whose merits had placed him at the head of this colony for the last fifty years.[110] He invited me to dine the next day. He had learnt about my situation, and seemed sensitive about it.

I went for a stroll in the company's garden: it is divided into four quarters, watered by a stream. Each quarter is bordered by a hedgerow of twenty-foot high chestnuts. These palisades shelter the plants from the wind, which is always strong: they have even taken the precaution of protecting the young avenue trees with a screen of reeds. In this garden I saw plants from Asia and Africa, but especially European trees covered with fruit in a season when I have never seen them in leaf.

I remembered that an officer of the King's marine called Viscount de Chaila had given me, when I left Mauritius, a letter for M. Berg, Secretary of the Council. I had that letter in my pocket, not having had time to leave it with my other papers on the *Indien*: I went to call on M.

Berg, and gave him my friend's letter. He received me well and offered me his purse. I made use of his credit to buy those things that were indispensable. I suggested that he procure me a passage on one of the Indies vessels: six were about to leave for Holland and six more at the start of March.

He assured me that this was impossible as the Dutch Company had expressly forbidden it. The main reason he gave me was that those Frenchmen who had travelled in the Company's ships had published hostile accounts. Such actions showed a lack of gratitude towards hospitality, and this consideration has stopped me from publishing my thoughts on how this colony might be attacked, making me more inclined to write something that would increase its prosperity.

The governor had said as much to me. I had to wait at the Cape as long as fate decreed. I had been led there by an unpredictable event, and would have to hope for another to take me out. For me it was a very agreeable distraction to be in such a quiet society of happy people in a land rich in all sorts of provisions.

M. Berg's son invited me to go to Constantia, a famous vineyard some four leagues away.[111] We slept at his country house, situated behind the Table Mountain, two short leagues from town. We arrived through a beautiful avenue of chestnuts. We saw grapes about to be harvested, orchards, chestnut groves, and plenty of fruit and vegetables. The next day we continued our route to Constantia: it lies on a north-facing hill (which here receives the midday sun). As we approached, we crossed a wood of silver-trees that resemble our pines, while their leaves look like our willows, covered in a striking white down.

This forest seemed made of silver. When the wind shook it and the sun shone on it, each leaf sparkled like a metal blade. We passed under these rich and deceptive branches to see less dazzling, but more useful, vines.

A long alley of old oaks led us to the Constantia vineyard. On the house front you see a poor painting of Constantia, a rather ugly, strapping girl leaning against a column. I thought it was an allegorical figure of Dutch virtue, but was told that it was the portrait of Miss Constantia, daughter of a Cape governor. He had had the house built with deep ditches around it, like a strong castle. He had wanted to build more storeys, but orders from Europe halted the construction.

We found the master of the house smoking his pipe in his nightgown. He led us into his cellar and made us taste his wine. It lay in small casks called *alverames*, holding ninety pints in rows in a very clean vault. Thirty remained. His vines in normal years produce two hundred. He sells his red wine at 35 *piastres* the cask and the white at 30. His profits are his alone. He is only obliged to reserve some for the Company, which pays him. This is what he told us.

After tasting his wine, we went into the vineyard. The muscat grape we tasted seemed just like the wine I had just drunk. The grapes do not grow on vine-props and the bunches hang just above ground. They are left to ripen until they are half dried by the sun. We tasted another kind of very sweet grape, which is not the muscat type. A very expensive wine is drawn from them, which is an excellent cordial.

The quality of the Constantia wine derives from the soil it grows in. The same stocks have been planted with the same exposure a quarter of a league from there in a place called Lower Constantia; the wine has degenerated. I tasted that too. The price, as well as the taste, is very inferior, and is sold at only twelve *piastres* the cask; scoundrels in the Cape fool strangers with it. Close to the vineyard lies a vast garden, in which I saw most of our fruit trees in hedges and rows, laden with fruit. They are inferior to ours, except for the grape, which I preferred. Olive trees do not thrive here.

On our return from the walk we found an ample breakfast. Our hostess overwhelmed us with kindness. She was descended from a French refugee and seemed delighted to see a man from her country. The husband and wife pointed out, at the front of the house, a hollow oak inside which they sometimes dined. They were as united as Baucis and Philemon[112] and they seemed just as happy, but for the husband having gout and the wife crying when we talked of France.

From Constantia to the Cape you travel along an uncultivated plain, covered with shrubs and plants. We stopped at Neuhausen, the Company's garden, laid out like the one in town but more fertile. All this part is not exposed to the wind, unlike the Cape region, where it blows up so much dust that most houses have double sashes in the windows to make them secure. We reached town in the evening.

A few days later, my host, M. Nedling, invited me to his country place, situated near M. Berg's. We left in his carriage, drawn by six horses. We spent several days in a state of delicious peace. The land was strewn with peach, pear and orange trees that nobody harvested. The walks were shaded by the most beautiful trees. I measured an oak at eleven feet of circumference: they claimed it was the oldest in the country. However, I was told that this tree was not more than ninety years old.

On 3 February my host proposed to some Dutchmen to climb up the Tafelberg or Table Mountain, the steep mountain at the foot of which the town is situated. I joined them. We left on foot at two o'clock after midnight. The moon shone very brightly. We passed a stream on the right which runs down the mountain and directed our climb towards an opening in the middle and which, from the town, looks like a chasm in a great wall. As we were walking we heard wolves howl and we fired a few shots in the air to scare them off. The path was rugged up to the foot of the mountain cliff, but it became even more so after. This gap which appears in the table is an oblique separation of more than a musket shot width at its lower entrance; up above it is only two *toises*

wide. This ravine is a kind of very steep staircase filled with sand and loose rocks. We climbed it, with precipices on both sides reaching up some two hundred feet. Sticking out from it are masses of rocks about to fall down. Water seeps from cracks and feeds countless aromatic plants. We heard bavians howling in this passage, a kind of large baboon resembling a bear.

After three and a half tiring hours we reached the table. The sun was rising over the sea and to our right its rays whitened the steep summits of the Tiger and four other mountain chains, the most distant of which appeared the highest. To our left, a little behind us, we saw, as if on a map, Penguin Island, then Constantia, False Bay and Lion Mountain: in front of us, Robben Island. The town was at our feet. We could pick out even the smallest streets. The vast squares of the Company's garden, with its avenues of oaks and tall hedges, looked like flower-beds bordered with box. The Citadel was a little pentagon as large as a hand, and the vessels from the Indies were no bigger than almond shells. I was feeling a kind of pride at being so high when I saw eagles hovering above me, nearly out of sight.

It would have been impossible, after all, not to feel some contempt for such small objects and above all for men who seemed like ants, if we had not felt that we were all similar. But we were cold and hungry. We lit a fire and had lunch. After eating, our Dutchmen tied a cloth at the end of a stick as a signal that we were returning. But they took it down after half an hour in case it was taken for a French flag.

The summit of the Tafelberg is a flat rock, about half a league long and a quarter wide. It is a kind of white quartz, covered in places by an inch or two of black vegetable mould, mixed with sand and white gravel. We found some puddles of water, formed by the clouds that frequently linger here.

The strata on this mountain are parallel and I could find no fossils. The lower rock is a kind of sandstone, which when in contact with the air seems to crumble into sand. Some bits of it resemble pieces of bread with their crust. This resemblance is so striking that I put some pieces in my pocket and on my return I gave them to my hostess who took them for sea biscuits. She picked up a bit and put it in her mouth and almost broke a tooth, which caused her a lot of pain. She looked at me reproachfully for having tricked her, but I suffered for my poor joke because I have never seen such stones since. I have often thought about the good Mme. Nedling, and reproached myself for the harm I did her.

Although the soil on the summit has no depth, there was a prodigious quantity of plants there. I picked ten species of immortelle, little myrtles, a fern which smelt of tea, a flower similar to the imperial, of a fine flaming red and many others I could not identify. I found a plant with a red, odourless flower; it could be taken for a tuberose. Each stalk has two or three leaves turned up together and holding a little water. The oddest of all, because unlike any that I had seen before, was a flower round like a rose, the size of a shilling and completely flat. This flower glitters in the prettiest colours. It has no stalk and no leaf. It grows abundantly in the gravel to which it is held by imperceptible threads. When picked, you see nothing but a slimy substance. Here are five whole plants that seem to resemble in their configuration one part of another plant.

1. The nostoc, which is only a *bean*; 2. A hairy plant which grows on nettles and resembles root *filaments*; 3. A lichen like a *leaf*; 4. The isolated *flower* of the Tafelberg; 5. The European truffle which is a *fruit.* I could add the *root* from the cave in Mauritius, if it wasn't the sole example I found there. I am inclined to believe that nature has followed the same plan with animals. I know several, especially marine ones, which resemble parts of other animals in their shape.[113]

I walked to the end of the Table. From there, I greeted the Atlantic Ocean, for after passing the Cape one is no longer in the Indian Ocean. I paid homage to the memory of Vasco da Gama, who was the first to dare go round this promontory of tempests.[114] Sailors all round the world should have placed his statue there, and I would willingly have offered a libation of Constantia wine to such heroic patience. It is doubtful, however, that Gama was the first navigator to open this route to trade with the Indies. Pliny reports that Hanno went round from the Sea of Spain as far as Arabia, as can be seen, he says, in the written memoirs he has left of that voyage. Cornelius Nepos says he saw a ship's captain who, fleeing King Lathyrus' anger, sailed from the Red Sea to Spain. Long before, Coelius Antipater affirmed that he had met a Spanish trader who went by sea to trade in Ethiopia.

Whatever the truth, the Cape, so feared by mariners for its stormy seas, is a great mountain situated sixteen leagues from here, and which has given its name to this town, despite being so far away. It is the end of the most southern point of Africa. In treaties, it is a point of demarcation; beyond it naval captures are still lawful several months after the Princes have been at peace in Europe. Peace has often been seen to its right, while to its left there has been war between the same flags; but more often it has seen ships gathering in its roads and living in peace together while war troubled the two hemispheres. I admired this happy shore that had never been laid waste by war, and which is inhabited by a people useful to all others by the resources of their economy and the extent of their trade. It is not climate that makes man. This wise and peaceful nation does not owe its morals and customs to the territory it occupies. Piracy and civil war ravage the Regencies of Algeria, Morocco, and Tripoli, yet the Dutch have brought agriculture and peace to the far end of Africa.

I amused myself with these pleasing thoughts, so rare in any place on earth, as I strolled around, but the sun's heat forced me to find some shelter. There was none but in the entrance to a ravine. I found my companions by a small spring, resting. As they were bored, we decided to go home. It was midday. We climbed down, some sliding by sitting up, others on their hands and knees. Rock and sand gave way under our feet. The sun was almost vertical, and its rays, reflected by the rocks, made the heat unbearable. We often left the path and ran to hide in the shade of some point of rock to breathe. My knees failed; I was overwhelmed by thirst; we reached town towards the evening. Mme. Nedling was waiting for us. Refreshments were ready. It was lemonade with nutmeg and wine added. We drank it without danger. I went to bed. Never had a trip given me so much pleasure, and never had rest seemed so agreeable.

Cape of Good Hope, this 6 February 1771

Letter 22
Quality of the Air and Soil in the Cape of Good Hope; Plants, Insects and Animals

The air at the Cape of Good Hope is very healthy. It is refreshed by southeasterly winds that are so cold, even in the height of summer, that all year round you wear cloth. Its latitude is, however, thirty-three degrees south. But I am convinced that the South Pole is far colder than the North.

There are few diseases at the Cape. Scurvy is quickly cured, although there are no sea turtles. Against this, smallpox has caused ravages here. Many people are deeply marked. It is claimed that it was brought by a Danish ship. Most of the Hottentots who caught it died. Since then they have been reduced to a small number and hardly come to town.

The Cape soil is a sandy gravel mixed with white earth. I do not know if it contains precious stones. The Dutch used to find gold in Lagoa in the Straits of Mozambique. They even had a settlement there, but abandoned it because of its unhealthy air.

At the Fort-Major's house I saw samples of a sulphurous earth with bits of wood reduced to carbon in it; it was a veritable gypsum, with black cubes of all sizes, amalgamated without losing their shape. It is believed to be iron ore.

The only trees native to the country are the gold-tree and the silver-tree, whose wood is fit only for burning. The first differs from the second by the colour of its leaves, which are yellow. There are said to be forests of these trees inland, but here the earth is covered with an infinite number of shrubs and flowering plants. This confirms my opinion that they succeed only in temperate countries, their calyx being formed to thrive in a moderate heat. Among those plants that seemed to me to be most remarkable, whether I have described them before or not, are: a red flower which resembles a butterfly, with a tuft, legs, four wings and a tail. A kind of hyacinth, with a long stalk, all of whose flowers back on each other at the top, like the buds of the Imperial; another bulbous flower, growing in the marshes, which resembles a large red tulip, in the middle of which are many little flowers. A shrub whose flower resembles a large flesh-coloured artichoke. Another common shrub, which is used to make beautiful hedges; its leaves grow opposite each other on one side and it carries clusters of papilionaceous, pink flowers. They are followed by leguminous seeds. I have brought them back to France to grow. When I got back, I sent them to the King's Jardin des Plantes where they took very well in the summer of 1772.

Of insects I have seen a beautiful red grasshopper, marbled black, beautiful butterflies, and one odd insect, a small brown scarab which runs fast; when you try to catch it, it releases a noise of wind, followed by a little smoke; if it touches your finger, this vapour stains it brown and lasts for days. It reloads its artillery several times and it is called the *Gunner*.

Hummingbirds are not rare. I have seen one the size of a walnut, of a changing green on its belly. It had a necklace of red feathers, sparkling like diamonds on its stomach, and brown wings like a sparrow, not unlike an overcoat covering its beautiful feathers. Its beak was black, rather long and appropriately curved for finding honey in the bosom of flowers, and it darts out a long and thin tongue. It lived for several days, and I saw it eat flies and drink sugared water. But as it tried to bathe itself in the cup where the water had been poured, its wings became stuck together and the ants ate it overnight.

I saw some birds with a fire colour on their belly and a black velvet on their head: in winter they turn brown. Some change colour three times a year. There is also a Bird of Paradise, but I did not find it as beautiful as the Asian ones (I have not seen that species alive). The gardener's friend and a kind of finch are often found in the garden. The gardener's friend is worth being transported to Europe, where it would be very useful in our gardens. I have seen it busying itself catching caterpillars and hanging them on thorns on bushes.

There are eagles and another sort of bird that very much looks like one. It is called the secretary, because around its neck is a ruff of long feathers fit for writing with. Strangely, it cannot stand upright on its legs, which are long and covered in scales. It lives off snakes only. The length of its armoured claws renders it very able to snatch them, and its ruff of feathers protects its neck and head from snakebites. This bird should also be naturalized at home. The ostrich is very common; I was offered young ones for an *écu*. I ate their eggs, which are less good than hen's eggs. I have also seen the cassowary,[115] covered in coarse hair, not feathers. There are a prodigious amount of sea birds whose names and habits I do not know. The penguin lays eggs that are very sought after but I found nothing marvellous about them. What is special is that the white, after being boiled, remains transparent.

The sea abounds in fish, more so than on the islands, but less than in Europe. On the shore are to be found shells, paper-nautilus, Medusa heads, limpets and some beautiful lithophytes which, when arranged on paper, represent pretty brown, purple and pinkish trees. They are sold to visitors. I saw a fish of the size and shape of a Flemish knife. It was silver, and naturally marked on both sides with the impressions of two fingers. There are sea-calves, whales, sea-cows, cod, and a great variety of species of ordinary fish; but I won't talk about these because I lack sufficient knowledge and observations in ichthyology.

There is a very common little mountain tortoise with a yellow shell marked with black; it is not used for anything. There are porcupines and marmots that differ from ours, as well as a great variety of dear and roe deer, wild donkeys, zebras etc. Some years back, an English engineer killed a giraffe about 16 feet tall, an animal which browses off leaves on trees.

The bavian is a large monkey, looking like a bear. Monkeys seem to be linked in nature with all classes of animals. I recall seeing a *sapajou* monkey that had a mane like a lion's. The Madagascan monkey called *maki* looks like a greyhound; the orangutan like a man.

Every day a species new to Europe is discovered; it seems as if they have hidden in those parts of the globe least inhabited by man, whose proximity is always fatal to them. One could also say that they are more varied as the country is less cultivated. M. de Tolbac told me that he had sent to M. Linnaeus in Sweden some plants from the Cape that were so different from any known that the famous naturalist wrote to him: "you have given me the greatest pleasure; you have upset my system."[116]

There are good horses at the Cape, and excellent asses. The oxen have a large lump on their neck, formed of fat and laced with little blood vessels. At first glance, this excrescence seems monstrous, but you quickly see that it is a reserve of food that nature has given this animal that is destined to live in Africa in scorched plains. During the dry season it gets thin and its lump diminishes; it is filled with new juices when it pastures on fresh grass. Other animals which pasture in the same climate also have their advantages: the camel has a hump and the dromedary has two in the shape of buckets; the sheep has a long tail made like a hood which is nothing but a mass of suet weighing several pounds.

Oxen are trained here to run almost as fast as horses with the carts to which they are harnessed.

Mutton and beef are so common that the head and feet are thrown away and attract wolves at night into the town itself. I often hear them howling nearby. Pliny observes that the lions of Europe, found in Romania, are cleverer and stronger than the African ones, and that African wolves and Egyptian ones are smaller and not so strong. Indeed, the Cape wolves are far less dangerous than ours. I could add to that observation that this superiority spreads to the people of our continent. We have more spirit and courage than the Asiatics and blacks: but it would be a worthier praise if I could say that we surpass them in justice, goodness and social virtues.[117]

The tiger is more dangerous than the wolf. It is cunning like a cat, but without courage; dogs attack it fearlessly. You cannot say the same for the lion. Once the dogs have scented his tracks, panic seizes them. If they see him, they stop, and do not approach. Hunters shoot him with large-bored guns. I have tried them out myself. There is hardly a single farmer on the Cape who can use such a gun.

Lions are only found over sixty leagues away; this creature lives in forests in the interior. Its roar sounds from afar like the dull rumbling of thunder. He hardly ever attacks man, whom he neither hunts nor avoids, but if a hunter wounds him, he will pick on him among the others and hurl himself on him with implacable fury. The Company gives permission and rewards for this hunting.

My hostess' brother, native to the Cape, was over six feet tall and strong like a man who had been brought up in nature. As we were talking of lions, he told me that he had been on a hunt with one of his friends and having killed a lion with a rifle shot, another lion, which he had not noticed, came up behind and seized him by the shoulder. He had the presence of mind and strength to force his fist into the lion's throat, which suffocated the animal. He showed me his scarred shoulder and said that M. de Tolback was his witness.

I omitted this anecdote in the first edition, fearing to include unbelievable incidents, but later I became convinced that nature has given man the ability to naturally tame all animals, confirmed in the case of that Indian who tames bulls with a string.

Here is a fact guaranteed by the governor, M. de Tolback, M. Berg, the Fort-Major and the principal inhabitants of the area. One finds, some sixty leagues from the Cape, in the uncultivated lands, an enormous amount of small goats. I have seen them in the Company's menagerie: they have two small horns on their heads; their hair is fawn-coloured with white spots. These animals feed in such large numbers that those to the front of the herd devour all the grass and become very fat, while those that follow find hardly anything and become very thin. They walk in vast herds until halted by a mountain chain; then they turn back and those at the back find the new grass and build up their fat, while those who walked at the front lose it. Attempts have been made to capture herds, but they cannot be tamed. These innumerable armies are always followed by great troops of lions and tigers, as if Nature wanted to assure subsistence to the wild beasts. One can hardly doubt the word of the men I have named that there are armies of lions in the interior of Africa; moreover, the Dutch account is faithful to history. Polybius says that while with Scipio in Africa he saw a great number of lions that had been crucified to scare away the rest from the villages. Pompey, said Pliny, put some six hundred lions to fight in the amphitheatre, including three hundred males. There is some physical cause that seems to reserve Africa for animals. It could be lack of water that has prevented human beings from multiplying and forming strong nations as in Asia. In such a vast extent of coast, only a few rivers run out to sea. The animals that feed can spend a long time without drinking. I have seen sheep on board vessels that drank but once a week, although they lived off dried grass.

The Dutch have created establishments for three hundred leagues along the ocean and for one hundred and thirty along the Straits of Mozambique, but have scarcely moved more than fifty leagues inland. It is claimed that this colony could put 4,000 or 5,000 men under arms but that it would be hard to assemble them. They would soon increase the number if they allowed the free exercise of religion. Holland, perhaps for its own reasons, fears the expansion of this colony, preferable in every way to the metropolis. The air is pure and temperate; all provisions abound; a quintal of wheat only costs one hundred *sous*, ten pounds of mutton, twelve *sous*, two and a half barrels of wine, five hundred pounds. They tax the considerable profits on sales to foreigners; the inhabitants live far more cheaply.

This country also trades with sheep, oxen, sea-calves and tiger skins, with aloes, salt provisions, butter, dried fruits and further foods. They have tried in vain to plant coffee and sugarcane; Asian vegetables do not grow either. Oaks grow quickly, but are worthless for construction as they are too tender. Firs have not taken. Pines rise to moderate height. This land could have, by its position, become the warehouse for trade with Asia, but marine arsenals remain in northern Europe. Further, its harbour is not safe, and its entrance is always dangerous. In this, the best season of the year, I have seen many vessels forced to hoist sail and go to sea. After all, the Europeans should be grateful to nature for having provided them with all they need, without adding what might gratify their passions.

Cape of Good Hope, this 10 February 1771

Letter 23
Slaves, Hottentots, the Dutch

The abundance of this country extends to the slaves. They have bread and vegetables at discretion. A sheep is given to every two blacks each week. They do not work on Sundays. They sleep on beds with mattresses and blankets. Men and women are warmly clothed. I speak of this as a witness and after having spoken with several blacks whom the French had sold to the Dutch to punish them, so they say, but in fact to make a profit. A slave here costs as much again as in Mauritius. The man is thus doubly precious. The fate of these blacks would be preferable to those of our European peasants, if anything could compensate them for their loss of freedom.

Good treatment influences their character. You are amazed to find them as zealous and industrious as our own servants. These are, however, the same Madagascan islanders who are so inattentive to their masters in our colonies. The Dutch still bring slaves from Batavia. They are Malays, from a large nation in Asia little known in Europe. They speak their own language and have their own customs. They are uglier than blacks, but share some traits. They are smaller, their skin is ash black, their hair very long, but thin. These Malays can be passionately violent.

The Hottentots are the natives of the country, and are free. They do not steal, nor sell their children and do not enslave each other. Amongst them adultery is punished by death; the guilty are stoned. Some earn a *piastre* a year as servants, and serve the inhabitants with affection, and often risk their lives for them. As weapons they use the half-lance or *assegai*. The Cape administration looks after the Hottentots. When they lodge a complaint against a European, they are favourably heard, the presumption being in favour of those who have the least and are needy.

I have seen many come to town, driving carts harnessed sometimes to eight pairs of oxen. Their whips are extraordinarily long and are held in both hands. From his seat the driver hits the head or the tail of an ox with equal skill.

Hottentots are pastoral people, and all are equal; but in each village they choose, among themselves, two men to whom they give the titles of captain and corporal, to look after trade with the Company. They sell their flocks very cheaply. They give four or five sheep for a bit of tobacco. Although they have many beasts, they often wait for them to die before eating them. Those I saw had a sheepskin over their shoulders, a bonnet and a belt of the same material. They showed me how they sleep. They lie naked on the earth and their coat acts as a blanket.

They are not as black as the Negroes, but, like them, have a flat nose, large mouth and thick lips. Their hair is shorter and frizzier. They resemble a ratteen. I noticed that their language is very odd in that each word that they pronounce is preceded by a click of the tongue, which, no doubt, gave them the name Choccoquas, as on the old map by M. Delisle.[118] One would think that they always only said the word *choccoq*.

As for the Hottentot women's apron, it is a myth whose falsity is agreed by everybody. It was promoted by the traveller Kolben, whose account is full of fables.[119] The censor cut out an anecdote about the Hottentot apron from my first edition. Here it is now. I overheard M. Poivre say that the Duke d'Orléans, retired in Sainte Geneviève, had asked him to verify if Hottentot women had this apron and he had said no. The censor decided to cut this out when in the end it is a fact of natural history, and a refutation of an anatomical error.

A more trustworthy observation comes from Pliny, who noticed that the stupidity of an animal is in proportion to how thick its blood is. Strong animals have, he said, thick blood, and the more docile ones have thin blood. To this cause I willingly attribute the superiority of the whites over the blacks.

Independently of the slaves and Hottentots, the Dutch retain indentured servants. These are Europeans to whom the Company has advanced money and whom the inhabitants take home with them, having first paid the administration what it spent. They are usually employed in homes. For the first years the Dutch are pleased with their servants' work, but abundance soon makes them lazy.

There is no gambling at the Cape, and no social visits. Women look after the servants and the houses, whose furniture is extremely clean. The husband manages the outside business. In the evening, the family meets for a stroll and to breathe the fresh air, once the wind has fallen. Each day repeats the same pleasures and same business.

Tenderness reigns amongst relatives. My hostess' brother was a peasant of the Cape, come from some seventy leagues away. This man did not speak a word and was always sitting smoking his pipe. With him, he had his ten-year-old son always next to him. The father put his hand to his cheek, and caressed him without saying a word; the child was as silent as the father, held his large hands in his little ones, looking at him with an expression of filial tenderness. This little boy was dressed as one is in the country. In the house his relative, of the same age, was properly dressed: these two children went walking together, in great intimacy. The town-dweller did not despise the peasant, he was his cousin.

I saw Mlle. Berg, aged sixteen, manage a large house on her own. She receives strangers, looks after servants, and keeps order among a numerous family, always at ease. Her youth, her beauty, her graces, her character earned her everybody's esteem; yet I noticed that she did not pay any attention to compliments. I said to her one day that she had many friends; "I have one best friend," she said, "he is my father."

The main pleasure of this Councillor was to sit down at home after business, surrounded by his family. They jumped up to embrace him while the little one hugged his knees; they took him as judge of their quarrels and pleasures, while the eldest daughter forgave some, approved others, smiled at all, doubling the joy of her father's heart. It seemed to me that she was Antiope to Idomeneus.[120]

These people, content with their domestic happiness, a consequence of their virtue, have not yet set it in novels and or in the theatre. There are no spectacles at the Cape, and nobody wants them. Each one sees in his own house what touches him the most: happy servants, well brought-up children, faithful wives. Here are pleasures you cannot find in fiction. Such things do not enter conversation; in fact, they hardly talk at all. They are melancholic people who prefer to feel than to reason. Perhaps also, an absence of events leaves them with little to talk about; but what does it matter that the mind is empty if the heart is full and if the sweet emotions of nature can excite it, neither stimulated by artifice nor constrained by false decencies!

When Cape girls fall in love, they naively admit it. They say love is a natural feeling, a sweet passion that calms their lives and compensates them for the dangers of becoming mothers. But they want to choose the person whom they will always love. They will respect, they say, being women, the bonds that they prepared whilst unmarried. They do not turn love into a mystery: they express what they feel. Are you loved? You are accepted, entertained, and publicly distinguished. I saw Mademoiselle Nedling cry when the man she loved left. I saw her sighing as she prepared the presents that were to be the pledges of her tenderness. She did not seek out witnesses, but did not hide from them.

This good faith is usually followed by a happy marriage. Young men are equally frank in their proceedings. They return from Europe to carry out their promises; they reappear having survived danger and with emotions that have overcome absence; esteem is joined to love and nourishes, all their lives, the desire in these constant souls to please, a desire that moreover extends to all those around them.

However happy they may be with such simple manners and in such an abundant land, all that comes from Holland is always dear to them. Their houses are covered with views of Amsterdam, its public squares and its countryside. Holland is their real motherland and even foreigners in their service do not speak in any other way. I asked a Swede in the Company's service how long the fleet would be on its return to Holland: "We shall be," he said, "at least three months before we get home."

They have a very strict Church, where the divine service is carried out with great decency. I do not know if religion increases their happiness, but you see among them men whose fathers sacrificed everything most dear to it. They are French refugees. They have, some leagues from the Cape, a settlement called La Petite Rochelle. They are overjoyed when they meet a compatriot, bring him to their homes, present him to their wives and children, like a happy man who has seen the land of their ancestors, and who has the right to return. They talk ceaselessly about France, admire it, praise it, and lament it like a mother who has been too severe with them. They thus spoil the happiness of the country they are living in by bemoaning their exile from a land they have never seen.[121]

At the Cape, great respect is given to the magistrates and especially the governor. His house is only distinguished from the others by a sentry and by the use of a trumpet to announce when he dines. This honour goes with his position; otherwise no pomp attends his person. He goes out without a retinue and he is easily approached. His house is situated on the banks of a canal, shaded by oaks planted in front of his door. You see portraits of Ruiter, of Van Trump and of illustrious men from Holland. It is small and simple, and apt for the few who come to him with business matters. But he who lives inside is so loved and respected that people who pass by always stop to greet him.

He gives no public feasts, but from his purse helps those honest families who are in a poor way. He is not paid court. If justice is wanted, it is obtained from the Council; if it is help, those are his duties; injustice only can be solicited.

He is nearly always master of his own time and uses it to keep order and peace, convinced that these are what make societies flourish. He does not believe that the authority of a chief depends on the division of his people. I heard him say that the best policy was to be straight and just.

He often invites strangers to his table. Although aged eighty, his conversation is lively: he knows our intellectual works and likes them. Of all the Frenchmen that he has met, the one he misses most is the Abbé de la Caille.[122] He had built an observatory for him. He appreciated his learning, his modesty, his disinterestedness, his social graces. I have only known the works of this learned man; but in reporting the tribute that foreigners have paid to his ashes, I am proud to complete the portrait of these worthy people with their praise for a man of my nation.[123]

Letter 24
Continuation of my Cape Journal

I was invited by M. Serrurier, first minister of the Church, to go and see the library. It is a very appropriate building. I noticed, above all, many theological works that have never lent themselves to dispute, as the Dutch never open them. At the end of the Company's garden is a menagerie where you can see many kinds of birds. The pelicans that I had seen on my arrival were the boarders of this house, but they had been chased away as they ate too many ducklings. In the daytime, they would go off and fish in the bay and return to sleep on land.

On 10 February a French ship was signalled; it was the *Alliance*, one of those that the cyclone had forced to set sail at Réunion. She had lost her mizzen-mast in the storm. They could give us no news about the *Indien*. They took on some supplies and continued towards America without repairing the loss of their mast. The Dutch preserve a number of masts by burying them in the sand, but they sell them very expensively. The *Normande*'s mizzen-mast cost one thousand *écus*.

On the 11th the *Digue*, a King's pink that had left Mauritius one month before, came into the Cape to get some provisions. I knew the captain, M. Le Fer. He said that he would not be more than a week at anchor and would then be sailing to Lorient. I could not count on seeing the *Indien* nor my effects, and as this opportunity seemed a favourable one, I decided to take it up.

I told M. Berg and M. de Tolbac of my decision: both repeated their offers of their purses. One evening, dining at the governor's, we talked about the Constantia wine. M. Berg asked me if I would take some back to Europe. I answered, naturally, that the problems with my finances did not allow me to make this purchase, as I had set aside a sum to make a present to a lady to whom I was strongly attached. He told me that he would relieve me of that embarrassment by giving me an *alverame* of red or white wine, or both if that pleased me more. I replied that one would suffice and that I would present it in his name to the person to whom it was intended. "No," he said, "I am giving it to you, so that you will remember me. I only ask as acknowledgment that you write and tell me of your safe arrival." He sent it to me the next day. M. Berg, for his part, with whom I had often spoken of how decently I had been treated by M. and Mlle. de Cremon, told me that he would take care of my gratitude towards them by sending them two dozen bottles of Constantia wine.

In a situation in which I lacked everything, I found that I had been fortunate to have met such obliging men among strangers.

I agreed with the *Digue*'s captain to pay 600 *livres* for my passage. He would leave two days later. I used M. Berg's credit very cautiously. I had a suit made, and some underwear. That was all the luggage an Officer returning from the East Indies had with him. Not only had I lost all my effects, but I was also indebted by more than 400 *livres*.

I had hardly made my arrangements, when the vessel the *Africain* anchored in the Cape; it had come to fetch provisions. It had left Mauritius half way through January. It brought news about the *Indien*. This is what we learned.

This ill-fated vessel had lost all its masts in the cyclone and after having been at sea for more than a month, had returned on its own to Mauritius in such a poor state that it had been disarmed. The rough seas had soaked part of its cargo and flooded the powder room so that the passengers' luggage floated about. A good man named M. de Moncherat wrote to tell me I would be able to see my luggage when it arrived and that, except for what was in my room, little had been damaged. However, I later found that everything inside my trunks had rotted. The worst damage was to my large volume of Plutarch, which had accompanied me in my solitude.

We were told about a very strange event that happened on the *Indien*. Among the convicts who were sent to Mauritius was a man from a good family called M. de ... In France he had murdered his brother-in-law. On the journey, he quarrelled with the supercargo of the vessel. Arriving on land, in daylight on the public square, without further formalities, he pierced him with his sword and broke the blade in the body. He rushed off into the forest where he was caught and brought to prison. His trial over, he was about to be condemned to death when during the night he dug a hole in the prison wall and escaped.

This incident happened two months after my departure.

During the cyclone endured by the *Indien*, the mizzen-mast broke and fell into the sea. The rigging was hurriedly cut away when they saw a sailor in the middle of the waves, hanging on to the floating mast. He was shouting, save me, save me. In fact, it was this same wretch. When the *Indien* returned to Mauritius, he again escaped. M. de Tolbac said about this man: "he who should be hanged will not drown." We had no news of the *Alliance*, which had probably sunk.

It was a great joy to take possession of my effects on the eve of my departure and not to be on the *Indien*, which would probably wait for a long while in Mauritius. The *Digue* postponed its departure until 2 March. I paid all my expenses with my bill-of-exchange upon the treasury of the colonies, at six months, by which I lost twenty-two per cent discount.

I bade farewell to the governor and to M. Berg, who gave me many natural history curiosities. I had presented him with some of mine. Mlle. Berg gave me three parrots with grey heads, large as sparrows that came from Madagascar. My hostess provided me with fruit, and wished me, weeping, as was her family, a happy voyage.

I left these good people and these gardens of European fruit trees, which in March were laden with fruit, with much regret. I rejoiced, however, at the thought of seeing these same trees in flower in Europe and at the idea that in a year I would have had two summers without winter. But even better than a beautiful country and sweet seasons, I was soon to see my country and my friends again.

Letter 25
Departure from the Cape, Description of Ascension Island

On 2 March, at two in the afternoon, we set sail with six vessels from the Batavia fleet. The six others had left a fortnight before. We left by the second opening in the bay, leaving Robben Island to the left.[124] We soon outsailed the Dutch ships. They sail together as far as the Azores, where two Dutch warships wait to accompany them back to Holland.

Sailors regard the Cape as a third of their way from Mauritius to Europe; they count the second third from the Cape to the Equator; the last third is the rest of the route.

A week after our departure, while we were on the deck after dinner, in perfect safety, we saw a great flame issue from the kitchen chimney; it rose as high as the mizzen's sail. Everybody rushed forward. It was panic; a clumsy cook had spilt some fat on the kitchen fire. We were told that a fire on another boat had burnt all the forward sails in a moment. The officers and crew had lost their heads and rushed in a crowd to warn the captain. He came out of his room and said coldly: "My friends, this is nothing. Turn the boat into the wind." And indeed the fire, driven by the wind, quickly died out after burning all the sails. This cool-headed man was called M. de Surville and was a captain in the Company.

We had a constant southeasterly wind and a good sea until Ascension Island. On 20 March we were near its latitude, which is 8 degrees south, but had gone too far east. We were obliged to sail down the longitude as our intention was to anchor there and hunt turtles.

On the morning of the 22nd we caught sight of the island. We could see it from ten leagues away, although it is only a league and a half wide. It is distinguished by its pointed hill called the Green Mountain. The rest of the island is formed of black and russet hills, and the rocks close to the sea were white with bird dung.

As you approach, the landscape becomes hideous. We hugged the coast to reach our anchorage at the northwest. We saw at the foot of the black hills what looked like the ruins of a large town. These are molten rocks, which have rolled down from an ancient volcano. They are scattered over the plain and down to the sea in bizarre shapes. The entire coast on this part is formed of these rocks. There are pyramids, grottoes, half-vaults; waves break against these craggy rocks, sometimes covering them, and as they retreat form white sheets of foam; sometimes finding raised plateaux, pierced with holes, they smash them from below and throw up jets of water. These black and white shores are covered with sea birds. Masses of frigate birds surrounded us and hovered above the rigging where we could catch them by hand.

We anchored in the evening in the entrance of the great bay. I climbed down into the boat with the men who were going to hunt the turtles. The landing-place is at the foot of a mass of rocks seen from the anchorage, at the extremity of the bay on the right. We landed on a beach of beautiful coarse-grained sand. It is white, mixed with red, yellow and many other coloured grains, like the aniseed called *mignonette*. At some paces from there we found a cave with a bottle inside where passing ships leave letters. You break the bottle to read them, after which you place them in another one.

We walked forward about fifty paces on the left behind the rocks. There we encountered a small plain where the soil broke under our feet, as if frozen. I tasted it. It was salt, which seemed strange to me, as the sea did not appear to reach so far in.

We brought wood, a kettle, and a boat's sail on which the sailors lay down to await night. It is only at eight o'clock in the evening that the turtles climb up the beach. Our men were relaxing, when one of them jumped up shouting, "There's a dead man, a dead man!" Indeed, a small cross stood above a pile of sand and we could see that someone had been buried there. This sailor had lain down on top without realizing; none of our sailors wanted to remain in this place; to please them we had to move some hundred paces on.

The moon rose and lit up this solitude. Its light makes agreeable places more moving, but here it made the scene more frightening. We were at the foot of a dark hill, at the top of which sailors had placed a large cross. In front of us the plain was covered with rocks that rose to a man's height. The moon made the tops, whitened by bird droppings, sparkle. These whitened heads on black bodies, with some standing and some leaning over, seemed like ghosts wandering among tombs. Profound silence reigned in this deserted place; from time to time all one heard was the noise of the sea on the coast or the vague cry of some frigate-bird, frightened at seeing people.

We went to the great bay to wait for the turtles. We lay down on our bellies in utter silence. At the slightest sound this animal flees. At last we saw three come out of the waves; we could make them out as dark shapes climbing slowly up the sandy shore. We ran towards the first of them but our impatience made us lose it, for it turned back down the slope into the sea. The second was further up and could not turn back. We threw it over on to its back. Through the night and in the same bay, we threw over fifty of them on to their backs, some weighed more than five hundred pounds.

Holes had been dug into the shore all over the place where they lay up to three hundred eggs, then cover them with sand so that the sun hatches them. We killed one turtle and made a soup; after this, I went to rest in the cave where letters are left, so as to enjoy the rock's shelter, the sound of the sea and the soft sand. I had ordered a sailor to bring my nightclothes, but he refused to cross over the place where the dead man was buried. There is no one as brave nor as superstitious as a sailor.

I slept very well. When I awoke I found a scorpion and some crabs at the entrance to the cave. I saw no other herbs but a kind of milk-thistle or celandine. Its juice was milky and very bitter; the plant and the animals were worthy of this island.

I climbed the side of a hill where the ground resounded under my feet. It was a reddish and salty cinder. It is perhaps from here that the salt pan where we spent the night comes from. A booby came and landed heavily a few steps from me. I pointed my stick at it and he seized it in his beak without flying away. This bird lets itself be caught by hand, as do all species who have not yet come into contact with man; which proves that there is a kind of good will and natural trust in all creatures towards animals which they believe will do them no harm. Birds are not scared of oxen.

Our sailors killed many frigate-birds to cut out a little portion of fat they have near the neck. They believe that it cures gout because this bird is very swift, but nature, which has attached this illness to our intemperance has not placed the remedy in our cruelty.

At six in the morning the boat came to load the turtles. As the waves were high, it anchored outside and pulled them aboard with a rope, one after another. This manoeuvre took all day. In the evening we freed the turtles that we did not need. When they have been a long time on their backs their eyes turn red like cherries, and pop out of their heads. There were several on the shore which other vessels had left to die this way. It is a cruel act of negligence.

Letter 26
Conjectures on the Antiquity of the Soil on Ascension Island, on Mauritius, on the Cape of Good Hope and in Europe

While our sailors were working to embark the turtles, I went to sit in one of the cavities of those rocks that cover the plain. The sight of this terrifying chaos led to a few reflections. If these ruins, I said to myself, were those of a city, how many memoirs we would have about those who built it and those who laid it waste! There is not a column in Europe that does not have its historian.

How is it that we who know so much, know nothing about where we come from or who we are? All learned men agree about the origin and duration of Babylon, now uninhabited, but nobody agrees about the nature and antiquity of the earth, which is the fatherland of all men. Some claim it is formed by fire, others by water, some by the laws of movement, others by crystallization. People in the West believe it is six thousand years old; those in the East that it is eternal.

If the rest of the earth resembled this island, there would be only one system. These pumice stones, these hills of cinder, these molten rocks which have bubbled like clinker, prove that its origin was volcanic, but how many years ago did it explode?

It seems to me that if that moment occurred ages ago, these heaps of cinders would not be pyramids; rain and sun would have flattened them. The angles and contours of these rocks would not be so sharp and cutting because a long action by the atmosphere destroys all projecting parts; statues carved by Greeks have become shapeless blocks when left outside.

Would it then be so difficult to judge the age of a body by its degree of decay, as one judges the antiquity of a medal by its rust? An old rock, isn't it a medal of earth struck by time?

Moreover, if this island was very old, these blocks of stone on the surface of the earth would have been buried by their own weight; it is a slow process, but the effect of heaviness is sure. The piles of cannon balls and cannons placed on the ground in arsenals slowly sink down over the years. Most Greek and Italian monuments have sunk deeper than their base. Some have even disappeared.

If I could find out how long it takes for a body with its shape and weight known to sink into a ground whose resistance is known, I would then have the equation that would let me find what I am seeking. The calculation would be easy once the experiment has been made. Meanwhile, I can safely reason that this island is very recent.

I can assume the same about Mauritius; but as its pointed mountains already have some ridges, as its rocks are a third or a quarter buried in the ground and their angles are somewhat blunted, I am persuaded that its age goes centuries further back than here.

The Cape of Good Hope seems far more ancient. The rocks that have fallen off the mountain summits are completely buried in the earth at the Cape, where they are found when digging. The mountains have at their feet raised embankments formed by the rubble of the upper parts. This rubble has been broken off by the long action of the atmosphere, so visible that most of the rubble lies where the wind is at its most powerful. I have observed this on Table Mountain where the part facing the southeast wind has much more of an embankment than the part looking on to the town.

While on Table Mountain I also noticed that stones the size of large casks had well-rounded angles. Even fragments no longer have sharp edges and form a white, smooth gravel, like flattened almonds. These stones are very hard and by their colour and texture resemble porcelain tablets.

The decomposition of these bodies announces their great antiquity; however, on the Table Mountain I found that the layer of organic mould was no more than two inches deep, although plants are common there. In many places the rocks are bare. So plants have not been growing there for a long time. However, no conclusion can be reached because the summit is not made of sand or of porous rocks, but of a kind of hard, white, polished pebble. Plant seeds would have had to be borne for a long time by the wind before germinating.

The layer of organic mould in the plains is far deeper, but this does not allow any conclusions about the soil's age because when this layer is deep, it could have been brought there from neighbouring mountains by rain, or conversely when it is thin, carried further away.

If there was a high, isolated mountain in Europe whose summit was flattened like Table Mountain, without being of a matter hostile to vegetation, you might compare the depth of its mould with that of some newly formed and equally isolated land, for example the surface of some of those islands which after hundreds of years are formed in the River Loire's mouth. Until we have more experiments I presume that Europe is far older than the Cape because the summits of its mountains are not so steep and their sides have gentler slopes and the rocks still on the earth's surface are blunted and round.

It is not a question here of those rocks that appear on mountain sides cut by the sea, torrents and out-flowing rivers, nor of stones that rain has exposed in the plains by washing away the earth, and even less of stones in fields covered and uncovered every year by ploughing. I speak of those that by their weight and situation obey only the law of gravity. I have seen none like that in the Russian and Polish plains. Finland is paved with rocks, but of a very different configuration; there one sees hills and valleys of solid rock. In some way, it is the earth that has petrified. However, as pines grow on the tops of these hills, it seems that they have been a long time in the air, which has decomposed them. It even seems that in a less cold temperature this decomposition would be quickly accelerated, but snow covers them for six months from the atmosphere's action and the cold, which hardens the earth and slows down the effect of their gravity.

The kind of rock that I believe is fit for experiments is that found near Fontainebleau. These are masses of rounded sandstone, separated from each other. Some are half or three-quarters buried in the earth, others lie in heaps on the surface as if for building something. They could be the summits of some stony mountains that have not completely sunk. It is likely that each century manages to sink them further into the soil and that there were many more two thousand years ago. The action of the elements and gravity tends to make the globe round. One day European mountains will be far less steep, one day the sea will have dissolved the coastal rocks against which it breaks today, as it has destroyed those of Scylla and Charibdis.

I then opened a history book in order to daydream. I fell on a place where the author said of some European families that their origins *are lost in the darkness of time* as if their ancestors had been born before the sun. He spoke in another part of Northern people as the creators of the human race, *officina gentium*: that torrent of barbarians, he said, that the North could no longer contain.

I have lived for some time in the North and have travelled over 800 leagues and do not recall seeing one ancient monument. However, populous societies leave durable traces; and from the little village bell-tower to the Egyptian pyramids, all land that has been cultivated has left testimony of its settlement. Greek and Italian fields are covered in ruins, so why aren't there any in Russia and Poland? It is because human beings only multiply with the fruits of the earth; it is because the North of Europe was uncultivated while the South was covered with vineyards, olive groves and harvests. These people, in their abundance, raised altars to all kinds of gods. Ceres, Pomona, Bacchus, Flora, Pales, the Zephyrs, the Nymphs were divine pleasures. A young girl would offer doves to Love, garlands to the Graces and prayed to Lucina to give her a faithful husband. Religion had not been separated from Nature, and as this knowledge lay in every heart, the earth, under such a favourable Heaven, was covered with altars. One saw the god of gardens in every orchard, Neptune on shores, Love in all the groves; naiads in grottoes, muses in porticoes, Minerva in peristyles; an obelisk to Diana appeared in every copse, and a temple to Venus raised its dome above the forests.

But when one inhabitant of these beautiful countries was forced north to a new home, once he had found himself under the frozen constellation of the Bear with his unhappy family, my God, how he must have been shocked as winter approached! The sun hardly rose above the horizon, its disk red and gloomy. The howling wind split the pine trees; fountains froze and rivers stopped. A thick snow covered the fields, woods and lakes. Plants, seeds, springs, all that supports life, was dead. You could hardly breathe, nor touch anything as death was in the air, and pain in your bodies. Ah, when that hapless man heard the cries of his children devoured by the climate, when he saw tears freeze on their cheeks and their outstretched arms stiffen... he must have been horrified at these death-like retreats! Dared he hope for posterity from nature and harvests from such iron-like fields? His hand must have trembled as he tried to dig open a soil that killed its farmers. He could share his misery with the flocks; seek, like them, moss on trees, and wander about a land where rest meant death. He could only dig a lair and if later you saw any monument rise from the snow, it would have been a tomb.

It is likely that the North of Europe was populated only when the South was abandoned. The Greeks, so often tormented by tyrants, preferred freedom to the beauty of a sky. Some of them travelled to Hungry, to Bohemia, to Poland and Russia, with those arts which help man overcome the elements, and allow him, alone among the animals, to live in any climate. From the Morea to Archangel, on an extent of more than 500 leagues, you can only speak the Slavonic tongue, whose words and letters derive from the Greek; they must have become Barbarians, emerging late to develop their power under a better legislature. Peter the Great was the first to lay the foundations of their modern greatness and today a great Empress is giving them laws worthy of Areopagus.[125]

Reflection on Solitude on Ascension Island

God would not be pleased if I did not recognize the good which human beings owe each other. I think that nature has made us communicate all together around the earth and if men were virtuous, there would only be one language, one religion and all humans would share the same passions, the same outbursts of joy and pain. But in thinking about all the good things we owe to society, so much evil comes with it, the prejudices of the tribe, the unjust wars of nations, religious prejudices which are imposed from childhood and arm us against each other, family against family and neighbour against neighbour. In our societies, money rules the ranks to such a point that he who has nothing bears all the brunt and rather than share in what is good, has a full share only of misfortunes. Tributes fall on the pauper; he is taxed; he bears the weight of superstition, of pride; he is the one taken as a soldier or sailor for wars abroad. More, he is the one forced into depravity in a bid to escape so many evils; he is forced to become a flatterer to escape his tyrants and obtain his basic needs. He pretends, deceives and is obliged to ally himself to the very power that oppresses him.

On the other hand, all these evils vanish in solitude. Man can only be a man in solitude; he can be himself, he banishes prejudices, he is free, he is true; nobody can offend him and he will not offend anybody; he avoids ridicule. Doubtless it is to enable him to live alone and to restore each man to his real self that nature, for a third of the day, hands him over to sleep as if to a deep solitude where he may be relieved from his burdens. It is during solitude that we will find men concerned about the happiness of other people, Lycurgus, Moses... It is there that our humours are purged, far from prejudices. We plead with solitude to let us indulge in our passions. Indeed, love is dangerous for solitary people and it is only among them that you find the great passions; but it is because solitude makes us people again by restoring nature's laws. Now, the first of these laws is to have a companion. In solitude all the prejudices of childhood, all that is mechanical in our schooling, all that dupes us and makes us fall asleep, is dissolved by nature. Nature reclaims its dues, night and day. Thus, the temptations of anchorites and the monsters that the ancients saw in the desert, monsters born in their imaginations, deriving from two contrasts; on the one hand, from the opinions and evils of society which have constrained them from seeking refuge in the deserts, and from their doctrine which blames their harmful minds rather than the aberrations of a society cut off from the laws of nature; and on the other hand, these same laws of nature present them ceaselessly with images of a woman, so that monsters, composed of a devil and of a Venus, are formed in their minds from these two contrasts.

A woman, then, is the solitary man's first need. But where in our societies can you find such a companion, as natural institutions have all been overturned? Woman should be brought up to please one man, as happens in the East where they have kept their natural customs, but with us we bring them up to please everybody. It is she who does the honours of the house to strangers; she enriches public feasts, outings, spectacles. How then to find a natural friend, someone to console us naturally against the ills of society when she is the very one who ties us to society? Thus in a depraved society, we are made unhappy by the same good that nature has prepared for our happiness. What can be done, then, when it is up to us to create an inner solitude which nobody can invade and where we break the affections or prejudices acquired from childhood, or rather create a society like the ancients had, with an ideal people among whom we all talk and communicate?

These ideas rolled around in my mind. To these general ills, I added some more personal ones. I remembered my ambition, so flattered with hope in Russia when I was loved by my superiors, the military honours I was meant to attain, all the hopes that my patriotism had given birth to in Poland, the high opinion people had of me in Paris, my desire to establish a new life in Madagascar. And now, rejected, let down by my superiors, without a position, fortune or contacts, I was falling back into seeking a living in Paris, still without a love to help me, without the family I had hoped to help and that I was forced now to abandon because I could not even look after myself. It was then that I reproached myself for not having a self-sufficient talent. I resolved to give up my status of engineer forever, as it had been the perpetual source of all my misfortunes.

These misfortunes came about, without a doubt, to strip me of all hope; but our future is like a mountain of several levels; when we are obliged by some flood to leave the bottom, we reach the summit in order to escape.

I reminded myself of so many people more unfortunate than myself, that all that scared me would pass. I realized that Providence rules everything, that it had saved me from many dangers, that at this very moment I enjoyed two great blessings, health and freedom. I raised my eyes up and felt consoled. I thought about life so rapidly passing and so fragile, of those few days of existence in which pleasure or pain are immaterial. And I thought that God would pull me through these awkward moments, that I had never foreseen what was to happen to me, that what I had taken for happiness had often been the source of unhappiness, and that what I had decided was a calamity could become a source of happiness and joy. I placed all my trust in that Supreme Being who makes so many beautiful constellations glide silently above my head. I resolved to live as nature commanded, day by day, although I was on one of the most desolate islands on the globe. With a secret pleasure, I enjoyed the roar of the sea smashing on the rocks. I thought of Philoctetes abandoned on the island of Lesbos, and said to myself: far from deceiving men, I, like Philoctetes, have been wounded, not by an arrow dipped in Hydra blood, but by arrows of calumny which fly in the dark and whose wound is incurable.[126] Like him I want to see my country again, but at least I am far from lying men. The roar of the sea pleased me, I felt myself to be within ramparts, protected against its fury. The storm gives pleasure to those who are safe on the shore; sheltered from danger, one enjoys a negative happiness. I stared at the magnificent constellations, so brilliant, rolling above my head in the gentle moonlight and thought of the intelligence that governs such grand objects. I thought that my feeble destiny would not be overlooked by such an intelligence and fell asleep in this understanding, sensing that God is everywhere and that the sight of the night-sky can beautify the most awful of deserts.

Letter 27
Observations on Ascension Island, Departure, Arrival in France
My thoughts on Ascension Island had led me astray; the truth is that one enjoys agreeable objects while sad ones make you think. Also, a happy man seldom reasons; only he who suffers meditates, to at least find some useful lessons among the evils that surround him. So true is it that nature has made pleasure man's well-spring; when she couldn't place it in his heart, she put it in his head.

Although Ascension Island has no soil or water, it does not occupy a useless place on the globe. Turtles go there for three months of the year to lay their eggs, far from noise. This is a solitary animal that flees crowded shores. A vessel anchoring here for twenty-four hours will drive it away from the bay for several days, and if the ship fires a cannon, it will stay away for several weeks. The frigate-birds and boobies are tamer because less experienced, but on the inhabited coasts they pick the most inaccessible peaks and cannot be approached. Ascension Island is a republic for them; primitive customs have lasted and the species multiplies because no tyrant can live there. Without a doubt, the common mother of all beings has ordained that there be barren sands in the middle of the sea, and desolate lands, but protected by the elements as a refuge and sacred asylum where animals can enjoy the good things also dear to man, namely, tranquillity and freedom.

How can it be that so many birds which fly so far away from Ascension Island during the day, that plane so high up in the sky, return at sunset and find the exact rock? I have posed this problem in my notes without having resolved it. Do they understand latitude and longitude? For a start, I think the sun is their guide, and leaving at dawn, they go to known localities in the sea. I believe that they guide themselves by the aquatic plants which the sea drags along and that confirm ocean currents. Out at sea I have observed that you find tidal currents like long strips of foam which cross the sea in a single line and that often the sea foams there and the tide advances towards you. As these birds have very acute sight, from high up they spot tiny fish that they catch as well as the seaweed that guides them and reveals where it is best to feed. Their speed is such that they fly more than sixty leagues an hour; indeed the swallow, I am told, flies at fifty leagues and the frigate-bird even more. The frigate-birds follow, then, these currents and seaweed. Another consideration is that frigate-birds, following certain seasons, can be found more to the North or to the South and this proves that the Atlantic currents change; according to the season the birds move right into the temperate regions, confirming that currents alternate from one pole to the other. Anyhow, this instinctive ability of birds to cover such prodigious distances to find the rock they left in the morning cannot compare to what we see in our gardens. The bee leaves its hive and flies sometimes a league away, displaying an instinct to find the hive again crossing rivers, fields, woods, and passing fifty similar hives. I have noticed that bees acquire knowledge like human beings, bit by bit and moving from what they know to the unknown, for after carrying to my house the two hives I had bought, the uprooted bees flew all around the garden, entered my house, visited all the floors, as the seller warned me they would; they learned to recognize the place and its surroundings, then, on the following days, they only flew around my house and then managed to fly as far as the King's garden, as they brought back orange dust from the Indian chestnut trees. These trees grow far from my house. Thus the bee gets to know its hive in the garden over the first days, then the neighbouring gardens, then the area, and moves with the rising and the setting of the sun, knowing well the wind's directions, for when the weather is bad, they do not go out. I think that bees acquire their geographic sense by degrees. The same goes for the frigate-birds which at first hardly leave the island, then fly further off, guiding themselves by the seaweed and tidal currents, so much so that I have never seen solitary frigate-birds, but always in flocks. But the bee far exceeds the frigate-bird with its hive. Here it brings its booty, here it constructs its intricate hexagons and yet it works without seeing anything, at least in terms of our eyes, for the hive entrance is just a tiny hole that does not let in any light. I do not think that naturalists have paid enough attention to this particularity for which one can draw a lesson about Providence, for what appears to be darkness to us is enough light for small animals. Their eyes are admirably made, for not only do they see the nectar in flowers in bright sunlight and can lead botanists there, but they can also see enough in the dark to make their fine hives.

This island has its natural freedom, which many beautiful countries have lost. Although situated between Africa and America, it has escaped slavery, which is the disgrace of two vast continents. It is common to all nations and belongs to none. It is rare to see any but English and French vessels anchor here on their way back from India. The Dutch who stock up at the Cape do not need to find fresh provisions here.

The air is very pure. I slept two nights out in the open without blankets; I have seen rain fall and clouds gather around the Green Mountain's peak, which is no taller than Montmartre. It is doubtless an effect of attraction, which is stronger at sea than on land.

When you land a sailor with scurvy on this island, he is buried in sand and experiences great relief. Although I was very well, I held my legs for some time in this dry bath and felt an extraordinary agitation in my blood for several days after and do not know why. I think, however, that this sand, being composed of calcareous particles, attracts and sucks out internal humours from the skin, rather like those absorbent stones that are placed on poisonous bites and suck out the venom. It would be worthwhile for some clever doctor to treat other illnesses with this remedy, which instinct alone led scorbutic sailors to try.

We spent another night on land. At ten in the evening I went for a swim in a cove between the bay and the landing-place. It is surrounded by a chain of rocks in a semi-circle. At the back of the cove, the sand rises to 15 feet and slopes down to the sea. As you enter the water there are several layers of rock at water level. The sea, which was very rough, broke noisily and carried over into the little bay. I held on to angles on the rocks and the waves rolled over my head.

On the 24th the barometer was very high. The *Digue* hoisted its flag, and signalled that it was to set sail. It was no longer possible for the sloop to land at the usual place. It went to pick up a dozen turtles in the bay that had been left there and returned to anchor with a grappling iron half a musket's shot from where we were. The strongest sailors stripped naked, waited for the wave to recede from the shore and, running, carried the passengers and their belongings out.

I remarked to the Officer that the boat was sufficiently loaded. There were still twenty men on land, and as many on board. He wanted to save the trouble of a second trip, so continued loading. At this moment, a monstrous wave lifted the sloop, broke the grappling and threw it on to the sand. Eight or ten men, who were in the water up to the waist, expected to be crushed. Had it come sideways, it would have been lost; luckily it ran aground from behind. Two or three following waves lifted it almost upright and then it set off from the front, shipping a great of water. Fear gripped several passengers on board and they jumped into the sea, thinking they would drown. Then all our sailors together, heaving at the same time, managed to refloat it. The boat came back a little later to embark those still on shore, and the same accident almost happened again.

If this double calamity had happened, we would have deserved pity. The ship would have sailed, and we would not have found water or wood on the island. They claim that you can find puddles in the rocks at the foot of the Green Mountain; it is also believed that skinny goats live off a kind of dog's tooth. Coconut palms had once been planted but had not survived. It's probable that famished goats would have eaten the seeds.

I noticed that the southeast of Ascension Island was formed completely of lava and the northwest of cinder hills and concluded that the winds blew from the southeast when this volcano rose from the sea and that they blew gently, otherwise they would have scattered the cinders away from these hills, rather than gathering them together. I presumed also that the volcano's furnace had not been lit by the air and that storms in the earth are independent of those in the air. They would seem, rather, to depend on water. Of all the volcanoes that I know, not one is far from the sea or a great lake. I have made this observation before, trying to explain the cause, and my opinion might be right, as it is confirmed by nature.

On Ascension Island rocks I found a kind of oyster called the leaf. The sand, as I have said, is composed of debris of coral and shells some of which I recognized. Off the rocks we caught sharks and *bourses* of all colours. There are also king-fish and moray eels, a kind of sea snake, said to be excellent to eat, with blue bones.

We set sail on the same day, 24 March, at five in the evening. We lived off turtles for over a month. They are kept alive all that time, sometimes on their backs, sometimes on their fronts, and are sprinkled with sea water several times a day. The flesh of the turtle is healthy, but you soon tire of it. The flesh is always hard, and its eggs without taste.

We crossed the Equator after calms and some storms. The currents were carrying us perceptibly northwards; some days, without winds, we made ten leagues in twenty-four hours. On 28 April we saw a lunar eclipse at eleven at night on the 32nd degree of latitude north. There we spent several days becalmed. They say that these calms are like the limits between different kingdoms of wind. From the 28th degree north to the 32nd, we found the sea covered with seaweed called grape clusters. They were filled with little crabs and tiny fish. This is perhaps nature's way of carrying to island shores animals that could not get there any other way; coastal fish are never found in the main sea.

With great joy we saw the pole star reappear on the horizon and each night we watched it rise with renewed pleasure. This view made strolls at night very pleasurable. One night at ten, as I was strolling the quarter-deck, I saw the quarter-master speaking agitatedly with the officer on watch. The latter made him light a lantern and followed him along the forecastle. I walked with them. We were surprised to see a cloud of thick black smoke issue from the hatchway. The sailors on watch were lying quietly on the mizzen-mast's sail and when we called them, they were seized with panic. The more intrepid climbed down the hatch with a candle, shouting that we were lost. We ran about looking for buckets, but could not find one. Someone wanted to sound the alarm to call everybody, another to work the aft pump to bring water below.

We were all gathered around the hatch, heads down, awaiting our sentence. The smoke increased and we even saw some flames. A moment later, a voice called up from the abyss and said it was merely fire from some wood left in the oven to dry. This moment of panic seemed to last a century. What a sad life sailors have! In the middle of fine weather, at perfect peace, soon to see our country again, a miserable accident could bring us the most dreadful of deaths.

On 16 May the crew exercised themselves by firing at a target, a bottle hanging from the end of the yard; we tried the cannons, we had five of them. This military exercise was done out of fear of being attacked by pirates called *Saltins*. Luckily we never met them. We had such poor guns that one next to me, on first being fired, burst apart in a sailor's hand and badly wounded him.

On the 17th, at midday on the high seas I saw a long, greenish band leading north and south. It was stationary and about half a league wide. The vessel passed it at its southern tip. There was no swell on the sea. I called the captain, who decided, as did his officers, that it was a shallow not marked on the map. We were level with the Azores.

On 20 May we saw an English vessel on its way to America: it told us we were at 23 degrees longitude, about 140 leagues further west than we expected. On the 22nd at 46 degrees 45 minutes north we thought we saw a reef over which the sea was breaking. As it was calm, we sent a boat off. It was a bank of foam formed by the tide beds. Two hours later we found a complete mast with its rigging. We thought it belonged to an English vessel, which had been forced by a storm to cut its masts. We hauled it aboard with pleasure for we lacked cooking wood, and worse, provisions. For the last week we had been having one meal every 24 hours. Our greatest privation was water; we tried to save it by cooking vegetables in salt water, but it was impossible to eat beans cooked that way; they were hard and bitter.

For several days the sky was covered at midday, so that we didn't know our latitude. On the 28th foul weather blew up. The vessel could only use its lower sails. At eleven in the morning we caught sight of a small ship in front of us. We steered towards it and passed it on its leeward. On its deck seven men were pumping with all their might, and water ran out of all the scuppers. We were rolling, hardly making headway, and a few times waves almost crashed over the rails. The master, in a red cap, shouted to us with a loud-hailer that he had left Bordeaux twenty-four hours earlier on his way to Ireland, and then tried to move away. We guessed that he was a smuggler, the custom being at sea as well as on land, to have a low opinion of untidy-looking people.

About one after midday, the wind died down; the clouds separated into two long ranges and the sun appeared. We set all the sails and placed sailors as lookouts on the main-top sail and kept the ship's head northeast to try and spy land before the evening.

At four we saw a small coastal lugger and asked questions it could not answer, as bad weather had forced it off its route. At five somebody shouted, "Land, land, to leeward!" We all ran to the deck. Some climbed the shrouds. We could clearly see some rocks on the horizon that seemed to turn white: we were told they were the Penmare rocks. At dawn we saw the coast some three leagues off, but nobody could recognize it. It was calm: we were burning with impatience to land. At last we saw a sloop; we hailed it and it answered us: it was a pilot. What joy to hear a French voice on the high seas! Everybody crowded to the side to watch the pilot climb aboard. "Good morning, friend," said the captain, "what land is that?' "It's Belle Isle, my friend," the old pilot answered. "Shall we have a breeze?" "If it pleases God, yes."

He had a large barley loaf with him that we ate greedily because it had been baked in France.

The calm lasted all day: towards evening the wind rose. The crew spent the night on deck; we put out our small sails. By morning we sailed along the Ile de Groix and reached anchorage. The custom officer, as is usual, climbed on board the vessel after which countless small fishing boats approached. We bought fresh fish and hurried to prepare our last meal, but we stood up, sat down, hardly ate, could not stop admiring the land of France.

I wanted to disembark with my luggage; in vain we called the sailors, but none answered. They had dressed in their best clothes, and were gripped by mute joy; they did not say a word, some were talking to themselves.

I decided to go my own way and entered the captain's cabin to say goodbye. We shook hands and he said to me, tears in his eyes, "I am writing to my mother." All around me I saw people in great emotion. I called a fisherman and climbed into his boat. Stepping on land, I thanked God for restoring me to a natural life.[127]

Letter 28[128]

On Voyagers and Voyages

It is the custom to seek, at the start of a book, to win the goodwill of the reader, who very often does not even read the preface. In my opinion it is far better to wait until the end when the reader is about to form his opinions. Then he will not be able to escape paying attention to the writer's excuses. Here are mine.

I have written this work to the best of my abilities; I have given everything I have to make it as good as possible. If it is poorly written, then it is not my fault. One should only be blamed for doing badly when one can do better.

If there are faults in my style, I would be grateful for my errors to be pointed out and I will correct them. During the ten years I have been absent from my country, I have forgotten how to speak French, and I have also noticed that it is often more useful to speak well than to think or even act well.[129]

My speculations and my ideas about nature are materials that I aim to use to build a vast edifice, but until I am able to carry this out I submit them here to criticism.[130] Good criticism is like a thaw that dissolves soft stones and hardens masonry blocks. I can add only one observation. It is said that a saint began a building with one quarry stone that ended up as a magnificent abbey. He carried out this miracle with time and patience, but I could have lost both.

I have talked about myself enough; let us pass on to more important matters.

It is remarkable that not one of our writers, so famous for their literature and philosophy, has published any travel book. We lack a model in such a fascinating genre, and we shall long lack one, for Messieurs Voltaire, d'Alembert, Buffon and Rousseau, have not written one. Montaigne and Montesquieu have written travel accounts, but did not publish them. It cannot be that they judged those countries in Europe through which they travelled sufficiently well-known, since they have made so many new observations about our own manners, with which we are quite familiar. I think that the travel genre, so little attempted, is packed with problems. You need universal knowledge, order in your plan, warmth in your style, and sincerity. You must speak about everything. If you skip some subjects, your work is imperfect; if all is said, it becomes diffuse, and interest wanes.

Yet we do have worthy travel writers. Addison seems to me to be outstanding, but unfortunately he is not French. Chardin[131] is philosophic but prolix; the Abbé de Choisy[132] saves his reader from the irritations of a sea-journey; he is always agreeable; Tournefort[133] describes learnedly the monuments and plants of Greece, but one would like to have seen a man with more feeling among the Grecian ruins; La Hontan speculates, and sometimes gets lost in the empty spaces of Canada; Léry paints the manners of the Brazilians and his own adventures in a very naive way.[134] From these different works you could compose one excellent one; but each one is limited: witness this sailor who wrote in his journal "that he had passed Tenerife by at a distance of four leagues, and whose inhabitants seemed very affable."

Some travellers have only one aim, namely to seek out monuments, statues, inscriptions, medals etc. If they meet some distinguished scholar, they ask him to sign his name and write a witty phrase in their album. Even if this habit is commendable, it would be better, it seems to me, to inquire into the characteristics of those people met, their probity, their virtues, their greatness of soul; one good example of this is worth any aphorism. If I had written my voyages around the north of Europe, you would have seen in my pages the names of d'Olgorouki, of Munich, the Palatine of Russia Czartorinski, Duval,[135] Taubenheim [136] etc. I would also have written about monuments, especially those that serve the public good, like the Berlin arsenal, the St. Petersburg academy etc. As for antiquities, I confess that they depress me. I see in a triumphal arch but proof of human weakness: the arch remains, and the conqueror has disappeared.

I prefer the tendril of a vine to a column; and I would have rather enriched my homeland with one nutritious plant than with Scipio's silver shield.[137]

The more familiar we become with the arts, the more nature appears foreign: we are even so artificial that we call natural objects *curiosities*, and seek the proof of Divinity in books. All we find in books (apart from Revelation) are vague reflections and general indications of universal order. However, to show an artist's intelligence, it is not enough to point to his work, it must be broken down. Nature offers such ingenious relations, such beneficent intentions, mute scenes that are so expressive and yet hardly noticed that whoever could present even a feeble picture of this to the least perceptive of persons would make him then cry out: "There is somebody here!"

The art of conveying nature is so new that the terms have not even been invented. Try to describe a mountain so as to make it recognizable: when you have talked about its base, its flanks and the summit, you have said it all. But what varieties in these curved, round, long, flat, hollowed-out forms etc.! You can only find roundabout phrases. The same goes for plains and valleys. But to describe a palace is not at all a problem. It is related to one or several of the five orders: it is subdivided into a sub-foundation, a main body, entablature; and, in each of its masses, from the plinth to the cornice there is not a single moulding that does not have a name.

It is not surprising, then, that travellers render natural objects so poorly. If they paint a country, you will see towns, rivers, mountains; but their descriptions are arid like geographical maps: India is no different to Europe. The peculiar characteristics are not there. If they mention a plant, they give precise details about its flowers, leaves, bark and roots; but the way it stands, its overall sense, its elegance, its hardiness or grace—that nobody can convey. Yet the likeness of an object depends on the harmony of its parts; you might have the measure of all the muscles on a man, but will still not have portrayed him.

If travellers, in writing about nature, fail by poverty of expression, they fail even more by excess of speculation. For a long time I believed, on the basis of the accounts I read, that wild man could survive in the forests. But in the forests of Mauritius I did not find one single edible fruit; and I tasted them all, even risking being poisoned. There were some seeds that were passably good in small amounts; in certain seasons you could not gather enough for a monkey's meal. There is only the dangerous onion from a kind of water lily, but this grows in mud under water, and it is unlikely that natural man would have found it there. I thought that man was better served at the Cape; I found shrubs covered with large, flesh-coloured artichokes, but they were of an unbearable bitterness. In French and German woods, all that is edible are the nuts of the beech and chestnuts; and these have a short season. We are told, it is true, that in the golden age of the Gauls, our ancestors lived off acorns; but the acorns of our oaks constipate us. We can only digest acorns from the green oak, which is very rare in France and only common in Italy, from where we get that tradition. A little natural history would serve to re-write the history of man.

In northern woods, we only find pine-cones, which squirrels devour, but it is unlikely that men could live from them. Nature has treated the king of animals badly, for the table is laid for all except him; fortunately, she has given him universal reason that makes use of everything, and sociability without which his strengths could not serve reason. From this one natural observation I can prove: 1) that the most stupid of peasants is superior to the most intelligent animal, which could not be taught to sow seed or work itself; 2) that man is born for society, without which he could not survive; 3) that society owes, in turn, a subsistence to all its members who can expect nothing outside of it.

Travellers fail even more by another excess: they nearly always situate happiness outside their own country. They give such agreeable descriptions of foreign countries that we spend all our life bad-tempered with our own.

If I dare say so, nature has its compensation for everything; I do not know which is better, a very hot climate or a very cold one. The latter is healthier; moreover, cold is a suffering that can be easily remedied while heat cannot be avoided. For six months I saw the white landscape of St. Petersburg; for six months I saw the black one of Mauritius; add the voracious insects, the cyclones that blow everything down, and choose. It is true that in the Indies trees never lose their leaves, that trees bear fruit without needing grafting, and that birds are more brightly coloured.

> But I prefer our nature
> Our fruits, our flowers, our greenness.
> A nightingale before a parrot,
> Feeling before gossip:
> And even more I prefer
> the scent of a rose and thyme
> to the amber that a Moor's hand
> collects on the shores at dawn.

One must also count the spectacle of an unhappy society as a great misfortune, for the sight of one single person in misery can poison happiness. Can one think without shivering that Africa, America and nearly all of Asia are under slavery? In India, people are forced into action with rattan whips, so much so that the stick has been called the *king of India*, the same in China, a country so praised, where most trivial punishments are inflicted physically. With us, laws are a little more respected by people. Moreover, however harsh our climate may be, the wildest nature can please me in some small corner. There are touching places even in the rocks of poor Finland. I have seen there more beautiful summers than those in the tropics, days without night, lakes so packed with swans, ducks, woodcocks, plovers etc. as if birds had left all other rivers to make their nests there. The sides of rocks are frequently covered with a shining, purple moss, and red carpets of kloueva[138] climb up the tall birch trees, whose green, supple leaves release scents and mingle with the sombre pyramids of the pine trees, offering shelter for lovers and philosophers. At the end of a little valley at the edge of the forest, far from envy, you can find the mansion of a good man whose mind is at rest, while you can hear the din of a torrent which your eyes can follow with joy as it falls and foams over the black ridge of rocks. It is true that in winter the greenery and the birds disappear. The wind, the snow, the frost and hail surround and shake the small house; but inside can be found hospitality. People come and visit from 15 leagues away and the arrival of a friend is a week-long party; the health of the guests, princes and their ladies is toasted and drunk to the music of horns and drums. The old men, around the fire, smoke and talk of ancient battles; the boys, in boots, dance to the melody of a fife or drum, around the young Finnish women in fur petticoats, who look like Pallas surrounded by Spartan youth.

If their modes and habits appear coarse, their hearts are sensitive. They talk of love, of giving pleasure, of France and especially Paris; for Paris is the capital of the world for all women. It is there that the women of Russia, Poland and Italy come to learn the art of ruling men with ribbons and laces; it is there that Parisian woman reigns, with wild good moods and graces always renewed. She watches the Englishman lay at her feet his gold and melancholy, while she, skilled in the arts, laughingly prepares a garland to bind all the people of Europe together in pleasure.

I prefer Paris to all other cities, not because of its feast days, but because the people are good, and you live in freedom. What do I care about its coaches, its grand houses, its din, its crowds, its gambling, its meals, its visits, its friendships, all so impetuous and vain? So many pleasures are superficial. Life should not be a spectacle. Only in the country can one enjoy genuine feelings, be oneself, with wife and children and friends. The country seems better to me than any town. The air is pure, the sights uplifting, walking is sweet, living is easy, customs are simple, and people are better. Passions develop without hurting anyone. He who loves freedom depends on nobody but heaven itself. The miser receives new presents all the time, the warrior gives himself up to hunting, the voluptuary satisfies himself with his garden and the philosopher can meditate without having to leave his home. Where can one find an animal more useful than the ox, nobler than the horse, and more lovable than the dog? Do we need to import from the Indies a more necessary plant than wheat and a more gracious one than the vine?

Of all landscapes I prefer that of my own country; not because it is beautiful, but because I was brought up there. In one's birthplace there is a hidden attraction, something indefinably moving, that no fortune could give you, and no other country supply. Where are the games we played when children, those days without end, without cares or bitterness? Trapping a bird overwhelmed me with joy. What greater pleasure than caressing a pheasant, feeling its beak peck at me, its heart throb in my hand and its feathers shiver! Happy the man who revisits the places where he was loved, where everything was pleasant, and the meadows he ran across, and the orchards he ransacked! Happier still he who had never left you, paternal roof, sacred retreat! Travellers return and find that their retreat has vanished, their friends dead and scattered, their family split up, without protectors... But life itself is but a short journey, and the age of man a fleeting day. I want to forget the storms, in order to recall the virtues and constancy of my friends. Perhaps these letters will preserve their names, and make them outlast my gratitude. Perhaps they will reach you, good Dutch people of the Cape. For you, unhappy black slave weeping on the rocks at Mauritius, if my hand, which cannot wipe away your tears, could at least make the tyrants regret and repent, then I would not ask any more of the Indies; I shall have made my fortune!

Paris, this 1 January 1773

NOTES

1   Fénelon, François de Salignac de la Motte (1651-1715), a theologian, writer and thinker, who ended up as the Archbishop of Cambrai. He wrote several treatises, including a *Dialogues sur l'éloquence* (1718), which argued for simplicity and for making more use of the Bible. He wrote on young girls' education, and published his *Explication des maximes des saints* in 1697. He hated despots, and predicted a Christian future based on brotherly love. He felt that a simple heart led to divine grace, an experiential sense of disinterested or ego-free love, strands of his thought developed by Bernardin de Saint-Pierre. Turenne, vicomte de, Henri de la Tour d'Auvergne (1611-1675), a French marshal-general, also a Protestant, who fought battles and skirmishes all his life and was particularly famous for his strategic intelligence. He was killed in action. His *Mémoires* were published in 1735. Henri IV (1553-1610), King of France from 1589 on. He was educated as a Protestant, became King of Navarre in 1571 after his mother's death, married in 1571, but soon after, following the 1572 St. Bartholomew massacre, was forced to become a Catholic. He then recanted, and later again converted to Catholicism. His was the famous phrase "Paris vaut bien une messe." Once he had assured his kingdom, Henri set about reforming the army, and ushered in an economic boom. He transformed Paris, including the great gallery at the Louvre. He was known as Henri le Grand, famous *inter alia* for his lover's antics. An extremely popular king with all his subjects, he was assassinated in Paris in 1610.

2   See Chaudenson, pp.29-34. I have severely edited this text for a reader of today's needs.

3   Maurice Souriau has detailed these court-cases. For example, Bernardin took his bookseller and publisher, Merlin, to court in 1773 concerning 600 *livres* owed to him and won his case, pp.148-149. Souriau also details the problem of pirate editions, pp.310-311.

4   In many ways, as Ngendahimana has argued, Bernardin wrote one long, ongoing work titled *Etudes de la nature* with *Paul et Virginie* and *La chaumière indienne* as volumes or appendices. As a genre, it could loosely be called an inter-connected essay.

5   Bénot claims that this is a reference to Frédéric-Melchior Grimm (1723-1807), a German-born friend of Diderot and rival to Rousseau, whose gossip was collected as *Correspondance littéraire*, 1812.

6   See Bernardin de Saint-Pierre, *Empsaël et Zoraïde ou les blancs esclaves des noirs à Maroc*, Présentation de Roger Little, University of Exeter Press: Exeter, 1995. Little calls it "antiesclavagiste", and argues that Bernardin sided with members of the abolitionist Société des Amis des Noirs but was the only one to have actually known blacks in Mauritius and Africa (pp.v-vi and pp.xvii-xxii). It was not published in Bernardin's lifetime, though he read it aloud at literary

evenings. The first edition was edited by Maurice Souriau in 1905, restoring the cuts made by Aimé-Martin in Bernardin's complete works.

7   According to Chaudenson's study of the Le Havre documents, what follows was prepared by Bernardin as an addition for his second edition.

8   Souriau misreads this passage (p.158); Bernardin would have used the journal form had he *re-written* his *Voyage*, but he had no intention of re-writing it, just adding to the first edition.

9   When Bernardin asked Mme. Poivre, the *intendant's* young wife he was trying to seduce while on Mauritius, to list his faults, she wrote and begged "a little less susceptibility." Souriau, p.104.

10   After Souriau quoted this passage, he remarked that Bernardin's second wife, "citoyenne Désirée Pelleporc", was 43 years younger than he when they married in Paris in 1806.

11   This landowner was Louis Laurent Faidherbe, Comte de Maudave (1725-1778). He arrived in Mauritius in 1763, and built up debts. Back in Paris, he agreed to colonize Madagascar, and reached Port Dauphin in 1768. His mission failed in 1770, with the loss of many lives. See Chaudenson, p.468. Before reaching Mauritius, Bernardin had decided to leave him.

12   Chaudenson also includes a long passage about Bernardin being left on shore by Maudave's party, and only just making his ship as it was leaving on the tide, as well as squabbles about cabins and rank. Bernardin finally got the tiny cabin his rank merited. These affronts were not taken lightly by the susceptible Bernardin.

13   Bernardin refers here, and many times elsewhere, to Pliny the Elder (AD23/24-AD79), prefect of the Roman Fleet, stationed at Misenum when Vesuvius erupted in AD79 and killed him. His sole surviving work is his famous *Historiae Naturalis*, in 37 books, a vast compendium of lore and fact about the natural world. Later, Buffon called his on-going work *Histoire naturelle* to honour Pliny.

14   From Homer's *The Odyssey*, Book XVII, in E.V. Rieu's Penguin translation: "All-seeing Zeus takes half the good out of a man on the day when he becomes a slave."

15   Lorient was built by the Compagnie des Indes Orientales in 1709, though the company had been there since 1666. It became an official town in 1738, hence Bernardin calling it a new town.

16   Bernardin included an "Avertissement", a detailed chart of the measurements of this 130-foot long ship, with an 85-foot high great mast in the first edition, as well as day-to-day nautical positions and meteorological observations. Chaudenson located the ship's log in the Archives Nationales in Mauritius, so that Bernardin's trip can be tracked (p.367).

17   This dog, a spaniel, was given to Bernardin by his sister; it was called Favori and accompanied him in Mauritius until it was stolen just before he left for

home. Bernardin wrote a satire about his dog entitled *Eloge de mon ami*, collected in volume XII of his *Oeuvres Complètes*, 1826.

18   King Juba II of Mauritania wrote an account of his expedition to the islands around 40BC, preserved by Plutarch and by Pliny. Juba married Cleopatra Selene, daughter of Mark Antony and Cleopatra. He was a Roman citizen and a prolific writer.

19   Bernardin included his sketches in the first edition of his travel account.

20   As noted in my introduction, Bernardin was well-travelled before he set off for Mauritius, and worked in St. Petersburg, Moscow, Warsaw and Berlin between 1760 and 1767 (and wrote about these places). The Danish island of Bornholm lies south-west in the Baltic Sea; in the Middle Ages it was an important trading post.

21   All that follows up to the section April 1768 was added to later editions, and included in the second edition of the anonymous English translation, as well as in Chaudenson.

22   Capt. James Cook (1728-1779) led the first modern scientific expedition on board the *Endeavour* in 1768, accompanied by a young Joseph Banks, to observe the transit of Venus from Tahiti for the Royal Society; he made two further voyages in 1772 and 1776 in the *Resolution* and was killed in Hawaii. His voyage overlaps with Bernardin de Saint-Pierre's and justifies the latter's plea about his trip not being scientific. Cook had his ghost-written *Account of a Voyage Round the World...* published in 1773, the same year as Bernardin's travel book.

23   This understated ritual is more vividly evoked in du B's earlier voyage of 1674, pp 29-31. An old sailor was dressed in a dressing gown, his face was dirtied, several bottles were tied to him, he held a map open and a cutlass; he made those crossing the line kneel, dripped some water from a silver cup on their heads and made them swear they would do the same to novices the next time they crossed the line. Sometimes they soaked those first-timers.

24   The *galère* is, of course, the Portuguese man-of-war (*Physalia*), an apt name as Portuguese ships were the first to take the route that Bernardin followed to Mauritius.

25   Barnacles, from the class *Cirripedia*.

26   The Latin name for the flying fish is *Excoetus volitans*; and there are over 100 species. They glide over the water and do not fly.

27   Bernardin refers to Pierre Chirac (c1650-1732), a doctor who while working for the Catalonian army cured an outbreak of dysentery. He later followed the Duc d'Orléans in Spain, became superintendant of the Jardin des Plantes, and doctor to Louis XV.

28   It is hard to know exactly which kind of tuna Bernardin is referring to, the Yellowfin Tuna (*Thunnus albacares*), the Skipjack Tuna (*Euthynnus pelamis*) or the Bluefin Tuna (*Thunnus thynnus*), all known in tropical seas.

29   This was the squabble between *Intendant* Poivre and Governor Desroches, as outlined in my introduction.

30   The cause of scurvy—a deficiency of Vitamin C—was not discovered until 1932, though Banks thought vitamin deficiency might be the cause during his trip with Cook. The British Navy issued lemon juice to its sailors from 1795, and then lime juice from 1865 (thus British sailors were known as limeys). Bougainville was forced to eat rats on his world journey and finding that none of his sailors developed scurvy thought that eating rats was the answer. Years later it was found that rats store vitamin C in their livers, unlike human beings who pass it out in their urine. Scurvy was the scourge of all long voyages. For an earlier, vivid description see, du B, *Les Voyages*, 1674. For the link between eighteenth-century theories of disease and scurvy on Cook's voyages see Christopher Lawrence in Miller & Reill, 1996, pp.80-106.

31   Charles Castel de Saint-Pierre, known as the Abbé (1658-1743), was at the Congress of Utrecht, and as a reformist, was elected into the Académie Française in 1695 but was ejected for being too critical of Louis XIV. His work includes *Project de paix perpétuelle* (1713), suggesting a supranational tribunal, forerunner of the United Nations, and a *Perfeccionement de l'éducation* that Bernardin refers to.

32   Confirmed by Robert Graves, in his *The Greek Myths*, vol. 2, p.300, where Palamedes, before being betrayed and stoned outside Troy, invented dice, as well as scales, measures, the alphabet etc.; his name meant "ancient intelligence".

33   I have omitted the technical details in Letter 5, but not what Bernardin wanted to add in the second edition about his arrival on the island, following Chaudenson.

34   Spelt van Neck in Barnwell, pp.7-10.

35   See Robert Barnes, "New Light on a 400 Year Old Mystery", in Evers and Hookoomsing, pp.31-50.

36   Le Pouce, meaning the thumb, stands at 811 metres, not quite the highest mountain on the island (the Piton de la Petite Rivière Noire stands at 828 metres). Charles Darwin climbed it on 2 May 1836 on his way home, when he stayed in Mauritius between 29 April and 9 May (see Darwin, 1845, pp.484-485). It was on the Pouce that Labourdonnais wanted to build an impregnable citadel; on its western slope Bernardin placed the huts of Paul and Virginie. See Toussaint, 1936, p.23. Today it is the Pouce Nature Reserve.

37   A *toise* is an archaic measurement of six feet. L'Abbé Nicolas Louis de la Caille, (1713-1762), was not a priest but an astronomer, who was allowed to wear priests' cassocks. He left France in 1750 and stayed two months in Mauritius from July 1753. He made a complete triangulation of Mauritius, which led to Bellini's map of 1763. Caille published his factual *Journal historique du voyage fait au Cap de Bonne Espérance*, 1763. See Nagapen, also Hollingworth, pp.21-

27.

38 Named after a Dutch governor-general from the Dutch East Indies whose ship was wrecked on the reefs at Mauritius on his way back home to Holland during a storm, and who drowned at sea in the Baie du Tombeau in 1615. See Toussaint, 1936, p.5. This distinctive mountain, 823 metres high, was first climbed in 1790 by Claude Peuthe.

39 *Tournefortia argentea*. Milbert complained that such a "sad" tree (though why he called it sad defeats me) should not have been named after the great French botanist and traveller Joseph Pitton de Tournefort (1656-1708), author of a *Voyage au Levant* (1717). Tournefort also created a now dated classification scheme.

40 Bois de natte (*Mimusops angustifolia*), illustrated in *The Medicinal Plants of Mauritius, Reproduced from the Original Water-Colours by Malcy de Chazal, 1803-1880.* The Schoolhouse Gallery: Abbey St. Bathans, 1989, p.116.

41 The bois d'olive (*Elaeodendron orientale*, renamed today *Pleurostylia leucocarpa*) is a native of the Mascarenas Islands, with red wood, and leaves and bark whose medicinal properties can cause violent reactions.

42 Milbert (vol. 2, p.125) repeats Bernardin's description, giving its Latin name, *Calophyllum coloba*, an indigenous tree.

43 The vacoa has given its name to a town, the most Indian in Mauritius, up on the plain. Buffon called this tree, perched on its exposed roots, the "indecent tree" because the roots looked like the natural parts of man (i.e. his penis). See Sonnerat, p.271.

44 The latan palm, or *latanier* in French (*Latania lontaroides/borbonica/loddigesti*) is native to Mauritius, the Île Ronde and Réunion. It was at the source of the Lataniers river that Paul and Virginie were brought up in shacks made from latan leaves.

45 The *coeur de palmiste* is a delicacy today in Mauritian cuisine. Also known as "chou", its Latin tag is *Dictyosperma album*. In *Paul et Virginie* we read how this jungle food sustains the two children when lost: "The cabbage contained inside the top of this tree, amongst its leaves, is very tasty to eat." Paul has to burn the palm-tree down; then they eat this white ambrosia raw and cooked, both equally "delicious" (pp.35-7).

46 The Mauritian government today is re-planting mangroves along the coast to prevent erosion.

47 In Latin *Calidium esculentum*, an edible species of water plant. A variety is the *brède songe* (*Colocasia antiguoram*), which like *brède martin* (*Solanum nigrum*) and *brède cresson*, common watercress, is eaten in soups and as an accompaniment to local Mauritian curries and other dishes.

48 In 1709 de la Merveille saw more than 4,000 monkeys attack a sweet potato field. Barnwell quotes from Hebert, 1708, p.132, on the Dutch who were "tormented by monkeys, who uproot all they sow and eat the crops." The

Mauritian monkey, *Macaca fascicularis*, is a crab-eating macaque from Indonesia, probably introduced by the Portuguese. Quammen calls it "skinny and smart", p.269.

49   According to Pridham, 830,000 rats were caught and destroyed in 1826 (p. 373). Earlier, de la Merveille wrote that "an infinite multitude of monkeys and rats destroyed everything" (Barnwell, p.123). Ducros in 1725 wrote: "This island might be called the kingdom of the rats" (Barnwell, p.143) and adds: "I have seen them myself, at nightfall, swarm out of the earth as numerous as ants, and spread desolation everywhere... You wrap yourself up like a corpse, and try to grow accustomed to feeling them running, jumping and fighting upon you."

50   The Mauritian *pigeon hollandais* (*Alectroenas nitidissima* [Scopoli]) became extinct in about 1830. See Hachisuka, pp.176-178.

51   Chaudenson identifies this "mangeur de poules" as *Circus maillardis*, a disappearing species.

52   These are termites.

53   Plutarch, or Plutarchus, was an immensely popular Greek writer-philosopher and tutor in Rome, born c.AD 46 and dying around AD119. He was famous for his biographies of Romans and Greeks known as *Parallel Lives* and for his moral treatises known as *Moralia*, with essays on subjects as diverse as friendship, exile, listening to poetry, conjugal love and eating flesh. Plutarch was a great influence on Montaigne, and, through Sir Thomas North's 1579 translation, on Shakespeare. Bernardin brought his volumes of Plutarch to Mauritius with him.

54   Rodrigues, a dependency of Mauritius, is a small volcanic island some 563 km east, about 18 km by 8 km, with a coral reef and roughly 35,000 inhabitants today. Named after its discoverer, Diego Rodríguez, in 1528, it was where Leguat tried to set up his utopia. The British occupied the island in 1809 as a base from which to take Mauritius in 1810. J.M.G Le Clézio wrote a novel, *Le Chercheur d'or* (1985) and a travel book, *Voyage à Rodrigues* (1986) about his grandfather and lost treasure in Rodrigues.

55   Literal translation, "monk's prick".

56   D'Argenville wrote a *Histoire naturelle éclaircie dans une de ses parties principales la Conchyliologie*, Paris, 1752, which Bernardin followed closely, according to Chaudenson.

57   I have translated the French *porcelaine* as cowrie. Professor Malcolm Cook published a description of the *porcelaine* found at the back of the manuscript of Bernardin's *Voyage* where Bernardin links the cowrie to the sea-shell Venus was born from and which "resembles that part of a woman's body that decency does not let me name" (p.854). Bernardin adds a bit about its mouth, its living flesh and a clitoris, then links this shell to the general property of sea-shells to "incite to making love", once prohibited by Rome, ending on his admiration

for nature's "games" and "power" that had created life itself. A fascinating glimpse into Bernardin's self-censorship. See Malcolm Cook, "Bougainville and One Noble Savage: Two Manuscript Texts of Bernardin de Saint-Pierre", *The Modern Language Review*, October 1994, pp.842-855.

58 Ile d'Ambre is one of the northern offshore islands, where the survivors of the *St Géran* wreck climbed ashore in 1744.

59 In the dialogue between a Traveller and a Lady (which I have omitted from this edition), Bernardin develops this critique of nature as a *machine*, based on the Cartesian/Newtonian model of nature as a well-oiled machine, within a "vast celestial contrivance", with God as the supreme engineer. Thus, a perfectly rational but static and determined world can be understood by whoever applies reason. This God-ordained, well-designed world was popularized in Britain by Bishop Paley in 1806. Such a pre-Darwinian world was shared by Bernardin, though his feelings prompted him to invent a more vital theory of matter as living Republics, close to how cells would later be seen. Bernardin develops Rousseau's discriminations about nature as a machine. Rousseau: "I see in all animals only an ingenious machine to which nature has given senses in order to keep itself in motion." But free-will makes man different: "Man receives the same impulsion, but he recognizes himself as being free to acquiesce or resist; and it is above all in this consciousness of his freedom that the spirituality of his soul reveals itself." In *A Discourse on Inequality*, pp.87-88.

 Bernardin writes of his plant-dwellers in the dawn of the microscope age, which revealed a new, unclassifiable world of "animalcules", made popular by Louis Joblot in 1718. See Barbara M. Stafford, "Images of Ambiguity: eighteenth-century Microscopy and the neither/nor", in Miller and Reill, 1996, pp.230-257.

60 Bernardin's experience of a cyclone entered *Paul et Virginie* twice; once, up in the hillside a storm devastates their garden, uproots all the trees except for the two "cocotiers", and terrifies all of them, although Paul, like the man cited by Bernardin in Port Louis, goes about propping up walls. The second time, the cyclone smashes the *St Géran* and Virginie drowns.

61 Bertrand François Mahé, Comte de La Bourdonnais. See my introduction.

62 The French East Indian Company (Compagnie des Indes), founded in 1664, ran Mauritius from 1725 to 1767, the year before Bernardin de Saint Pierre sailed out. The company was abolished in 1769. It appointed governors like La Bourdonnais. From 1767 to 1790 the island became a crown colony, with a royal governor and an *intendant*.

63 Banian, or Banyan, comes from the Gujarati for a man from the trading caste and not to the banian or Indian fig tree (*Ficus benghalensis*) associated with the Buddha and very common in Mauritius today.

64 Bernardin transfers this view to *Paul et Virginie*, where all references to Port

Louis are negative and critical. Up in their hillside nest there is no envy, no social ambition, no torments over reputation, no libraries, no philosophers. In town "one is only curious about malicious anecdotes" (p.49). The novel is an elegy to living in solitude, away from "le malheur social", money and moral corruption.

65 Steinhauer was temporary governor of Mauritius from 1768 to 1769, and later governor of Réunion, following the squabble between Governor Jean Daniel Dumas and *Intendant* Poivre, each one accusing the other, one of embezzlement, the other of absolute incapacity, and both famous for being "touchy", according to Sornay (pp.43-44). Finally Dumas was relieved of his post, and Steinhauer stood in until M. le Chevalier Desroches arrived in 1769.

66 Charles Henri Nassau-Siegen (1745-1805) travelled with Bougainville around the world, fought for Spain and Russia, became an admiral and destroyed the Turkish fleet in 1788.

67 René Magon was governor of Mauritius from 1756 to 1759, built the church at Pamplemousses, introduced cattle from Madagascar, cut down too much of the forests and squabbled with the East Indian Company. He is buried at Pamplemousses. See Sornay, p.41.

68 On Poivre, see my introduction.

69 Pondicherry was the centre of French India and headquarters of the Compagnie des Indes Orientales which ran Mauritius as a staging post between Pondicherry and France. Founded in 1673, it was occupied by the English in 1778, was returned to France in 1816 and finally became part of India in 1954. The Malabar coast was the west coast of India. After the Seven Years War, France had to give up its Indian colonies, and Mauritius became a French crown colony in 1767. The "malabars" were mostly Roman Catholic. In 1806 they numbered some 1,615. The Muslim slaves and freemen, who also lived in the Camp des Malabars in Port Louis and were called "Lascards", were often sailors and numbered some 200 in 1806. See Abdool Cader Kalla in Evers and Hookoomsing, 2001, pp.158-159.

70 On the *Code Noir*, see my introduction.

71 De Cossigny (1690-1780), a royal engineer, was sent out to Mauritius to report on which of the two main harbours should be developed and fortified. He arrived in June 1732, and decided that Port Louis was the better of the two ports. He made many enemies, could not get his work started, and was ordered to leave in 1735. Back again in 1736, he built warehouses, and planned defences. His third visit lasted from 1753 to 1757. According to Hollingworth, he "perfected quarrelling to a fine art" (p.13). His son, Charpentier de Cossigny, born in Mauritius, was appointed the island's governor for two years from 1790 during the revolutionary period. Hermans set up a forge, and exploited veins of iron ore at Pamplemousses in the 1750s. François Etienne Le Juge arrived as the Councillor to the Conseil Supérieur,

lived in Pamplemousses and imported several trees, having planted over 800 by 1763. For more on Poivre, see my introduction.

72   This aphorism is carved into the side of the white marble obelisk, known as the Colonne Liénard and donated by Liénard in 1860, which stands in the Botanical Gardens at Pamplemousses.

73   Marcus Terentius Varro (116-27 BC), known as the wisest of the Latin writers, was also a great scholar and prolific writer whose *Res rusticae* has survived in the form of a dialogue about practical matters in country life. Varro also wrote Menippean satire, treatises on law, astronomy, history, grammar etc.

74   Bernardin possibly refers to Gnaeus Pompeius Magnus (106-48BC), Pompey the Great, about whom Plutarch wrote a biography, *Pompey*.

75   "Cold" as used here is one of the ways of describing the property of matter (dry, moist, hot) and suggests indifference and apathy. Cossigny *fils* called the pineapple "the one-eyed king of blind fruits, which tears the stomach and gives you indigestion into the bargain, unless you are a creole, an ostrich or a *trompette de cuirassiers*." Cited in Barnwell, p.134. According to historian Keith Thomas, the pineapple was the most highly esteemed fruit in England at the start of the eighteenth century because it was so expensive and difficult to grow.

76   Again, Milbert (vol. 2, p.123) simply repeats Bernardin's description, calling it the shoemaker's flower, *hibiscus rosasinensis*.

77   The red jasmine tree (*Plumiera rubra*).

78   Within ten years of the arrival of French settlers (1735), there were some sixty sugar estates. By 1779 John Buncle noted: "There is much sugar-cane upon the island. They make some rum of a very indifferent quality..." De la Merville wrote earlier in 1709: "We saw the press-house where they make what is called in Mauritius cane-wine and elsewhere frangourin, a whitish liquor strong and sweet." In Barnwell, pp.134, 125 and 172.

79   Mocha, a port in Yemen, from where this coffee comes. Bernardin refers to *Coffea arabica*.

80   *Fêtes bananes*: C. Thomi Pitot, a fierce Mauritian critic of Bernardin, accused him of mishearing "bonne année" for "banane" (p.166) and using this to attack the slave-owners. See my introduction on Pitot.

81   In Latin, *Carica papaya*, a Carib word, transplanted to Mauritius from the Americas.

82   *Terminalia edulis*.

83   John Parish, the first English translator, adds a note in the 1800 edition: "This may be considered as a promise of what has been since so very ably performed by our author in his masterly *Studies of Nature* which... has no parallel among the French writers of the present century, posterior to the days, at least, of the good Fénelon, and the romantic Citizen of Geneva." (p.143). He refers to Bernardin's *Etudes de la Nature*, 1784, and in the last line, to Rousseau.

84   Bernardin left this last passage in Latin: *mulieris corporis bifurcationem cum natura et pilis repesentat,* but added his own footnotes: "Which means more or less that this coconut resembles a natural woman. Why is the French language more reserved than Latin? Are we more chaste than the Romans?" This double *coco de mer* is a palm (*Lodoicea maldivica*). For years it was thought to come from an underwater tree, until in 1743 the palm was found growing in the Seychelles.

85   Sago, a Malayan word, is a starch extracted from the pith of several palms, including the *Metroxylon rumphii.*

86   Milbert claimed that the mangosteen (*Garcinia mangostana*) was brought to Mauritius from India in 1754 and again in 1770.

87   "According to Ammien Marcellin, it was Lucullus who brought the first cherry tree to Rome from Cerasonte," M.-N. Bouillet, *Dictionnaire d'histoire et de geographie,* Hachette: Paris 1871, p.1133.

88   The martin (*Acridotheres tristis*) is not a native of Mauritius, but of India.

89   Bernardin gave his reader detailed measurements of the cave, which I have omitted.

90   This scene was transposed into the later *Paul et Virginie* when the two children, lost in the forest, find some "cabbage" to eat (palm heart) and need to make a fire to burn down the palm-tree. Bernardin wrote: "Necessity leads to industry, and often the most useful inventions come from the most wretched people. Paul decided to light a fire the negro way." (p.36) He places a bit of wood into a hole in a branch and turns it fast in his hands until the friction creates sparks. Another debt to the black slaves?

91   The highest of the Trois Mamelles is La Montagne du Rempart at 545 metres. Palma lies on the road from Flic en Flac to Quatre Bornes.

92   The Corps de Garde mountain reaches 720 metres and is today a nature reserve.

93   Côte means "hill", i.e. small. Côte became a source of information for Bernardin: "I accustomed Côte to speak to me with the greatest frankness." See Chaudenson, p.240. The naming of slaves, rather than the using of their real names, was part of the humiliation attached to the system, from which Bernardin was not free. Anthony Barker lists some of the names used in the 1820s in Mauritius; these run from Rousseau to Beaux Yeux, Dodo and Loco. Every member of a kitchen workforce on a plantation was named after a vegetable: Salade, Asperge, Oignon etc. Barker, pp.56-57.

94   Guillaume de Séligny (1727-1797), in charge of military defences near his plantation at Petite Rivière.

95   The Morne Brabant is one of Mauritius' most visible landmarks and is inscribed with legends. In 1772, for example, a ship was wrecked on the reefs; in 1835, when slavery was finally abolished, some slaves supposedly threw themselves off its summit thinking they were being chased as maroons. It has

long been associated with runaway slaves, a real danger in Bernardin's time, as he noted. Today it has a long public beach and some of the island's most luxurious hotels. Malcolm de Chazal called the Morne a "mountain-fairy". Professor Vinesh Hookoomsing, in an unpublished paper, has examined the legend about the maroon slaves on the rock mentioned by Bernardin, who creatively added to it as "an oral narrative in an endless amplification".

96 This is still named the Baie du Jacotet, and the island is Îlot Sancho.

97 This became Souillac Harbour, used to load sugar on barges to be taken to Port Louis before trains, and now lorries, did it. It remains a pretty fishing-port. De Souillac was governor from 1779-1787.

98 Stags (*Cervus timorensis*) were introduced by the Dutch in 1639 from Batavia, Indonesia. They are hunted during the winter; the meat has been essential for the island.

99 This is the beautiful area known as Blue Bay.

100 The River Créole now passes through the town of Mahébourg.

101 The unnamed island is the Île de la Passe, with a ruined lighthouse and fort. The nearby Île aux Fouquets has a disused lighthouse, now a national monument. The Pointe du Diable had a battery from 1750 to 1780 to prevent ships entering. The Dutch settled here in 1589. It was in this bay that the French defeated the English in a sea-battle in 1810. For a contemporary version, see the "anonymous officer's" account in my bibliography.

102 This was Bernardin's mistaken pet-idea. See my introduction, note 112.

103 The *piastre* was Spanish and in 1771 one *piastre* was worth six *livres*. It was translated into English as a dollar. The money circulating on the island was the result of so many ships of different nationalities passing through and paying for goods of all sorts mainly with silver *piastres*. Only after the English conquered was uniformity imposed with the pound sterling, minted in Britain, adopted in 1860. In 1875 the Indian rupee became the official currency. See de Sornay, 1950, pp.299-304.

104 Literally, horses from Friesland, a kind of barbed wire first used in 1688 to stop cavalry charges.

105 There was some urgency in Bernardin's plan as England had her eye on the island as a post on the way to India. In December 1810 the English finally landed on shore near Cap Malheureux, opposite the Coin de Mire island, and easily marched past Grande Baie on to Port Louis, which they took.

106 Seneca the Younger, Lucius Annaeus (c.4BC-AD65) was born in Córdoba, Spain, and became tutor to Nero, who turned against him and ordered him to commit suicide. Seneca was a stoic, who wrote against tyranny and was famous for his *Epistulae morales* and several tragedies.

107 Volume Two opens with Letter 19.

108 Autourou was a Tahitian brought back to Europe by Louis-Antoine de Bougainville after his two-year round-the-world voyage. Autourou was

presented to the King and his court at Versailles, and met philosopher-friends of Bougainville like d'Alembert, Helvétius, Buffon etc. He passed through Mauritius in 1769 while Bernardin was there. In 1770 Bougainville sent Autourou home via his friend, *Intendant* Poivre in Mauritius, where he arrived in October 1770, where Bernardin saw him again, and where he stayed a year until October 1771. He caught smallpox and died at sea off Madagascar. He was woman-mad, and called Mauritius "Enora erao piri piri", which meant "country miserly with cunts". See Rennie, 1995, pp.109-140.

109   This protected valley was recreated as the place where the untouchable and his wife lived in Bernardin's *La chaumière indienne*. See appendix.

110   This was Ryk Tulbach, governor of the Cape from 1751 to 1772. See Bénot, 1983.

111   Captain Cook: "The Constantia wine which is made here is excellent, but the genuine sort is made only at one particular vineyard a few miles from the town" (p.111). Nicholas Pike, in 1873, continued to praise this wine: "The lovely village of Constantia lies in this neighbourhood, famous for its delicious Constantia and Pontac wines, which, to be thoroughly appreciated, should be drunk on the spot" (p.47).

112   Baucis and Philemon were a happy old peasant couple who put up and fed Jupiter and Mercury, disguised as travellers, when nobody else would. Jupiter created a flood and saved the couple, who became priests of the temple that was once their cottage. They died together and became two trees, as told by Ovid in book VIII of his *Metamorphoses*.

113   Another example of Bernardin's invented taxonomy, based on visual analogies between parts of flowers and animals, which he would develop later in his *Etudes de la nature*.

114   Vasco da Gama, the Portuguese sailor, continued the journey carried out by Bartolomeu Dias, the first to reach the Cape in 1488. Da Gama left Lisbon with four boats on 8 July 1497, reached the Cape on 20 March 1498, and went on to India, to return on 9 September 1498. He returned to India in 1502-1503 and died in Cochin in 1524, having just being made Viceroy of India. Camões (1524-1580), who also sailed to India, turned Gama's life into the epic of Portuguese literature, *Os Lusiadas* (1572).

115   How did Bernardin see this New Guinean flightless bird at the Cape? Is he mistaken in the name?

116   Linnaeus was the Latin version of Carl von Linné, a Swedish botanist and doctor, born in 1707, who revolutionized taxonomy with his binomial system. In 1735, in Latin, he published his *Systema naturae*, and in 1737 his *Genera plantorum*. He died in 1778. See my introduction.

117   In a later note Bernardin retracted this comment: "It was doubtless a European prejudice and Montesquieu's opinion that led me to place us above other nations. I said that we had more spirit and courage than the Asians and Blacks,

and I was completely wrong. To begin with spirit, it is a fact that our religion, our laws, our arts, our industry come originally from Asian people, to whom we owe everything. As for the Blacks, there is a kind of ferocity that comes from their government. As for courage, which country does not have its heroes? If the Asians have been wise enough not to attempt conquests, look at the intrepidity of the Turks and the Persians. Look at the history of China. So it is not climate but government that shapes human beings and it is education that prepares them..." See Chaudenson, p.282.

[118] Guillaume Delisle (1675-1726), Geographer to King Louis XV, published many maps, based on the latest astronomic and travellers' observations.

[119] Peter Kolb or Kolben, *The Present State of the Cape of Good Hope*, 1719 in Germany; translated into English in 1731 and French in 1741. See Pratt, 1992, chapter 3. Hottentot was a generic name for a group of nomadic pastoralists, today called the Khoikhoi. Mary Louise Pratt has analysed how these Khoikhoi have been represented by selected travel writers to the Cape and comments in a footnote on the "endless, usually pornographic discussion of an 'extra' genital part", the apron. Stephen Jay Gould has written on this *sinus pudoris*, or "apron", in relation to Cuvier's dissection in 1817 in Paris of the "Hottentot Venus": "Cuvier resolved the debate with his usual elegance: the *labia minora*, or inner lips, of the ordinary female genitalia are greatly enlarged in Khoi-San women, and may hang down three or four inches below the vagina when women stand..." See *The Flamingo's Smile: Reflections in Natural History*, Penguin: Harmondsworth, 1986.

[120] Antiope, Queen of the Amazons; Idomeneus, the good-looking Homeric hero, wise King of Crete, who survived the sack of Troy.

[121] These French were descendants of the 200 Huguenot refugees who landed at the Cape in 1687 from Holland, founded Cape viniculture, and inter-married. The French would later occupy the Cape for a few years from 1781-1784.

[122] See note 37 for details on the Abbé de la Caille.

[123] John Parish, the first translator, adds a footnote: "The late Dr. Goldsmith is said frequently to have spoke of this chapter as a master-piece of good sense and well directed attention and sensibility," (p.262).

[124] Robben Island was turned into a prison in 1657. Nelson Mandela was imprisoned there from 1964 to 1982.

[125] Bernardin met and worked with Catherine the Great of Russia (see my introduction). John Parish wrote: "The reader will please to recollect that the text was written when this celebrated Empress was in the zenith of her power and popularity" (p.285).

[126] Philoctetes, the archer who inherited Heracles' bow, was bitten by a snake and the smell from the wound was so offensive that he was abandoned on Lesbos. Later cured, he challenged Paris at Troy and won.

[127] This letter then contains an "Explanation of some marine terms for readers

who are not sailors" in the form of an alphabetical list. See Chaudenson, pp.317-326.

128 I omitted here a long philosophical dialogue about nature and Providence between a Traveller and a Lady as too dated, even too ridiculous to include. To give the curious reader a short sample of this dialogue, I cite the opening:

Lady:

You have given me some very curious things. What do you call those pretty stone trees with roots, stems and masses of leaves, and even peach-coloured flowers? If they were green, you could have taken them for plants from one of our gardens.

Traveller:

Madame, they are madrepores. Nothing is more common in the seas of the Indies. Nearly all the islands are surrounded by them. They grow under water and form forests covering several leagues. You can see fish of all colours swimming there, as birds fly about in our woods.

Lady:

That must be a charming sight. Have you brought fruits from those trees?

Traveller:

These plants do not bear fruit. They are not from the vegetable world but are the work of small animals working together in a society.

Lady:

I would never have guessed.

Traveller:

There is something even more marvellous. In my madrepores you can see shrubs that have veritable leaves and whose branches are flexible like wood: these are lithophytes. These lithophytes and corals are equally the work of little animals.

Lady:

But what proof have you?

Traveller:

You can see them under a microscope. Chemistry has conducted some experiments with them, which are still uncertain because chemistry can only reason about what it destroys. In fact, the conclusion is that such regular works must belong to beings gifted with an orderly mind and intelligence. After all, small shrubs are not harder to make than the hexagonal wax cells fashioned by bees. This has long been in dispute, but now everybody agrees.

Lady:

If everybody says so, one must believe it. I do not want to be the only person opposing all this.

Traveller:

Ah, if I dared, I could show you something even more difficult to believe.

129   Bernardin was out of France from 1760 to 1770. See my introduction.

130   Bernardin kept to his word and published his *Etudes de la nature* in 1784 in three volumes, with the fourth in 1787 being his *Paul et Virginie.*

131   J. Chardin, 1643-1713, travelled to Persia in 1670-71, then, due to persecution of Protestants, moved to London where he died. He published his *Voyage en Perse* in 1686.

132   The Abbé de Choisy, 1644-1724, moved in scandalous circles until he was about thirty, dressed as a nun and was known as *la comtesse de Barres.* Then he was sent as a missionary to Siam, where the King of Siam made him a priest. He wrote a *Journal du Voyage de Siam* (1687).

133   See note 39. Tournefort was given the chair of medicine at the Collège de France, and travelled widely around Europe and then to Constantinople. He published his *Voyage du Levant* in 1717.

134   Jean de Léry, *Histoire d'un voyage faict en la terre du Brésil* (1578). Claude Lévi-Strauss wrote on him in *Tristes tropiques,* 1955.

135   Louis Duval, a Genevan jeweller to the court of Catherine II, became a great friend. He lent Bernardin money when he was broke in Russia in 1765. Bernardin named his slave Duval after his friend; see Souriau, p.32.

136   Taubenheim was another devoted friend, a retired officer who looked after Bernardin in Berlin when he was depressed. See Souriau, pp.67-75.

137   Not in fact a shield, but an embossed silver plate 72 centimetres in diameter and weighing 10,300 grams, on view in Paris.

138   Bernardin's footnote: a creeper of a beautiful green, with leaves resembling the box tree. It produces a small red fruit that relieves scurvy.

Appendix: La chaumière indienne

Foreword

Here is a short Indian tale that contains more truths than many stories.[1] I had intended to add it to my travel book on Mauritius, published in 1773 and which I will reprint with additions. As I spoke of Indians from that island, I had wanted to link them with a picture of customs from India from some rather interesting notes that I had taken. I had thus created an episode tied to a historical anecdote that became the opening section. It was to do with a company of learned Englishmen sent, some thirty years ago, to different parts of the world to find enlightenment on several scientific matters. I speak of one of them who went to India to compete in this progress towards truth. But as this episode turned into a work in its own right, I decided to publish it separately.

I can assure you here that I had no intention of casting ridicule on the learned societies of Europe, although I have plenty to complain about, not in relation to any individual but to the interests of truth which they often persecute when it contradicts their systems.[2] I am also too indebted to several learned Englishmen who, without knowing me and solely through their love for science, have honoured my *Etudes de la nature* with glorious praise. The character I have drawn of one of their colleagues is unequivocal proof of my high esteem for them. Certainly I have come to see the importing of understanding from foreign countries, as much as the exporting of it from England to wild places through the travels of Cook and Banks, as a step forward which deserves the whole world's respect for that country. Denmark and then France have imitated England, but in unfortunate ways, since only one of the dozen Danish learned travellers returned home and there has been no news from two French warships employed on this human mission and captained by the unlucky La Pérouse.[3]

I intended an even more useful end: to remedy the ills afflicting humanity in India. My motto is to help the wretched and I extend this sentiment to all people. If in the olden days, philosophy came from India to Europe, why cannot it revert from civilized Europe to India, sunk again in barbarism. A society of learned Englishmen has just been formed in Calcutta, which one day will root out prejudices in India. This good deed would compensate for the evils that European trade and wars have brought with them. As for myself, who have no influence, I have tried to dress this up as a story in order to make it more graceful and agreeable. It is through stories that you can make people attentive to truth.

> We are all Athenians on this point, even myself
> at the moment that I create this moral tale.
> If a fairy-tale was told to me,
> it would give me a very great pleasure.

La Fontaine, book viii, fab. 4. [4]

It is said, with more wit than reason, that the fable was born in the despotic countries of the West, and that truth had been veiled so that tyrants might read it. But I wonder whether a sultan would not be more offended to see himself painted in the emblem of a screech owl or a leopard, than as himself; and if the reflected truths would not wound him as much as direct ones? Thomas Roe, English ambassador to Selim-Shah, the Mogul emperor, recounted that this very despotic prince had chests, arrived from England, opened for him in order to see what presents he had been sent, and was utterly surprised to find a painting representing a Satyr being led by the nose by a Venus. "He imagined," he said, "that the painting was made to mock Asian people who were represented by the black, horned Satyr, being of the same complexion; and that the Venus pulling the Satyr by the nose was the enormous power that women have there over men."[5]

Thomas Roe, to whom the painting was sent, had great difficulty in destroying its effect in the Mogul's mind. He recommended to the directors of the East Indian Company in England that they never again send any allegorical picture to India because the princes there, he said, are very suspicious. It is in the nature of despots. I do not think that fables have been invented for them anywhere, unless to flatter them.

In general, a taste for fables is scattered around the world, but more so in free countries than in those ruled by despots. Savage people found their traditions on fables: in no country have they been more popular than in Greece where everything in nature, politics and religion is but the result of certain metamorphoses. There is no famous family that does not have some animal among its ancestors, and that does not count among its cousins some bulls, swans, nightingales, doves, crows or magpies. You may notice that the English, in their literature, have a special taste for allegory, although truth can be stated freely among them. Asians were in the same situation in Aesop's and Lokman's times,[6] but today we can no longer find fabulists, although their countries are full of sultans.

The people closest to nature, and thus the most free, are those who love to embellish. It is due to a love for truth, which is how nature's laws are felt. Truth is the light of the soul, as physical light is the body's truth. Both linked together give us the knowledge of what is: the former clarifies objects, the latter shows us their uses, and as at the beginning all light derives from the sun, so all truth derives from God, whose sensuous image the sun is. Few can withstand the sun's pure light. It is because of the weakness of our eyes that nature gave us eyelids, to open them to whatever degree suits us; for the same reason nature planted forests, whose green leaves give sweet and transparent shade; and nature spreads mists and clouds into the skies to soften the sun's over-powerful rays. Few people can seize the purely metaphysical truths. It is because of the weakness of our intelligence that nature made ignorance the eyelids of our souls; that is the way the soul opens by degrees to the truth, that it admits solely the truth it can bear, that it surrounds itself with fables which are so many arbours in whose shade it can contemplate nature. When it wishes to raise itself to Divinity itself, nature veils it with allegories and mysteries to withstand the glare.

We would not see the sunlight if it did not rest on bodies, or at least on clouds. It escapes beyond out atmosphere, it dazzles us at its source. The same goes for truth; we would not grasp it if it did not fix itself on sensuous events or at least on metaphors and comparisons which reflect it. It needs a body that reflects it back. Our understanding cannot grasp purely metaphysical truths; it is dazzled by those that emanate from what is divine, and can only grasp those that rest on its works. It is for this reason that the language of civilized countries cannot paint anything, because it is full of vague ideas and abstractions, while that of simple and natural people is very expressive, because it is full of similarities and images. The former are used to hiding their feelings; the latter extend them out. But often clouds, dispersed into a thousand fantastic shapes, break down the sun's rays into richer hues, more varied than those which colour nature's usual works; thus fables reflect a wider truth than that of real events. Fables carry truth into all realms by appropriating animals, trees and the elements, striking thousands of sparks. Thus the sun's rays play into the deepest water, but never die out, and reflect objects from the earth and the sky, highlighting their beauties by these consonances.

Ignorance is thus as necessary to truth as shadow is to light, because it is from the former that our intelligence creates its harmonies, as shadows allow us to see.

Moralists, as I have already observed in my *Etudes*, have nearly always confused ignorance with error. Ignorance, when we consider it on its own, apart from truth, with which it shares such sweet harmonies, is the name for our intelligence at rest. It allows us to forget the ills of the past, and hides the present and future ones; indeed it does us good as it comes from nature. Error, on the other hand, is always an evil; it is a false light that shines to lead us astray. I can best compare it to the light of a fire that burns down the rooms it lights up. It is remarkable that there is not one moral or physical ill that does not begin with an error. Tyrannies, slavery, and wars are based on political and even sacred errors;

for tyrants, who have propagated them to establish their power, have always derived them from Divinity or from some kind of virtue so as to make people respect them.

It is easy, however, to distinguish error from truth. Truth is a natural light, which lights itself everywhere on earth because it comes from God; error is an artificial glow which has always to be fed and cannot be universal, as it comes from men. Truth is useful for everybody; error only benefits a few and harms everybody because individual interest is the enemy of general interest, when it can be separated.

You must take care not to confuse the fable with error. The fable is a veil over truth, error its ghost. The fable was often invented to dissipate error. Yet, however innocent a fable might have been in its origin, it becomes dangerous when it assumes the main characteristics of an error, that is when it benefits one particular kind of person. It matters little that in the olden days the moon, under the name of Diana, was always a virginal goddess who presided over hunting. This allegory suggested that moonlight was favourable for hunters to set traps for wild beasts and that hunting banished love's passions. Not much harm was done when the pine tree in the forest was dedicated to her; this tree became a meeting-place during hunts. There was still not much harm done when a hunter, to attract Diana's protection, hung the head of a wolf from a branch. But when he hung the whole skin, there were people who wanted to profit from this and built a chapel to the goddess where not only wolf skins were offered, but also sheep skins in order to preserve the rest of the flock from wolves. Offerings multiplied to include the head of a giant boar that had crashed through the vines and which had chased all the dogs and local youths. Hunters attracted pilgrims and pilgrims merchants. Soon there was a village around the chapel, which, because people are credulous, quickly became an oracle. As victories were predicted, kings would send gifts, so the chapel became a temple and the village a town with pontiffs, magistrates, territories. Soon taxes were levied from the people to built magnificent temples, like those at Ephesus;[7] as fear has more power over the mind than trust, men were sacrificed there to make the Diana cult formidable. Thus an allegory imagined for human good led to evil because it benefited one town and one temple.

Truth is even harmful to human beings when it becomes the patrimony of one tribe. There is certainly a long way from the Gospel's tolerance to the Inquisition's intolerance, from the precept given by Jesus to his apostles to shake the dust from their feet when they left a city where they were refused entry, and of his indignation when they asked him to command fire from heaven, to the destruction of the ancient American Indians and the *auto-da-fe* pyres.

In the Tuileries, to the right as you enter the garden, is an Ionic column which the famous Blondel, professor of architecture, would show as a model to his students. He would make them aware that all the columns that succeeded it diminished its beauty more and more. The first one, he said, was the work of a famous sculptor and then the others were made successively by artists who deviated from its grace and proportion the further away in time they were. The person who sculpted the second one had imitated the first one well enough, but he who made the third one only copied the second one. Thus from copy to copy, the latest was far inferior to the original. I have often compared the Gospel to this beautiful column in the Tuileries, and the work of commentators to those in the rest of the gallery. And if you take into account commentators from then up to today, what shapeless columns their tomes would offer! And who in life's troubles would dare to rely on them?

As truth is a ray of heavenly light, it will always illuminate everybody, as long as their windows are blocked against it. But, as in everything, how many bodies are founded to propagate it, so that they benefit from it, and substitute it with their own candles and lanterns! Soon, when they are powerful, they will persecute people who find the truth, and even if they do not, they will oppose them with the weight of inertia, which prevents them disseminating the truth. That is why people who love truth often abandon towns and their fellow men and women. That is the truth I have wanted to prove in this short work. I will be happy if in my own country I can contribute to the happiness of one unhappy person by painting that of a pariah in his hut in India!

The Indian Hut

About thirty years ago a group of learned Englishmen[8] was established to go and seek, in different parts of the world, insights into all branches of learning in order to enlighten mankind and make it happier. It was funded by a company of subscribers from the same country, made up of merchants, lords, bishops, university dons and the Royal family, together with some sovereigns from the North of Europe. These learned men numbered twenty. The Royal Society of London[9] had given each one a volume containing the state of the questions whose solutions they had to bring back. The questions amounted to three thousand five hundred. Although the questions were different for each of the doctors of philosophy, and related to the country they were travelling to, they were linked, so that the light cast from one would necessarily spread to all the others. The President of the Royal Society, who had compiled them with help from his colleagues, had strongly felt that the clearing-up of a difficulty often depends on somebody else's solution, and that one follows on from a preceding one; which leads the search for truth far further than one thinks.

In short, to use phrases uttered by the president in his instructions, it was the most superb encyclopaedic edifice that any nation had yet raised to progress in human knowledge; which justified, he added, the necessity for academic bodies to pool the truths scattered around the world.

Apart from this tome of questions to clarify, each one of these travelling learned men had a commission to buy, on his travels, the most ancient copies of the Bible and the rarest manuscripts of all sorts, or at least not to spare anything to get hold of fine copies. To carry this out, the subscribers had obtained letters of recommendation for all the consuls, ministers and ambassadors to Great Britain whom they would come across on their route, and, even better, good letters of credit, endorsed by the most prestigious bankers in London.

The most learned of these doctors, who knew Hebrew, Arabic and Hindi, was sent overland to the East Indies, the cradle of all the arts and sciences. He started his journey in Holland and visited, in succession, Amsterdam's synagogue, and Dordrecht's synod;[10] in France, it was the Sorbonne and the Academy of Sciences in Paris; in Italy countless academies, museums and libraries, among them the Musical Library in Florence, St. Mark's library in Venice and the Vatican's in Rome. While in Rome, he weighed up whether to go west to Spain and consult the famous University of Salamanca, but fearing the Inquisition, he preferred to embark at once for Turkey. He reached Constantinople, where, with his money, Turkish holy men allowed him to finger through all the books in the Saint-Sophia mosque.

From there he went to Egypt and its Copts; then to see the Maronites of Mount Lebanon,[11] the monks of Mount Carmel and from there to Sana'a' in Arabia; then on to Isfahan, Kandahar, Delhi and Agra; at last, after three years on the road, he reached the banks of the Ganges at Benares, the Athens of India, where he conferred with the Brahmins. His collection of ancient editions, original books, rare manuscripts, copies, extracts and all kinds of annotations had become the most considerable that any individual had ever assembled. Sufficient to say that it was composed of ninety bundles weighing together one thousand, five hundred and forty-five pounds, in Troy weight.[12] He was about to embark for London with his rich cargo of wisdom, elated at having exceeded the hopes of the Royal Society, when a simple thought overwhelmed him with anxiety.

He realized that after conferring with Jewish rabbis, with Protestant ministers, with superintendents of Lutheran churches, with Catholic doctors in theology, with the Academicians of Paris, of La Crusca, of the Arcades and twenty-four more of the most renowned Italian academies, with the Greek popes, with Turkish mullahs, with Armenian Verbiesis, with Persian sayyids and casys, with Arab sheiks, with ancient Parsees, with Indian pandits, far from having clarified even one of the three thousand five hundred questions posed by the Royal Society, he had simply contributed to multiplying the doubts. And as they were all linked one to the other, it followed, contrary to what his illustrious president thought, that an obscure solution cast its shadows on the evidence of others; that the clearest truths had become completely problematic; and it was even impossible to unravel one of them in this vast labyrinth of answers and contradictory authorities.

The doctor of theology evaluated this from a simple survey. Among the questions, there were two hundred about Hebrew theology that had to be resolved; four hundred and ninety on the diverse communions of the Greek and Roman churches; three hundred and twelve on the ancient religions of the Brahmins; five hundred and eight on the sacred Sanskrit language; three on the actual state of the Indian people; two hundred and eleven on trade between the English and India; seven hundred and twenty-nine on the ancient monuments on Elephanta Island and Salsette, in the vicinity of Bombay Island; five on the age of the world; six hundred and sixty-three on the origin of ambergris and on the properties of diverse kinds of Arabic antidotes; one on the not yet examined causes of the tide of the Indian Ocean, which flows for six months westwards and six months eastward; and three hundred and seventy-eight on the sources and periodic floods of the Ganges. On this occasion, the doctor had been invited to collect, as he travelled, all that touched on the sources and floods of the Nile, which had been worrying Europe's learned men for many centuries. But he judged that this subject had been sufficiently debated, and was alien to his mission. Now, about each of the questions that the Royal Society had proposed, he had found, one after the other, five hundred further questions, which, considering the three thousand five hundred original questions, led to seventeen thousand five hundred answers: and supposing that each of his nineteen colleagues had done the same, it followed that the Royal Society would have three hundred and fifty thousand difficulties to solve before establishing any truth on a solid basis.

Thus, all that they had collected, far from making each proposition converge into a common centre, following the terms of their instructions, would make them, in fact, diverge one from the other, making it impossible to link them up. Another thought upset the doctor even more: and it was that, although he had shown *sangfroid* worthy of a Frenchman in his laborious researches as well as his own brand of courtesy, he had made implacable enemies with most of the doctors of theology with whom he had argued. "What will happen to the peace of mind of my compatriots," he said, "when, in my ninety bundles, I will have brought home new topics of doubt and dispute, rather than the truth?"

He was about to embark for England, his head full of confusion and worry, when the Brahmins of Benares announced that the most senior

Brahmin of the famous pagoda of Jagrenat[13] or Jagernet, situated on the Orixa coast, by the sea, near one of the mouths of the Ganges, was the sole person able to resolve all the Royal Society's questions.

He was in fact the most famous pandit or learned doctor that anybody had ever heard of: people came to consult him from all over India and from several Asian kingdoms.

In no time at all the doctor left for Calcutta and approached the director of the English East India Company who, to honour his country and to the glory of all learning, provided him with transport to Jagrenat in the form of a palanquin covered in crimson silk with gilded tassels, and two relays of strong coolies, in two teams of four men each; two porters, a water-carrier, a jug-carrier to offer refreshment, a hookah-carrier, a parasol carrier to keep out sunlight, a *malsachi* or torch carrier for night time, a wood-collector, two cooks; two camels and two carts loaded with provisions and baggage; two footmen or runners to announce his arrival; four armed sepoys on Persian horses to accompany him and a standard-bearer carrying the English coat of arms. You could have mistaken the doctor of theology, with such a splendid crew, for a clerk of the East India Company. There was, however, this difference: that instead of soliciting gifts the doctor was going to give them away. As in India you can never appear empty-handed before any person in an official category, the director had given him, at the expense of the British nation, a fine telescope and a Persian carpet for the head Brahmin, superb shawls for his wife and three pieces of Chinese taffeta, in red, white and yellow to make scarves for his disciples. The presents were piled on to the camels' backs and the doctor set off in his palanquin, with the Royal Society's book.

Along the way, he thought about which question he would ask the chief Jagrenat Brahmin first; whether he would open with one of the three hundred and sixty-eight questions dealing with the spring and flooding of the Ganges, or with the one dealing with the alternating and semi-annual currents in the Indian Ocean, which would lead to a discovery of the origin and periodic movements of the Oceans all round the world. But although this question interested students of physics infinitely more than all those that had been asked over the centuries concerning the origins and enlargements of the Nile, it had not yet attracted the attention of Europe's learned men. He preferred to ask the Brahmin about the universality of the flood, which has stimulated so many disputes; or, going further up, if it is true that the sun has changed several times during its life, rising in the West and setting in the East, following the tradition of Egyptian priests recounted by Herodotus; and even about the time of the earth's creation, which the Indians claim was several million years ago. Sometimes he thought it more useful to consult him about the best kind of government for a nation and even about the rights of man, for which no code exists anywhere; but these last questions were not in his book.

"However," the doctor said, "before all else, it seems most appropriate to ask the Indian pandit about the best way to find the truth: for if it is through reason, which I have applied up to now, reason changes according to the man: I should ask him also where I must seek truth: if in books, they all contradict each other; and, in the end, if one should communicate the truth, for as soon as they know it, they quarrel over it. Here are three preliminary questions that our august president did not think about. If the Jagrenat Brahmin can resolve them, I will hold the key to all the sciences, and, which means more, I would live in peace with everybody."

That is how the doctor of theology reasoned with himself. After a ten-day journey he reached the shore of the Bay of Bengal; on the road he came across many people returning from Jagrenat, all enchanted with the wisdom of the head pandit whom they had just consulted. The eleventh day, at sunrise, he caught sight of the famous Jagrenat temple. Built on the seashore, it dominated everything with its great red walls and galleries, its domes and white-marble towers. It rose at the centre of nine avenues of evergreen trees, leading to the same number of kingdoms. Each avenue was composed of a different species of tree: of palms, teaks, coconut palms, mango trees, latan palms, camphor trees, bamboos, banana trees and sandalwood trees, and led towards Ceylon, Golconda,[14] Arabia, Persia, Tibet, China, the kingdom of Ava, of Siam and the Indian Ocean islands. The doctor reached the temple by the bamboo avenue that follows the Ganges and the enchanted islands of its river mouth. This temple, though built on a plain, rises so high that, having spied it in the morning, he only reached it in the evening. He was truly struck by admiration when he inspected its magnificence and grandeur close up. Its bronze gates sparkled in the setting sun's rays and eagles planed above its rooftops, lost in clouds. It was surrounded by great ponds made of white marble whose transparent waters reflected the domes, galleries and doors: all around it were vast courtyards and gardens with large buildings adjacent where the Brahmins who worked there lived.

The doctor's footmen ran to announce him; immediately a troop of young *bayaderes*, or dancing girls, emerged from one of the gardens and led him on with singing and dancing to the sound of tabors. They wore *mougri* flowers as necklaces and frangipani flowers around their waists. The doctor, immersed in their scents, dances and music, advanced to the temple door, at the back of which he noticed, in the light of several silver and gold lamps, the Jagrenat statue, the seventh reincarnation of Brahman, shaped like a pyramid, without hands or feet, which he had lost while trying to carry the world to save it. Prostrate at his feet, face down, were penitents, some promising out aloud that, on his feast day, they would hang from his chariot by their shoulders; others wanted to be crushed under its wheels. Although the spectacle of these fanatics, who uttered loud groans voicing their horrible vows, inspired a kind of terror, the doctor was getting ready to enter the temple when an aged Brahmin, who was guarding the door, stopped him and asked what kind of person was being brought in. When he learnt who the doctor was, he said that given his state of *frangui* or impurity, he could not present himself in front of the Jagrenat nor the great priest without washing himself three times in the temple's baths, and that he should wear nothing that came from any kind of animal, especially cow hide, because cows are worshipped by Brahmins, nor pig skin, because it horrifies them. "What should I do?" asked the doctor. "I bring a gift of a Persian carpet, an Angora goat skin and Chinese silk to the leader of the Brahmins." "Everything offered to the Jagrenat temple," he was answered, "or to its great priest, will be purified by being a gift; but that does not apply to your clothes." The doctor had to take off his English wool coat, his goat skin shoes and his beaver hat. Then the old Brahmin, having washed him thrice, dressed him in a sandalwood-coloured cotton cloth and led him to the rooms of the chief Brahmin. The doctor was about to enter, holding the Royal Society's book in his hands, when the man leading him asked what the book was bound in. "It is bound in calf," answered the doctor. "Didn't

I warn you," said the Brahmin in a rage, "that the cow is worshipped by Brahmins! And you dare to present yourself to our leader with a book bound in calf skin!" The doctor would have had to go and purify himself in the Ganges, if he had not cut short all difficulties by offering some gold coins to the person speaking to him. He left the book in question in his palanquin and consoled himself by saying: "At the end of the day, I have only three questions to ask this learned Indian. I would be happy if he could teach me how to seek the truth, where it can be found and if it should be communicated to all men."

The ancient Brahmin presented the English theologian, robed in cotton, bareheaded and barefoot, to the Jagrenat's high priest in a vast room supported by sandalwood columns. The walls were green and trimmed with stucco mixed with cow dung so polished and shiny that you could look at yourself. At the end of the room was a platform made of ebony; on this platform, through lattice work of Indian cane varnished red, you glimpsed the venerable chief of the pandits with his white beard and three threads of cotton around his head, according to the Brahmin custom. He was sitting on a yellow carpet, his legs crossed, in a state of perfect immobility, without a flicker of his eyes. Some of his disciples chased flies away from him with fans made from peacock tails: others burned scent from aloe wood in silver perfume pans and others played drums in a very gentle manner. The rest, numbering many, among whom were fakirs, yogis and ascetics, lined both sides of the hall in deep silence, eyes staring down and arms crossed on their chests.

The doctor at first wanted to walk up to the principal pandit to pay his respects; but his presenter held him up some nine mats away, telling him that Omrahs, the grand Indian princes, stepped no nearer; that Rajahs, the Indian sovereigns, could only advance to six mats; that princes, sons of Moguls, to three, and that only the Mogul himself had the honour of approaching the venerable chief, to kiss his feet.

However, several Brahmins carried the telescope, the chintzes, the rolls of silk and the carpets that the doctor's people had deposited at the hall's entrance to the foot of the platform; the ancient Brahmin glanced at them without giving any sign of approval. They were taken inside to his rooms.

The English doctor was about to begin a fine, long speech in Hindi when his presenter warned him that he would have to wait for the high priest to question him. He made him sit down on his heels, his legs crossed like a tailor, following the customs of the country. The doctor grumbled about so many formalities; but what will a man not do to find truth after having gone all the way to India to find it?

Once the doctor had sat down, the music stopped, and after a few seconds of deep silence, the head pandit asked him why he had come to Jagrenat.

Although the great priest of Jagrenat had spoken in Hindi clearly enough to be understood by a part of the assembly, his word was carried by one fakir to another fakir, and this other one to a third one who spoke it to the doctor. He answered in the same language: "That he has come to Jagrenat to consult the chief of the Brahmins, because of his great reputation, to learn from him the best means to know truth."

The ancient chief of the pandits, after a moment's thought, answered: "Truth can only be known through the Brahmins." Then the whole assembly bowed in admiration at their leader's answer.

"Where should one go to seek the truth?" the English doctor briskly resumed.

"All truth," answered the Indian wise man, "is contained in the four vedas written one hundred and twenty thousand years ago in Sanskrit, which only the Brahmins can interpret."

With these words, the whole hall echoed with applause.

The doctor, regaining his self-control, said to the great priest of Jagrenat: "As God has hidden truth in books whose interpretation is reserved solely for Brahmins, it follows then that God has forbidden knowledge to the majority of men who do not even know that Brahmins exist. Now, if that was the case, God could not be just."

"Brahman wanted it that way," answered the great priest. "Nothing can oppose Brahman's will." The assembly's applause increased. Once it had died down, the Englishman put his third question: "Should truth be communicated to all men?"

"Often," said the ancient pandit, "it is wise to hide the truth from the world; but it is a duty to tell it to the Brahmins."

"Do you mean," the Englishman shouted angrily, "that one should tell the truth to the Brahmins who do not tell anybody else! It seems that the Brahmins are very unjust."

At these words, there was a dreadful uproar in the assembly. They had heard, without complaint, God accused of injustice, but they could not contain themselves when they heard this last reproach. The pandits, the fakirs, the ascetics, the yogis, the Brahmins and their disciples wanted to argue with the English theologian, all at the same time; but the high priest of Jagrenat silenced them by clapping his hands and said in a very clear voice: "Brahmins do not argue with European doctors of theology." Then, having stood up, he left the room to the whole assembly's acclamations, while they continued to criticize the doctor loudly and might have done him some harm if they had not feared the English, whose prestige is all-powerful on the banks of the Ganges. When he had left the room, the man looking after him said: "Our very venerable father would have given you, following the custom, water-ice, betel and scents, but you have angered him." "I'm the one who should be angry," said the doctor, "having spent so much effort in vain. Tell me, what is your chief complaining about?" "What?" answered the man, "you want to argue with him? Don't you know that he is India's oracle, and that every one of his words is a ray of enlightenment?" "I never doubted it," said the doctor, picking up his coat, his shoes and his hat. A storm was building up and night was approaching; he asked if he could spend the night in one of the temple's lodges but they refused to let him sleep there because he was unclean. As the ceremony had upset him, he asked for something to drink. They brought him water in a bowl, but once he had drunk from it they smashed it, because, being unclean, he had soiled it by drinking from it. So the doctor, vexed, called his people, who were prostrate in adoration on the steps of the temple, and climbing back into his palanquin, he set off again along the bamboo alley by the sea as night fell and under a sky covered with clouds. On the road he said to himself: "The Indian proverb is quite right: all Europeans who come to India learn patience if they didn't have it, and lose it if they had it. As for myself, I have lost mine. I just couldn't find out which was the best way to find truth, where it should be sought and if it should be communicated to men! Man is thus condemned all over the world to error and dispute: so much for coming to India to consult the Brahmins!"

As the doctor was reasoning with himself in his palanquin, one of those storms called typhoons in India burst out. The gale came from the sea, and forced the Ganges waters upstream, so that waves broke into foam against the island in the river's mouth. It lifted columns of sand from the shore and clouds of leaves from the woods, which it blew about all over the place, along the river and around the countryside and high into the air. Sometimes it rushed along the bamboo alley, and although these Indian reeds were as tall as large trees, it shook them like grass in a meadow. Through whirlwinds of dust and leaves one could see the long avenue undulating as a part was flattened on the right and then on the left, while the other part lifted itself back up, creaking. The doctor's retine, scared of being crushed or drowned in the Ganges waters flooding the banks, took a route across fields, going haphazardly towards some hills. But night fell and they had been walking for three hours in the deepest darkness, not knowing where they were going when a bolt of lightning, splitting the clouds and whitening the horizon, let them see far away to the right the Jagrenat temple, the Ganges islands and the rough sea, and close by, in front of them, a little valley and wood between two hills. They ran there to take refuge and as they arrived at the valley's entrance thunder rolled lugubriously. The entrance was flanked by rocks and filled with old trees of prodigious girth. Although the tempest bent their tops with terrible din, their gigantic trunks remained still like the rocks surrounding them. This part of the ancient forest seemed to be an asylum of tranquillity, but it was hard to penetrate it. Rattan snaked around its edge covering the feet of the trees, and liana, leaping from trunk to trunk, turned the forest into a solid wall of leaves whose green openings allowed no exit. However, the rajpoots had cut open a passage with their sabres and everybody entered, with the palanquin. They were thinking they had escaped the storm when suddenly the rain fell straight down in thousands of torrents. Bemused, they saw a light and a cabin in the narrowest part of the little valley. The Indian servant ran to light his torch, but turned back soon after, out of breath, shouting: "Don't go any nearer, a pariah lives there!" Then all the troop shouted in panic: "A pariah! A pariah!" The doctor, thinking it was some kind of wild animal, put his hand on his pistols. "What is a pariah?" he asked his torchbearer. "It is," he was answered, "a man without faith or law." "It is," answered the head of the guards, "an Indian of such low caste that it is permissible to kill him if he touches you. If we enter his house, for nine moons we cannot put a foot in any pagoda, and to purify ourselves we must bathe nine times in the Ganges

and be washed by a Brahmin as many times, from head to toe in cow's urine."[15] All the Indians shouted: "We will not enter a pariah's home." "How did you know," the doctor asked the torchbearer, "that your compatriot was a pariah, without faith or law?" "Because," answered the torchbearer, "when I opened the door to his hut I saw that he was sleeping with his dog on the same mat as his wife, to whom he was giving something to drink in a cow's horn." All the doctor's retinue repeated: "We will not enter a pariah's home." "Stay here if you want to," said the Englishman, "for me all the castes of India are the same when it comes to taking shelter from the rain."

Saying these words, he leapt from the palanquin, and taking his book with questions under his arm and carrying his night case, pistols and pipe, he went alone to the door of the hut. Hardly had he knocked when a man of gentle appearance opened the door and stepped back immediately, saying: "Sir, I am but a poor pariah, not worthy of receiving you; but if you think it right to take shelter in my home, you would honour me very much." "My brother," said the Englishman, "I accept your hospitality without a qualm." Then the pariah went outside with a torch in his hand, a load of dried wood on his back, and a basket of coconuts and bananas in his hand, and approached the men in the doctor's retinue who were some distance from there, under a tree, and said to them: "As you do not want to honour me by entering my home, here are fruits wrapped in their skins that you can eat without fear of pollution, and here is fire to dry you and protect you from tigers. May God preserve you!" He immediately entered his hut and said to the doctor: "Sir, I repeat, I am but a wretched pariah, but as I see by the whiteness of your skin and by your clothes that you are not Indian, I hope that you will not be disgusted by the food this poor servant will offer you." At the same time, he placed on a mat some mangoes, custard apples, yams, sweet potatoes cooked in ashes, grilled bananas and a pot of rice seasoned with sugar and coconut water; after which he retired to his own mat next to his wife and child, asleep next to her in a cot. "Virtuous man," said the Englishman, "you are worth far more than me, because you do good to those who despise you. If you do not honour me by sitting on this mat with me, I will think that you take me for an evil man and I will leave this hut on the spot, even if I am to be drowned by the rain and devoured by tigers."

The pariah got up and sat on the same mat as his guest and both began eating. The doctor enjoyed the pleasure of being safe in the middle of a tempest. The hut was unshakeable; apart from its situation in the narrowest part of the valley, it was built under a banian or fig tree whose branches grow roots at their tips and form many arcades supporting the main trunk. The leaves of this tree are so thick that not a drop of water can pass through; and although the storm made its terrible roars heard, mixed in with the din of lightning, the smoke from the hearth which rose through the middle of the roof and the light of the lamp hardly flickered. The doctor admired the Indian and his wife's tranquillity, more profound even than that of the elements. Their child, black and polished like ebony, slept in his cot; his mother rocked him with her foot while she amused herself making a necklace of red and black beads. The father cast his tender glances first on one and then on the other; a cat lay by the fire, half-opened its eyes and sighed looking at its master.

As soon as the Englishman finished eating, the pariah gave him some charcoal to light his pipe, having similarly lit his own. He made a sign to his wife who brought to their mat two cups of coconut juice and a gourd full of punch, which she had prepared while they ate, with water, lemon juice, arrack and sugarcane juice.

While they smoked and drank, the doctor said to the Indian: "I think you are one of the happiest men I have ever met, and thus, one of the wisest. Let me ask you some questions. How are you so tranquil in the middle of a terrible storm? You are protected only by a tree and trees attract lightning." "Lightning has never struck a banyan fig tree," he answered. "That is most curious," said the doctor, "could it be that this tree has negative electricity, like the laurel?" "I don't understand you," countered the pariah, "but my wife thinks that it's because the god Brahma once took shelter under these leaves; as for myself, I think that God, in these stormy regions, having given the banyan fig trees such thick leaves and branch-like arches to shelter people under, does not allow them to be struck by lightning." "Your answer is very religious," said the doctor. "So it is your trust in God that keeps you so calm. Conscience reassures you more than science. Tell me, I beg you, which sect do you belong to, for you are not from an Indian one, because no Indian wants to talk to you? In the list of learned castes that I have consulted while travelling, I did not come across pariahs. In which region in India lies your temple?" "Everywhere," answered the pariah, "my temple is nature; I adore its author at sunrise, and I bless him at sunset. Taught by misfortune, I never refuse help to someone more unfortunate than I am. I try to make my wife, my child, even my cat and dog happy. I wait for death at the end of my life, like a sweet sleep at the end of a day." "In which book did you find these principles?" asked the doctor. "In nature," answered the Indian, "I know no other." "Ah! That is a great book," said the Englishman, "but who taught you to read it?" "Misfortune," said the pariah, "coming from a caste reputed to be vile in my country, not able to be Indian, I made myself a human being; rejected by society, I found refuge in nature." "But in your solitude, you have at least some books?" asked the doctor. "Not one," said the pariah, "I don't know how to read or write." "You have spared yourself many doubts," said the doctor rubbing his forehead. "As for myself, I was sent from England, my country, to seek out the truth among learned men in numerous nations, so as to illuminate men and make them happier; but, after many vain enquiries and serious arguments, I have reached the conclusion that truth is folly, because when you find it, you would not know who to confide in without making many enemies. Tell me sincerely, don't you think like me?" "Although I am but an ignorant man," answered the pariah, "as you ask me to give my opinion, I think that all men are obliged to seek the truth for their own good: otherwise they remain covetous, ambitious, superstitious, evil, cannibalistic even, following the prejudices or interests of those who have raised them."

The doctor, who was thinking all the time of the three questions that he posed to the chief pandit, was delighted by the pariah's answer. "Since you believe," he told him, "that all men are obliged to seek the truth, tell me then what means one should use to find it; for our senses delude us, and our reason leads us even further astray. Reason differs among men: that is why it is so variable around the world. It is, I believe, in the end, merely the particular interest of each one of us: that is why it is so variable around the world. There are not two religions, two nations, two tribes, two families, what am I saying, two men who think the same way. How should you then seek the truth, if intelligence cannot help?" "I believe," answered the pariah, "that it is with a simple heart. The senses and the mind may err, but a simple heart, although it can be fooled, never fools you."

"Your answer is profound," said the doctor. "You must first look for truth with your heart and not with your mind. Men all feel the same way and reason differently, because the principles of truth are found in nature, and it is in their interest to draw the consequences from it. It is thus with a simple heart that you should seek truth; a simple heart has never pretended to understand what it does not understand or believe what it does not believe. It does not contribute to self-deceit, nor to deceiving others; thus, a simple heart, far from being feeble like those of the majority of human beings seduced by their own interests, is strong, such as it should be to seek truth and hold on to it." "You have developed my idea far better than I could," took up the pariah. "Truth is like dew from heaven: to keep it pure, you must collect it in a pure vase."

"Very well said, sincere man," answered the Englishman, "but it is the hardest thing to find. Where should you go to seek truth? A simple heart depends on us, but truth depends on other people. Where can it be found, if those who surround us are seduced by their prejudices and corrupted by their interests, as most people are? I have travelled among many people, I have combed their libraries, I have consulted their doctors and I have found everywhere nothing but contradictions, doubts and opinions a thousand times more varied than their languages. If you do not find truth in the most famous stores of human knowledge, where must you go to find it? What use would a simple heart be among people with false minds and corrupt hearts?" "Truth would be suspect to me," answered the pariah, "if it came only to me through other people; it is not among them that you should seek it, but in nature. Nature is the source of all that exists; its language is not unintelligible and variable like than of men and their books. To base truth on a book is like basing it on a painting or a statue, which is the creation of a single country and subject to change every day. All books are the art of man, but nature is the art of God."

"You are quite right," took up the doctor, "nature is the source of natural truths, but where, for example, is the source of historical truths if not in books? How can one make sure about the truth of a fact that happened some two thousand years ago? Were those who passed it down without prejudices or fixed views? Did they have a simple heart? Moreover, the books themselves, which passed all this down, don't they need copyists, printers, commentators and translators? And all these people, don't they more or less alter the truth? As you very well say, a book is but the art of a man. You must then give up historical truth, as it reaches us through men liable to making mistakes." "What does the history of past things," said the Indian, "matter to our happiness? The history of what is now is the history of what was and what will be."

"Very well," said the Englishman, "but you would agree that moral truths are necessary for the happiness of human beings. How to find them in nature? Animals wage wars, kill each other and eat each other; the very elements fight the elements; will not men act the same way with each other?" "Oh, no," said the good pariah, "for each man will find the rule of his actions in his own heart, if his heart is simple. Nature has placed this law there: Do not do to others what you would not do to yourselves." "It is true," said the doctor, "that nature has arranged the interests of the human race along our own ones; but how can you find religious truths among so many traditions and cults which divide nations?" "In nature itself," answered the pariah. "If we consider it with a simple heart, we would see God in His power, His intelligence and His goodness; and as we are frail, ignorant and wretched, there is enough to commit us to worship Him and love Him all our lives without arguing."

"Admirably put," said the Englishman, "but now, tell me, when you have discovered a truth, should you pass it on to other people? If you publish it, you will be hounded by countless people who live with the contrary error, assuring us that this same error is the truth, and all that tries to destroy it, is the error itself." "You must," said the pariah, "tell the truth to men who have a simple heart, that is, to good people who are seeking it, and not to the evil people who push it aside. Truth is a fine pearl, and the evil person is a crocodile who cannot put it on his ear because he does not have one. If you throw a pearl to a crocodile, instead of wearing it, he will want to devour it; he will break his teeth and in his fury will hurl himself on you."

"There is only one objection to make to you," said the Englishman, "and that is that it follows from what you have just said that men are condemned to error, though truth be fundamental for them, for, as they persecute all who speak it, what doctor would dare enlighten them?" "The one," answered the pariah, "who himself persecutes those men to make them learn through sorrow." "Oh, this time, natural man," said the Englishman, "I think you are mistaken. Sorrow throws men into superstition; it crushes the heart and mind. The more men are miserable, the more they are vile, gullible and grovelling." "That is because they are not wretched enough," said the pariah. "Sorrow resembles the black mountain of Bember, at the limits of the burning kingdom of Lahore; if you climb it, you will see sterile rocks ahead of you, but when you reach the summit, you see the pure sky above your head and at your feet the kingdom of Kashmir."

"A just and charming comparison!" exclaimed the doctor. "Each one of us has a mountain to climb in his lifetime. Yours, virtuous solitary man, must have been tough for you have climbed above all the people I have known. You must have been very wretched! But tell me first why your caste is so vilified in India and that of the Brahmins so honoured? I have just come from the chief of the Jagrenat temple, who does not think any further than his idol and is worshipped like a God." "This," answered the pariah, "is because the Brahmins say that, at the beginning, they sprang from the god Brahma's head and the pariahs from his feet. They add, what is more, that one day Brahma, while travelling, asked a pariah for something to eat and was given human flesh: since this tradition, their caste is honoured and ours is cursed all over India. We are not allowed to approach towns and any rajpoot guard can kill us if we so much as breathe over him." "By St. George!" cried out the Englishman, "how mad and unjust! How could the Brahmins have persuaded Indians of such a folly?" "By teaching them from infancy," said the pariah, "and repeating it to them ceaselessly: men are taught like parrots." "You are unfortunate!" said the Englishman. "How did you pull yourself out of the abyss of infamy where the Brahmins had thrown you when you were born? I think that nothing is more desperate for a man than to vilify him in his own eyes; it is to strip him of the first consolation of all; for the surest of all consolations is the one where we can retreat into ourselves."

"I first asked myself," said the pariah, "whether the history of the god Brahma is true. Only the Brahmins, keen to give themselves divine origins, tell it. They have doubtless imagined that a pariah had wanted to turn Brahma into a cannibal to take revenge on the pariahs for refusing to believe what they uttered about their saintliness. After that, I said to myself: suppose that fact was true: God is just, He cannot make a whole caste guilty of the crime of one of its members when the whole caste did not take part in it. But even supposing that the whole caste of pariahs had taken part in the crime, their descendants were not accomplices. God does not punish the children for the sins of their ancestors, whom they have never seen, just as He doesn't punish the elders for the faults of their grandchildren who are not yet born. But suppose that I have to pay for the punishment of a pariah, perfidious towards his God, some thousands of years ago, without having participated in the crime. Could something have lasted that long, hated by God, without also being destroyed? If I was cursed by God, nothing that I planted would survive. So at last, I told myself: suppose that I am hated by God, who does me good; I would want to try to make myself agreeable to Him by following His example, by doing good to those I should hate."

"But," the Englishman asked him, "how do you manage to live, being rejected by everybody?" "First," said the Indian, "I say to myself: if everybody is your enemy, be a friend to yourself. Your misfortune is not beyond the strength of a man. However heavy the rainfall, a little bird only gets one drop at a time. I was walking in the woods and along the river looking for food, but would usually only find some wild fruit, and I was scared of the ferocious beasts. Thus I realized that nature had hardly done anything for solitary man, and that nature had tied my existence to that same society which had rejected me from its womb. I haunted abandoned fields, which abound in India, and always found some edible plant that had survived the ruin of its planters. I travelled from province to province, assured of finding everywhere some subsistence in the leftovers of harvests. Then I found the seeds of some useful vegetables and I would plant them, saying, if it's not for me, it will be for someone else. I felt less miserable seeing that I could do some good. There was one thing I passionately desired: it was to enter into towns. I admired their ramparts from afar, and their towers, the prodigious throng of boats on the riverbanks, the caravans on their roads, packed with goods arriving from all points of the horizon, the troops of warriors who came from deep in the provinces to guard the town, the arrivals of ambassadors with their numerous retinues coming from strange kingdoms to report on happy events, or to make alliances. I got as close as I could to their avenues, contemplating with amazement the long columns of dust raised by so many travellers and I trembled with desire at that confused din that came from the great cities, and which from the neighbouring countryside resembles the murmur of waves breaking on the shore. I said to myself: a congregation of men of so many different types who work together, who share their riches and their joys, must make a town a place of delights. But if I was not allowed to approach during the day, who would stop me at night? A feeble mouse, which has so many enemies, goes and comes where it wants thanks to the dark; it moves from the shack of the poor to the palace of kings. To enjoy life, it only needs starlight; why did I need the sun? I reflected thus outside Delhi; I was emboldened to the point where I entered the town at night, through the Lahore gate. First, I walked along a solitary road, formed on both sides by houses with terraces, with arcades where merchants had their shops. I found the great stores and bazaars closed, and complete silence reigned. As I approached the town's interior, I passed the superb Omrah neighbourhood, full of palaces and gardens along the Gemna. All was echoing with the noise of instruments and dancing girls who sang and danced on the riverbank, lighted by torches. I stood by the door of a garden to enjoy such a sweet spectacle, but was pushed away by slaves who were chasing some wretch with a stick. As I left the neighbourhood of the powerful, I passed by several temples of my religion, where a great number of wretches were howling, lying on the ground. I hurried to escape these monuments to superstition and terror. Further on, the mullah's piercing voice announced the hours of the night from high up and revealed that I was at the foot of a mosque's minaret. Nearby were the European factories, with their pavilions and their guards who ceaselessly cried out: '*Kaber-dar!* Watch out!' I hugged the side of a huge building that I recognized as the prison because of the noise of chains and groans that emanated from inside. I soon heard the screams of pain in the vast hospital, from which emerged carts piled high with corpses. Making my way on, I met thieves fleeing along the road; patrols of guards chased them; gangs of beggars who, despite being beaten by rattan whips, begged at the doors of palaces for some leftovers from the feasts, and everywhere women prostituted themselves publicly to get something to eat. At last, after a long walk on the same road, I reached an immense square surrounded by the fortress in which the Great Mogul lives. It was covered with the tents of the Rajahs and Nabobs of his guard and their squadrons, distinguished one from the other by their burning torches, standards and long canes with cow tails from Tibet on their tips. A large moat filled with water and bristling with artillery surrounded the fortress, like the square. In the light of the guards' fire I considered the castle's towers, which rose to the clouds, and the length of the ramparts, which were lost in the horizon. I would have loved to enter but great *korahs* or whips, hanging from stakes, snuffed the very desire to put my foot inside. I stayed thus at one of its extremities, near some black slaves, who let me rest near a fire around which they were sitting. From there I could admire the imperial palace, and said to myself: 'Here is where the happiest man alive lives! So many religions preach his authority; so many ambassadors arrive for his glory, so many provinces exhaust their wealth for his treasures; so many caravans travel for his sensual satisfactions, and so many armed men watch in silence over his safety!'

"While I was thinking these thoughts, great cries of joy were heard all over the square and I saw eight camels decorated with streamers pass by. I learned that they were loaded with the heads of rebels, sent to him by Mogul generals from Decan province, where one of his sons, whom he had named governor, had been waging a war against him for the last three years. Soon after, at full speed, a courier arrived on a dromedary; he had come to announce the loss of a border town in India, betrayed by one of its commanders who had given in to the Persian king. Hardly had this courier passed by when another, sent by the governor of Bengal, brought the news that the Europeans, with whom the Emperor had arranged a warehouse at the mouth of the Ganges for the benefit of trade, had built a fort and had taken control of navigation in the river. A few moments later, after the arrival of two couriers, we saw an officer leave the castle at the head of a detachment of guards. The Mogul had ordered him to go to the district of the Omrahs and fetch the three leaders, in chains, accused of being spies for the enemy of the state. The evening before he had arrested a mullah who was preaching sermons praising the king of Persia and who had said aloud that the Emperor of India was an infidel, because, contrary to Mohammed's laws, he drank wine. Finally, I heard that he had just had one of his wives and two captains of his guard strangled and thrown into the Gemna, convinced that they had plotted with his rebellious son. While I mulled over these tragic events, a long column of smoke rose suddenly from the kitchens in the brothel, its swirls of smoke mixing with the clouds and its red glow lighting up the fort, the ditch, the square, the mosque's minarets and spreading to the horizon. At the same time, the great copper kettledrums and the guards' *karnas* or large oboes sounded the alarm with a terrifying din. Squadrons of cavalry spread round the town, rushing through the doors of the houses near the castle and forcing the inhabitants with violent strokes of their *korahs* to help with the fire. I experienced myself how dangerous it is for small fry to live near to the great. The great are like a fire which burns even those who throw incense on to it, if they get too near. I wanted to escape but all the avenues off the square had been sealed. It would have been impossible for me to get out had it not been for God's providence, for the side where I stood was that of the brothel. As the eunuchs moved the women on to elephants, they made our escape easy; for if the guards everywhere forced people with whips to help out at the castle, the elephants, with their trunks, forced them to keep away. Thus, chased by some and then by others, I left that awful chaos and in the light of the fire reached the other side of the suburb where in their shacks, far from the great, the people rested in peace after their work. It was there that I began to breathe. I said to myself: I have now seen a town! I have seen where the masters of the nation live! How many masters are themselves slaves! They obey, even when they should be resting, sensual pleasure, ambition, superstition; they fear, even asleep, a crowd of wretched and evil-doing people who surround them: thieves, beggars, courtesans, firebrands, even their soldiers, their fellow grandees and their priests. How would a town be in the daytime if it was like that at night? Man's woes increase with his pleasures; how the emperor, who gathers them all together, must complain! He must fear civil and foreign wars, the objects that are his consolation and defence; his generals, his guards, his mullahs, his women and his children. The ditches around his fort cannot stop the ghosts of superstition, nor his elephants, however well armoured, keep his dark worries away from him. As for myself, I have none of those fears; no tyrant has control over me nor over my body nor over my soul. I can serve God following my conscience, and have nothing to fear from anyone as long as I do not torment myself; the truth is that a pariah is less unhappy than an emperor. Saying these words, tears come to my eyes and falling on my knees, I thank heaven that by learning to support my own calamities, I have been shown more intolerable ones than mine.

Since that time I have only travelled around the outer districts of Delhi. From there I could see the stars light up people's homes and blend with their fires, as if the sky and the town were but one domain. When the moon lit up this landscape, I saw new colours from those of daytime. I admired the towers, the houses, the trees, both silvered and covered in crepe, reflected far off in the waters of the Gemna. I wandered freely through the great and silent neighbourhoods and thought that the whole town was mine. And yet humanity would have refused me a handful of rice, so odious had religion made me! Not being able to make friends among the living, I sought them among the dead; I went to cemeteries to eat on the tombs the food left by pious relatives. It was there that I loved to think. I said to myself: this is the city of peace, here power and pride have vanished; innocence and virtue are safe; here all life's fears are dead, even the fear of dying; here is the inn where for ever the carrier has unharnessed his cart, where the pariah can rest. During these thoughts, I found death desirable and I came to despise the earth. I pondered about the west from where thousands of stars would appear. Although their destiny was unknown, I felt that they were linked with those of man, and that nature, which has supplied his needs with so many objects that he cannot see, had at least attached us to what she has offered that we can see. My soul rose into the sky with the stars and when dawn's pink hues joined their sweet and eternal light, I felt as if I was at heaven's gate. But as soon as its fires gilded the tops of the temples, I vanished like a shadow; I went far from men to rest in the fields at the foot of a tree where I fell asleep as birds sang."

"What a sensitive and unlucky man," said the Englishman, "your story is very moving; believe me, most cities are only worth seeing at night. After all, nature has its nocturnal beauties that are no less touching; a famous poet of my country has only celebrated that aspect.[16] But, tell me, how did you manage to make yourself happy when day broke?"

"It was already a great deal to be happy at night," said the Indian. "Nature resembles a beautiful woman who, during the day, only shows the beauties of her face to the world, and who, at night, reveals her secrets to her lover. But if solitude has its pleasures, it has its privations; it seems to an unlucky man to be a tranquil harbour from which he watches other people's passions melt away, without being shaken up himself; but while he congratulates himself on his immobility, time itself drags him along. You cannot cast an anchor into the river of life; it carries away those who fight its current and those who flow with it, the wise man as well as the madman, and both reach the end of their days, one having abused life, the other not having enjoyed it. I did not want to be wiser than nature, nor find my happiness outside the laws nature has prescribed for man. I wanted above all else a friend with whom I could communicate my pleasures and pains. I looked for one among my equals, but I only found envious people. However, I did find one who was sensitive, grateful, faithful and free of prejudice; to tell the truth, not of our species, but in the animal one; it was that dog you see. He had been abandoned quite small on a street corner and was about to die of hunger. He awoke my compassion and I brought him up; he became attached to me and became my inseparable companion. But it was not enough. I needed a friend who was unhappier than a dog, who knew all human society's evils and who could help me withstand them; who only wanted nature's bounties and with whom I could enjoy them. It is only by twisting round each other that two feeble shrubs can resist the storm. Providence exceeded my desires by giving me a good woman. It was in the depths of my misfortunes that I found my happiness. One night when I was at the Brahmins' cemetery I saw in the moonlight a young Brahmin woman half covered under a yellow veil. At the sight of a woman with the blood of my tyrants, I stepped back in horror, but I reproached myself, moved by compassion and seeing the care with which she busied herself. She was laying food out on a mound that covered the ashes of her mother, who had been burned alive, with her father's corpse, following her caste's customs, and she was burning incense, to call the shade of her deceased.[17] Tears came to my eyes seeing a person sadder than myself. I said to myself: "Alas, I am tied by bonds of infamy, but you by those of glory. At least I live peacefully in the depths of my precipice and you, always trembling at the edge of yours. The same destiny that stole your mother from you threatens you also one day. You have received but one life and you will have to die two deaths; if your own death does not drag you into a tomb, your husband's will while you are still alive. I cried and she cried; our eyes, bathed in tears met and communicated like all who are unhappy; she turned her eyes away, wrapped herself in her veil and withdrew. The following night, I returned to the same place. This time she had placed a larger amount of food on her mother's tomb; she had realized that I needed it and as Brahmins often poison their funeral food, to stop pariahs eating it, she had only brought fruit. I was touched by this sign of humanity, and to show her the respect I brought to her offering, instead of taking the fruit, I added flowers; they were poppies, which expressed how much I felt for her suffering. The following night, I saw with joy that she had approved of my homage; the poppies had been watered and she had put a new basket of fruit some distance from the tomb. Piety and gratitude emboldened me. Not daring to speak to her as a pariah, scared of compromising her, I undertook, as a man, to express all the affection that she had sparked off in my soul: following the custom in India, to make myself understood I borrowed the language of flowers and added marigolds to the poppies. The next night I found my poppies and marigolds bathed in water. The following night, I became even bolder; I added to the poppies and marigolds a dark *foulsapatte* flower, which shoemakers use to dye their leather black, to express my humble and hapless love. The next day, at dawn, I ran to the tomb, but found my dark flower dried out because it had not been watered. The following night, I tremblingly placed a tulip with red leaves and a black heart to express the fire that consumed me; the next day I found the tulip in the same state as the *foulsapatte*. I was struck with grief. Two days later, I brought a rose bud with its thorns, as a symbol of my hopes mixed with many fears. But imagine my despair when I saw, in the first light of day, my rose bud far from the tomb! I thought that I was losing my mind. Whatever might happen to me, I resolved to speak to her. The following night, as soon as she appeared, I threw myself at her feet, but remained abashed as I presented her with my rose. She spoke the first word and said to me: "Wretched man, you speak to me of love, and soon I will be no longer. Like my mother, I have to accompany my husband, who has just died, to the funeral pyre: he was old and I married him still a child;

goodbye, leave me and forget me; in three days I will be no more than a pile of ashes."

At those words, she sighed. I was flooded with sadness and said to her: "Unhappy Brahmin woman! Nature has broken what binds you to society: break those of superstition; you can do that by taking me as your husband." "What!" she cried, "I would escape death by living with you in disgrace! If you love me, you must let me die." "God would not be pleased," I cried out, "if I freed you from your fears to plunge you in mine! Dear Brahmin woman, let us escape together into the depths of the forest; it would be better to trust tigers than human beings. But heaven, in which I believe, will not abandon us. Let's flee: love, night, your calamity, your innocence, all will be on our side. Let's hurry, unfortunate widow, already your pyre is being prepared and your dead husband is calling you. Poor torn-down liana, lean on me and I will be your palm tree." Then, groaning, she threw a glance at her mother's tomb, then up to heaven, and, letting one of her hands fall into mine, with the other she took my rose. I immediately seized her by the arm and we set off. I threw her veil in the Ganges to make her parents think that she had drowned herself. We walked along the river for several nights, hiding ourselves by day in rice paddies. At last we arrived in this region that wars previously depopulated. I penetrated into the depths of the wood, where I built this hut and planted this little garden. We live very happily here. I revere my wife like the sun, and love her like the moon. In these depths of solitude we take the place of everything for each other; we were despised by the world, and as we held each other in esteem, the praises I heap on her or those I receive from her seem sweeter that the applause of a crowd." Saying these words, he looked at his child in the crib, and at his wife, who was crying with joy.

The doctor wiped his tears and said to his host: "In truth, what is held in honour by men is often worthy of their scorn, and what is scorned by them is often worthy of honour. But God is just: you are a thousand times happier in your obscurity than the head Brahmin of Jagrenat in all his glory. He is exposed like all his caste to all the changes of fortune; it is on the Brahmins that fall most of the scourges of civil and foreign war that have desolated your beautiful country for so many centuries. It is to them that one often calls for forced tributes because of the power they hold over people's opinions. But, most cruelly for them, they are the first victims of their inhuman religion. At the cost of preaching error, they have been so penetrated by it themselves that they have lost the feeling for truth, justice, humanity and piety. They are bound in the chains of superstition with which they wanted to capture their compatriots; they are forced all the time to wash themselves, to purify themselves, and to forego many innocent pleasures; in fact, what cannot be said without horror, as a consequence of their barbaric dogmas, is that they see their relatives, their mothers, their sisters and their own daughters burnt alive. Thus nature, whose laws they have violated, punishes them. For you, you are allowed to be sincere, good, just, welcoming, pious; and you escape the beatings of fortune and the ills of public opinion by your very humiliation."

After this conversation, the pariah took leave of his guest to let him rest, and withdrew, with his wife and the baby's cot, into a small room next door.

The next day, at dawn, the doctor was woken by birdsong from the branches of the Indian fig tree and by the voices of the pariah and his wife, who were together praying. He got up, and when the pariah and his wife opened their door to wish him good morning, he was vexed, for he saw that there was no other bed in the hut than the double bed and that they had stayed awake all night to let him have it. After they had made the welcoming salaam, they hurried off to prepare breakfast. While this was happening, he walked around the garden; he found it, like the hut, surrounded by the arches of the Indian fig tree, so interlaced that they formed an impenetrable hedge, even for his eyes. He could see above the leaves the red sides of the rock flanking the valley all around him: a small spring merged that watered the garden planted without any plan. He saw, all mixed up, mangosteen trees, orange trees, coconut palms, litchi trees, durian trees, mango trees, banana trees and other plants laden with flowers and fruit. Their trunks even were covered; the betel nut wound round the Areca palm, and the pear along the sugarcane. The air was fragrant with their scents. Although most of the trees were still in shade, the first rays of dawn already lit up their tops. You could see hummingbirds flit about, sparkling like rubies and topazes, while Bengali birds and *sensa-soules*, or five-hundred-voices, hidden in the damp leaves, made their concert heard from their nests. The doctor was strolling under these charming shades, far from his ambitious, scientific thoughts, when the pariah invited him to have breakfast. 'Your garden is delicious," said the Englishman, "its only defect is that it is so small; in your place, I would add a lawn and spread into the wood. "Sir," answered the pariah, "the less space you have, the more you are protected; one leaf is enough for the fly-bird." Saying these words, they entered the hut where they found the pariah's wife breast-feeding the baby; she had laid out breakfast. After a silent meal, the doctor got ready to leave. The Indian said: "My guest, the countryside is still flooded with last night's rain, the roads are impassable; spend the day with us." "I cannot," he said, "I have too many people with me." "I see," said the pariah, "that you are in a hurry to leave the country of the Brahmins to return to that of the Christians, whose religion allows everybody to live as brothers." The doctor stood up, sighing. Then the pariah made a sign to his wife, who, her eyes lowered and silent, presented the doctor with a basket of flowers and fruit. The pariah, speaking for her, said to the Englishman: "Sir, please excuse our poverty; we are unable to perfume our guests in the Indian manner, with ambergris and aloe wood; we only have flowers and fruit; but I hope that you will not scorn this little basket filled by my wife's hands. There are no poppies or marigolds, but jasmine and bergamots. By the lasting quality of their scent these are symbols of our affection, whose memory will remain, even if we will not meet again." The doctor took the basket, and said to the pariah: "I cannot thank you for your hospitality enough or show the esteem I hold you in; accept this gold watch, made by Graham, the most famous watchmaker in London; it only needs winding once a year." The pariah answered: "Sir, we do not need a watch; we have one that always works and never goes wrong: it is the sun." "My watch strikes the hours," added the doctor. "Our birds sing it," answered the pariah. "At least," said the doctor, "take these coral beads to make red necklaces for your wife and child." "My wife and child," answered the Indian, "will never lack red necklaces as long as our garden produces Angola peas." "Accept, then," said the doctor, these pistols to defend yourself from thieves in these solitudes." "Poverty," said the pariah, "is a rampart that keeps thieves away; the silver decorating your weapons would be enough to attract them. In the name of God who looks after us, and from whom we hope for recompense, do not take away the price of our hospitality." "Even so," said the Englishman, "I would like you to keep something of mine." "Well, dear guest," answered the pariah, "as you so wish it, I propose an exchange: give me your pipe and take mine. When I smoke in yours, I will remember that a European pandit did not scorn the hospitality of a poor pariah." The doctor immediately presented him with his English leather pipe whose mouthpiece was of yellow amber, and received in return the pariah's, with its stem of bamboo and its bowl of baked earth.

Then he called his people who were shivering from the bad night they had spent, and after embracing the pariah, he climbed into his palanquin. The pariah's wife, who was crying, stood at the hut's door, holding her baby in her arms; but her husband accompanied the doctor to the edge of the wood, showering him with blessings. "May God be your recompense," he said, "for your goodness to the wretched! May I be duty-bound to Him for you! May He bring you happily back to England, that country of learned men and friends who seek the truth around the world for the sake of man's happiness!" The doctor answered him: "I have travelled half way round the world and I have everywhere seen error and discord; I have only found truth and happiness in your hut." Saying these words, they parted and both men shed tears. The doctor was already far into the countryside when he could still see the good pariah at the foot of a tree, waving his arm in farewell.

The learned doctor, back in Calcutta, took a boat to Chandernagore, from where he sailed for England. When he arrived in London, he sent the ninety packages of his manuscripts to the president of the Royal Society, who deposited them in the British Museum, where researchers and journalists still today busy themselves translating them, praising them, mocking them, criticizing them, and writing pamphlets. As for the doctor, he kept the pariah's three answers about truth to himself. He often smoked his pipe and when he was questioned on what he had most usefully learnt on his travels, he answered: "You must seek truth with a simple heart; it can only be found in nature; you should only tell it to good people." To which he added: "You can only be happy with a good woman."

Notes

1. I have translated from Bernardin's *La chaumière indienne*, Chez P. Fr. Didot le Jeune: Paris, 1791, pp.1-130.

2. Bernardin included a note in the 1791 edition of *La chaumière indienne* complaining that the academicians ridiculed his *Etudes* because he did not possess a "long list of academic titles" (p.xxxv).

3. Jean-François de Lapérouse was born in Albi in 1741 and became a ship's captain in 1780. He sailed to America in 1782 and destroyed some English bases in the Hudson Bay. In 1785 Louis XVI sent him with two ships, the *Boussole* and the *Astrolabe*, on a voyage of discovery to the East. He reached Japan and from 1788 completely disappeared. Despite several searches, his wreck was found only in 1828 on the reefs of Vanikoro island. Milet de Mureau published an account of his travels in 1797, re-edited by Hélène Minguet for the Maspéro/La Découverte series.

4. Jean de la Fontaine, (1621-1695), published his first collection of fables, *Fables choisies et mises en vers* in 1668, with further collections in 1679 and 1693, adapting Latin and Indian sources.

5. Sir Thomas Roe (c.1581-1644) was the first English ambassador to the Court of the Great Mogul in 1615; he kept a *Journal* and later published an account of his negotiations in Istanbul, where he lived from 1621-1628.

6. Aesop was the supposed author of a collection of Greek fables, dating from the sixth century BC and made famous in the West in later prose translations. Erasmus popularized them in Latin in schools. Lokman, or Luqman, famous in the Arabian tradition and cited in the *Koran* for his fables, was known from thirteenth century for his *Fables of Luqman*, first edited in 1615.

7. On the Mediterranean coast of Turkey, not far from Smyrna, and famous for the magnificent temple to Diana built by Croesus. One of the seven wonders of the ancient world, it was burnt down by Erostratus in 356 BC, rebuilt and again sacked in 203 AD by Constantine. The philosopher Heraclitus was born there, and St. Paul preached there in 57 AD and wrote his famous epistle to its inhabitants.

8. The 1797 English translation, *The Indian Cottage or, a Search after Truth*, identified this as the Dilettanti Society. This society was founded in 1732 to encourage the study of classical archaeology.

9. The Royal Society of London (for the Improving of Natural Knowledge) was given its Royal Charter in 1662, with Dryden and Wren among its early members and Isaac Newton its president at the end of the seventeenth century.

10. Holland's oldest town, founded in 994 and the seat of famous Calvinist synods of 1618 and 1619.

11. Syrian Christians in Lebanon, so-called after Maro their fifth-century founder.

12. A system of weighing precious metals, with 12 ounces in the pound.

13. So Bernardin spells this Hindu temple. The 1797 English translation gives

Juggernaut (today Jagannath), where Krishna is dragged in a huge cart under whose wheels devotees are crushed (mentioned later by Bernardin).

14   An old name for Hyderabad.

15   While translating this parable, I read a story in the London *Guardian* of 4 August 2001. In a rural part of Uttar Pradesh, a 16-year-old boy from the Brahmin caste and his 18-year-old girlfriend from a lower caste had been murdered and cremated in front of their families for daring to flout the caste laws.

16   Bernardin's reference is to Edward Young's *Night Thoughts* (full title *The Complaint or Night Thoughts on Life, Death and Immortality*), 1742-1745, which was extremely popular all over Europe.

17   Bernardin disapprovingly refers to the ritual of widow burning, or *sati* or suttee (in English). Supposedly prohibited in 1829 by the British in India, it is still occasionally practiced (as recently as 1987), as Wendy Doniger noted in her review "Why Did They Burn?" in the *Times Literary Supplement*, 14 September 2001.

Bibliography

Main Text Consulted

Anonymous. [Jacques-Henri Bernardin de Saint-Pierre]. 1773. *Voyage à l'Isle de France par un Officier du Roi*, printed in Amsterdam and distributed by Merlin: Paris. Two volumes, 1-328 & 1-278.

Further Editions Consulted

1826. *Oeuvres Complètes de Jacques-Henri Bernardin de Saint-Pierre* (the *Voyage* is in vols. 1-2), ed. L. Aimé-Martin. P. Dupont: Paris.

1834. Armand-Aubrée, Editeur: Paris.

1885. Merchants and Planters Gazette: Port Louis.

1983. Edition d'Yves Bénot. La Découverte-Maspéro: Paris.

1986. Edited by Robert Chaudenson. Editions de l'Océan Indien: Rose Hill, Mauritius.

1996. *Ile de France. Voyage et Controverses*, by Bernardin de Saint-Pierre, Thomi Pitot and Abbé Ducrocq. Editions Alma: Mauritius.

Earlier Translation

1775. *A Voyage to the Island of Mauritius, (or, Isle of France), the Isle of Bourbon, the Cape of Good Hope, etc.* Translation by John Parish. W. Griffin: London.

1800. *A Voyage to the Isle of France, the Isle of Bourbon and the Cape of Good Hope; with Observations and Reflections upon Nature and Mankind.* Translated from the French, printed by J. Cundee: London [although the translator has removed his name and added passages, it is Parish's translation of 1775]. Translated into German in 1774 and into Italian in 1844.

Other Works by Bernardin de Saint-Pierre Consulted

Etudes de la nature, 1784.

Paul et Virginie. 1787. 4th volume of 3rd edition of *Etudes de la Nature*.

Paul et Virginie. With an "avant-propos", Paris, 1793 [the edition I quote from].

Paul et Virginie. Editions Nilsson: Paris, 1928.

Paul et Virginie. Edition de P. Trahard revue par E. Guitton, Classiques Garnier:

Paris, 1989.

La chaumière indienne, 1791, Chez P. Fr. Didot Le Jeune: Paris, 1-130pp. "Avant-propos", x-xxxiii.

Oeuvres choisies de Bernardin de Saint-Pierre, contenant Paul et Virginie, La chaumière indienne, Voyage à l'Ile de France etc. Librarie de Fermin Didot Frères: Paris, 1857.

Empsaël et Zoraïde ou les blancs esclaves des noirs à Maroc. Présentation de Roger Little, University of Exeter Press: Exeter, 1995.

Secondary Criticism and Background Reading

Aimé-Martin, L. 1826. "Essai sur la vie et les ouvrages de Bernardin de Saint-Pierre", in *Oeuvres Complètes de Jacques-Henri Bernardin de Saint-Pierre*, ed. L. Aimé-Martin. P. Dupont: Paris.

Allen, David Elliston. 1976. *The Naturalist in Britain.* Penguin Books: Harmondsworth.

Anon. 1811. *Account of the Conquest of Mauritius with Some Notices of the History, Soil, Products, Defences and the Political Importance of this Island ...* by an officer who served on the Expedition. Military Library: London.

Armstrong, Margaret. 1941. *Trelawny. A Man's Life.* Robert Hale: London.

Barker, Anthony. 1996. *Slavery and Antislavery in Mauritius, 1810-33. The Conflict between Economic Expansion and Humanitarian Reform under British Rule.* Macmillan Press: London.

Barker, Lady. 1897. "Mauritius", in W. C. Procter (ed.), *Round the Globe.* Wm. Isbister Limited: London.

Barnwell, P. J. 1948. *Visits and Dispatches (Mauritius, 1598-1948),* The Standard Printing Establishment: Port Louis.

Baudelaire, Charles. 1973. *Correspondance,* ed. Claude Pichois, Gallimard: Paris.

Baudry, Janine. 1989. "Un aspect mauricien de l'oeuvre de Bernardin de Saint-Pierre: la flore locale", *Revue d'Histoire littéraire de la France,* Sept-Oct, 782-790.

Beaton, Rev. Patrick. 1859. *Creoles and Coolies, or Five Years in Mauritius.* James Nisbet & Co.: London.

Bissoondoyal, Basdeo. 1968. *The Truth about Mauritius.* Bharatiya Vidya Bharan: Chowpatty, Bombay.

Bissoondoyal, U. 1990. *Promises to Keep.* Editions de l'Océan Indien/Wiley Eastern Ltd.: New Delhi.

Blair Allen, Richard. 1983. *Creoles, Indian Immigrants and the Restructuring of Society and Economy in Mauritius, 1767-1885.* University of London thesis.

Bory de St. Vincent, J. B. G. M. 1804. *Voyage dans les quatre principales iles des mers d'Afrique...* 3 vols. Chez F. Buisson: Paris.

Bougainville, Louis Antoine.1989. *Voyage de Bougainville autour du monde.* (1771) Editions La Découverte, Maspéro: Paris.

Buffon. 1984. *Histoire naturelle.* Choix et préface de Jean Varlout. Gallimard: Paris.

Burkhardt, Francis and Sydney Smith (eds.). 1985. *The Correspondence of Charles Darwin.* Vol. 1, 1821-1836. Cambridge University Press: Cambridge.

Chapuiset Le Merle, André de. 1950. *Précis d'Histoire de l'Île Maurice (XVe au*

XVIIIe siècle). Nouvelle Imprimerie Coopérative: Port Louis.

Chaudenson, Robert. 1986. "Introduction". In Bernardin de Saint-Pierre, *Voyage...* Editions de l'Océan Indien: Rose Hill, Mauritius.

Chelin, Antoine. 1948(?). *Une île et son passé: Île Maurice (1507-1947).* No date, no publisher.

Cook, Captain James. 1932. *Voyages of Discovery.* J. M. Dent: London.

Cook, Malcolm. 1994. "Bougainville and One Noble Savage: Two Manuscript Texts of Bernardin de Saint-Pierre", *The Modern Language Review,* October, 842-855.

Darwin, Charles. 1842. *On the Structure and Distribution of Coral Reefs.* Walter Scott: London.

—.1845. *Journal of Researches into the Natural History and Geology of the Countries visited during the Voyage of HMS Beagle round the World, under the Command of Captain Fitzroy, RN.* Heron Books Reprint: Geneva, no date.

—.1985. *The Correspondence of Charles Darwin.* See under Burkhardt.

D'Epinay, Adrien. 1890. *Renseignements pour servir à l'histoire de l'île de France, jusqu'à l'année 1810 inclusivement.* Nouvelle Imprimerie Dupuy: Port Louis.

Donovan, John. 1982. "Introduction". In *Paul and Virginia.* Peter Owen: London.

Dubois, le sieur. 1674. *Les voyages faits par le sievr D B aux isles Dauphine & Bourbon, 1669, 70, 71 & 72.* Claude Barbin: Paris.

Duchêne, Albert. 1935. *Les Rêveries de Bernardin de Saint-Pierre.* Librairie Félix Alcan: Paris.

Dumas, Alexandre. 1846. *George, or, the Planter of the Isle of France.* Translated by G. J. Knox. Simms and McIntyre: London.

D'Unienville, Alix. 1954. *Les Mascareignes. Vieille France en mer indienne.* Albin Michel: Paris.

—.1973. *Pour la bicentenaire du Voyage à l'Isle de France de Bernardin de Saint-Pierre. Etude comparative de textes des Harmonies de la nature relatifs à l'Isle de France.* The Mauritius Printing Company: Port Louis.

Elsner, Jas and Joan-Pau Rubies (eds.). 1999. *Voyages and Visions: Towards a Cultural History of Travel.* Reaktion; London.

Evers, Sandra J. T. and Vinesh Y. Hookoomsing (eds.). 2001. *Globalisation and the South-West Indian Ocean.* University of Mauritius: Réduit.

Fanchette, Régis. n.d. *Ile Maurice. Mauritius.* Editions Delroisse: Paris.

Guyot, Alain. 1997. "Bernardin de Saint-Pierre: du voyageur récalcitrant au voyageur immobile", *Revue des Sciences Humaines,* 245, Jan-March, 111-127.

Hachisuka, Masauji. 1953. *The Dodo and Kindred Birds, or the Extinct Birds of the Mascarene Islands,* H. F. & G. Witherby: London.

Heady, Sue. 1997. *Le Guide Spectrum de l'Ile Maurice.* Camerapix: Nairobi.

Hill, Anne.1956. *Trelawny's Strange Relations. An Account of the Domestic Life of Edward John Trelawny's Mother and Sisters in Paris and London, 1818-1829.* The Mill House Press: Stanford Dingley.

Hollingworth, Derek. 1965. *They Came to Mauritius. Portraits of the Eighteenth and Nineteenth Centuries.* Oxford University Press: Nairobi.

Hookoomsing, Vinesh Y. 2000. "Au visiteur lumineux", in Bernabé, Jean etc. *Des îles créoles aux sociétés plurielles: Mélanges offerts à Jean Benoist*. Ibis Rouge Editions.

—.2000. "Memory, Imagination and Identity encoded in Language and Literature: the Creole Experience", paper read at Cape Town, August.

—.2001. See under Evers and Hookoomsing (eds.).

Humboldt, Alexander von. 1995. *Personal Narrative of a Journey to the Equinoctial Regions of the New Continent*. Introduction by Jason Wilson. Penguin Books: Harmondsworth.

Lanson, Gustave. 1923. *Histoire illustrée de la littérature française*. Vol. 2, Librairie Hachette: Paris.

Leblond, Marius. 1946. *Les Iles Soeurs ou le paradis retrouvé. La Réunion-Maurice*. Editions Alsatia: Paris.

Leguat, François. 1720. *Voyages et aventures de François Leguat & de ses compagnons en deux isles desertes des Indes orientales*, 2 vols. David Mortier: London.

Little, Roger, "Présentation", Bernardin de Saint-Pierre, *Empsaël et Zoraïde*. 1995.

Ly-Tio-Fane, Madeleine. 1958. *Mauritius and the Spice Trade: the Odyssey of Pierre Poivre*, Mauritius Archive Fund, Esclapan: Port Louis.

Malim, Michael. 1952. *Island of the Swan: Mauritius*. Longmans, Green and Co: London.

Maurel, Martine. 2000. *Mauritius*. New Holland Publishers: London.

Milbert, M. J. 1812. *Voyage pittoresque à l'ile de France*. 2 vols. Neveu: Paris.

Miller, David Philip and Peter Hans Reill (eds.). 1996. *Visions of Empire: Voyages, Botany and Representations of Nature*. Cambridge University Press: Cambridge.

Mockford, Julian. 1950. *Pursuit of an Island*. Staples Press: New York and London.

Mourba, Suresh. *Misère noire (ou réflexions sur l'histoire de l'Ile Maurice)*. No publication details.

Nagapen, Amédée. 1996. *Histoire de la Colonie Isle de France-Ile Maurice, 1721-1968*. Port Louis. No publisher.

Naipaul, V. S. 1987. *The Overcrowded Barracoon and other Articles*. Penguin Books: Harmondsworth.

Ngendahimana, Anastase. 1999. *Les idées politiques et sociales de Bernardin de Saint-Pierre*. Peter Lang: Bern & Berlin.

Nwulia, Moses D. E. 1981. *The History of Slavery in Mauritius and the Seychelles, 1810-1875*. Fairleigh Dickinson University Press: London & Toronto.

O'Brian, Patrick. 1987. *Joseph Banks: A Life*. Collins Harvill: London.

Pichois, Claude and Jean Ziegler. 1996. *Charles Baudelaire*. Fayard: Paris.

Pike, Nicholas. 1873. *Sub-Tropical Rambles... in and around the Island of Mauritius*. Marston, Low & Searle: London.

Pitot, Albert. 1899. *L'Isle de France. Esquisses historiques (1715-1810)*. E. Pezzami: Port Louis, Mauritius.

Poivre, Pierre. 1769. *The Travels of a Philosopher, being Observations on the Customs, Manners, Arts, Agriculture, and Trade of Several Nations in Asia and Africa*.

London.

Pratt, Mary Louise. 1992. *Imperial Eyes. Travel Writing and Transculturation.* Routledge: London.

Pridham, Charles. 1849. *An Historical, Political and Statistical Account of Mauritius and its Dependencies.* T. and W. Boone: London.

Prosper, Jean-Georges. 1989. *L'Ile Maurice, ancienne Isle de France. Fille de la Révolution.* Proag Printing Company: Port Louis.

Quammen, David. 1996. *The Song of the Dodo: Island Bio-geography in an Age of Extinctions.* Hutchinson: London.

Racault, Jean-Michel (ed.). 1986. *Etudes sur Paul et Virginie et l'oeuvre de Bernardin de Saint-Pierre.* Publications de l'Université de la Réunion: Paris
—.1986. "Une relecture de *Paul et Virginie*", in *Etudes sur Paul et Virginie et l'oeuvre de Bernardin de Saint-Pierre.*

Rennie, Neil. 1995. *Far-Fetched Facts: The Literature of Travel and the Idea of the South Sea.* Clarendon Press: Oxford.

Robinson, Philip. 1986. *Bernardin de Saint-Pierre: Paul et Virginie.* Grant & Cutler: London.

Rousseau, Jean-Jacques. 1968. *The Social Contract.* Translated and introduced by Maurice Cranston. Penguin Books: Harmondsworth.
—. *A Discourse on Inequality.* 1984. Translated and introduced by Maurice Cranston. Penguin Books: Harmondsworth.

St. Clair, William. 1977. *Trelawny: The Incurable Romancer.* John Murray: London.

Smith Simmons, Adele. 1982. *Modern Mauritius: The Politics of Decolonialization.* Indiana University Press: Bloomington.

Sonnerat, Pierre. 1782. *Voyages aux Indes Orientales et à la Chine.* 3 volumes. Paris.

Sornay, Pierre de. 1950. *Isle de France. Ile Maurice. Sa Géographie, son histoire, son agriculture, ses industries, ses institutions.* The General Printing and Stationary Company: Port Louis.

Souriau, Maurice. 1905. *Bernardin de Saint-Pierre d'après ses manuscrits.* Société Française d'Imprimerie et de Librairie: Poitiers.

Sparry, E.C. 2000. *Utopia's Garden: French Natural History from Old Regime to Revolution.* University of Chicago Press: Chicago.

Stedman, John Gabriel. 1992. *Stedman's Surinam. Life in an Eighteenth-Century Slave Society,* edited by Richard Price and Sally Price. John Hopkins University Press: Baltimore.

Storey, William Kelleher. 1997. *Science and Power in Colonial Mauritius,* University of Rochester Press: Rochester.

Strong, L. A. G. 1954. *The Story of Sugar.* Weidenfeld & Nicolson: London.

Thomas, Hugh. 1997. *The Slave Trade: The History of the Atlantic Slave Trade, 1440-1870.* Picador: London.

Toussaint, Auguste. 1936. *Port Louis. Deux Siècles d'histoire (1735-1935).* Port Louis.
—.1939. "Une étude historique", *Cahiers Mauriciens,* 1, 175-182.

—.1956. *Bibliography of Mauritius (1502-1954)*. Co-edited with H. Adolphe. Escapon: Port Louis.

—.1977. *History of Mauritius*, Macmillan Education: Nairobi.

Trelawny, Edward John. 1974. *Adventures of a Younger Son*. (1831) Introduction by William St. Clair, Oxford University Press: London.

Twain, Mark. 1925. *Following the Equator. A Journey Round the World*. (1897) Harper and Brothers: New York.

Unnuth, Abhimanyu. 1988. *A Portrait of Professor Basdeo Bissoondoyal*. Editions de l'Océan Indien: Rose Hill, Mauritius.

Vissière, Isabelle. 1986. "Esclavage et négritude chez Bernardin de Saint-Pierre", in J-M. Racault (ed.). *Etudes sur Paul et Virginie*.

Wilson, Jason. 1995. See Humboldt, "Introduction".

—.2001. "Letter from Port Louis", *The Times Literary Supplement*, 12 January, 12, 15.

Worster, Donald. 1979. *Nature's Economy: The Roots of Ecology*. Anchor Books: New York.